Germany: The Third Reich 1933–45 THIRD EDITION

Geoff Layton

HODDER
EDUCATION
PART OF HACHETTE LIVRE UK

To my wife, Janet

Study guides revised and updated, 2008, by Sally Waller (AQA).

The publishers would like to thank the following for permission to reproduce copyright illustrations: AKG-images, page 64, 83; © Austrian Archives/Corbis, used on pages 18, 33 (bottom); © Bettman/Corbis, used on pages 6, 20, 35, 39, 47, 119, 179, 187; BPK Berlin, used on page 124; BPK Berlin/Kunstbibliothek, Staatliche Museen zu Berlin. Photo: Knud Petersen, used on page 54; © Corbis, used on pages 56, 69, 98, 128; © Hulton Deutsch Collection/Corbis, used on pages 113, 122, 146; Mary Evans Picture Library, used on page 37; Mary Evans/Weimar Archive, used on page 93; © Popperfoto.com, used on page 126; Punch Ltd, used on page 163; Yad Vashem Art Museum, Jerusalem/Mrs Simenhoff, S. Africa, used on page 97.
The publishers would like to acknowledge use of the following extracts: Routledge for an extract from *The Final Solution* edited by David Cesarani, 1994. **Every effort has been made to trace all copyright holders, but if any have been inadvertently overlooked the Publishers will be pleased to make the necessary arrangements at the first opportunity.**

Although every effort has been made to ensure that website addresses are correct at time of going to press, Hodder Murray cannot be held responsible for the content of any website mentioned in this book. It is sometimes possible to find a relocated web page by typing in the address of the home page for a website in the URL window of your browser.

Orders: please contact Bookpoint Ltd, 130 Milton Park, Abingdon, Oxon OX14 4SB. Telephone: (44) 01235 827720. Fax: (44) 01235 400454. Lines are open 9.00–6.00, Monday to Saturday, with a 24-hour message answering service. Visit our website at www.hoddereducation.co.uk

© Geoff Layton 2005
First published in 2005 by
Hodder Education,
a part of Hachette Livre UK
338 Euston Road
London NW1 3BH

Impression number	10 9 8 7
Year	2010 2009 2008

The front cover illustration shows a poster of Adolf Hitler reproduced courtesy of AKG Photo, London
Typeset in Baskerville 10/12pt and produced by Gray Publishing, Tunbridge Wells
Printed in Malta

A catalogue record for this title is available from the British Library

ISBN: 978 0 340 888 94 0

Contents

Dedication

Keith Randell (1943–2002)

The *Access to History* series was conceived and developed by Keith, who created a series to 'cater for students as they are, not as we might wish them to be'. He leaves a living legacy of a series that for over 20 years has provided a trusted, stimulating and well-loved accompaniment to post-16 study. Our aim with these new editions is to continue to offer students the best possible support for their studies.

1

The Creation of the Nazi Dictatorship 1933–4

POINTS TO CONSIDER
During the years 1930–3 Germany was a troubled country.
The onset of an economic crisis had resulted in the decline
of the young Weimar democracy, while the power and
influence of Nazism had grown enormously. The purpose of
this chapter is to consider why Hitler was eventually
appointed chancellor and how and why the Nazis changed
Germany into a brutal dictatorship in the years 1933–4.
These issues are explored through the following themes:

• The rise of Nazism and the failure of Weimar Germany
• The 'legal revolution', January–March 1933
• Nazi co-ordination
• From chancellor to *Führer*
• Conclusion: consolidation or revolution?

Key dates

1929–33		The Great Depression
1932	July	*Reichstag* election: Nazis emerged as largest party in *Reichstag*
1933	January 30	Hitler appointed chancellor
	February 27	*Reichstag* fire: Communists blamed
	March 5	Last elections according to Weimar Constitution
	March 21	Day of Potsdam
	March 23	Enabling Act passed
	July 14	All political opposition to NSDAP declared illegal
1934	June 30	Night of the Long Knives: destruction of SA by SS
	August 2	Death of Hindenburg: Hitler combined the offices of chancellor and president. Oath of loyalty taken by the army

1 | Weimar and Nazism

Several years after the event, the British correspondent of *The Times* described the scenes in Berlin on 30 January 1933, the day of Hitler's appointment as chancellor of Germany:

> Berlin was buzzing like a beehive from morning till night, the nerves of four million people were quivering like harp strings … The **Brownshirts** were hilariously jubilant … Hour after hour they poured with their torchlights through the once forbidden Brandenburg Gate … marching with the triumphant ecstatic air of soldiers taking possession of a long beleaguered city.

> Opposite me were two palaces, one a grey ponderous building in the Wilhelmian style of architecture, the other a clean-cut four-square building, a typical product of the Germany of 1918–33. Behind a lighted window of the old building stood a massive old man. I saw him nod his head continually as the bands blared and the Brownshirts marched past, throwing their heads back and their eyes right to salute him. But they were not there to honour him. His day was done. The salute to the old man was perfunctory. Fifty yards down the street in the new palace was another window, on a higher level, open, with the spotlights playing on it, a young man leaning out … A colleague found beauty in the scene. 'Hitler looks marvellous', he said. The old and the new. Field Marshall and Bohemian Corporal. Hitler and Hindenburg. Tramp, tramp, tramp, blare, blare, blare. Hour after hour they came.

The appointment of Hitler on 30 January 1933 was undoubtedly a crucial turning point. Indeed, it is often seen as the fatal day that marked the end of Weimar Germany and ushered in the **Third Reich**. However, it is important to remember two essential points:

- Weimar democracy was really dead *before* the establishment of the Nazi dictatorship in early 1933.
- Although Nazism rapidly developed into a mass movement in 1929–33, Hitler's political position was not one of absolute power at first.

The failure of Weimar Germany

Three major themes stand out as fundamental weaknesses in the Weimar Republic:

- the hostility of Germany's **élites**
- ongoing economic problems
- limited base of popular support.

The hostility of Germany's élites

From the very start, the Weimar Republic faced the hostility of Germany's established élites, though at first this opposition was

---

Key date

Hitler appointed chancellor: 30 January 1933

Key terms

Brownshirts
So called because of the colour of their uniform. They were the SA (*Sturm Abteilung*) and also became known in English as the Stormtroopers. They were organised and set up in 1921 as a paramilitary unit led by Ernst Röhm.

Third Reich
Third Empire: a term for the Nazi dictatorship, 1933–45. It was seen as the successor to the medieval Holy Roman Empire and Imperial Germany 1871–1918.

Key question
Why did Weimar democracy fail?

Key term

Élites
The conservative vested interests in society, e.g. the army, the civil service and *Junkers* (landowners).

Democratic republic
A political system opposing a monarchy, but based on democratic principles.

Imperial Germany
Germany from its unification in 1871 to 1918. Also referred to as the Second Reich (Empire).

Kaiser
German Emperor.

Hyper-inflation
Hyper-inflation is unusual. In Germany, in 1923, prices spiralled out of control as the government increased the amount of money being printed. This displaced the whole economy.

Great Depression
Economic crisis of 1929–33 marked by mass unemployment, falling prices and a lack of spending.

Centre Party
(Zentrumspartei, ZP) Major political voice of Catholicism, but enjoyed a broad range of support. In the 1920s it became more sympathetic to the right wing.

limited. However, a major problem for Weimar was the fact that so many key figures in German society and business rejected the idea of a **democratic republic**. They worked against the interests of Weimar, hoping for a return to the good old days of **Imperial Germany** and the **Kaiser**. This was a powerful handicap to the successful development of the Republic in the 1920s and, in the 1930s, it was to become a decisive factor in its final collapse.

Ongoing economic problems

The Republic was also troubled by a series of economic crises that affected all levels of society. It inherited the enormous costs of the First World War (1914–18) followed by the burden of post-war reconstruction, Allied reparations and the heavy expense of new welfare benefits, for example health insurance, housing and benefits for the disabled. So, even though the **hyper-inflation** crisis of 1923 was overcome, problems in the economy were disguised and remained unresolved. These were to have dramatic consequences with the onset of the **Great Depression** in 1929.

Limited base of popular support

Weimar democracy never enjoyed widespread political support. There was never total acceptance of, and confidence in, its system and its values. From the Republic's birth its narrow base of popular support was caught between the extremes of left and right. But, as time went by, Weimar's claims to be the legitimate government became increasingly open to question. Weimar democracy was associated with defeat and the humiliation of the Treaty of Versailles and reparations. Its reputation was further damaged by the crisis of 1922–3. Significantly, even the mainstays of the Weimar Republic had weaknesses:

- The main parties of German liberalism, the Democratic Party and the People's Party, were losing support from 1924.
- The **Centre Party** and German Nationalist People's Party were both moving to the political right.
- Although the Social Democrats were loyal and committed to democracy, they failed to join many of the coalitions and work with their left-wing partner, the Communists.

In short, a sizeable proportion of the German population never had faith in the existing constitutional arrangements and, as the years passed, more were looking for change.

Weimar's phases

These unrelenting pressures meant that Weimar democracy went through a number of phases:

- The difficult circumstances of its formation in 1918–19 left it handicapped. It was in many respects a major achievement that it survived the problems of the period 1919–23.
- The years of relative stability from 1924–9, however, amounted to only a short breathing space and did not result in any strengthening of the Weimar system. On the eve of the world economic crisis, it seemed that Weimar's long-term chances of survival were already far from good.
- In the end, the impact of the world depression, 1929–33, intensified the pressures that brought about Weimar's final crisis.

In the view of some historians, Weimar had been a gamble with no chance of success. For others, the Republic continued to offer the hope of democratic survival right until mid-1932, when the Nazis became the largest party in the July **Reichstag** election. However, the decision to rule by **emergency decree** from 1930 created a particular system of presidential government. This fundamentally undermined the Weimar system and was soon followed by the electoral breakthrough of the Nazis. From this time, the chances of Weimar democracy surviving were very slim indeed.

The rise of Nazism

In the *Reichstag* elections of July 1932 only 43 per cent of the German electorate voted for pro-democratic parties. In effect, the majority of the German people had voted in a free (and reasonably fair) election to reject democracy, despite the fact that there was no clear alternative. However, this outcome did not have to end in a Nazi dictatorship. So the key question is, why was it that Hitler assumed power just six months later?

The Great Depression

The economic crisis transformed the Nazis into a mass movement. Admittedly, 63 per cent of Germans never voted for them, but 37 per cent of the electorate did. Within four years the Nazis had been transformed from being just a splinter party to becoming by far the strongest in a multi-party democracy (see Table 1.1, page 5) The Depression had led to such profound social and economic hardship that it created an environment of discontent, which was easily exploited by the Nazi message and its political methods.

Key terms

Reichstag
The German parliament created in 1871. From 1919 it became the main representative assembly and law-making body.

Emergency decree
In Article 48 of the Weimar Constitution the President had the right in an emergency to rule by decree and to override the constitutional rights of the people.

Key question
Why did the Nazis, and not any of the other parties, replace Weimar?

Key date
Reichstag election – Nazis emerged as largest party in *Reichstag*: July 1932

Key terms

NSDAP
National Socialist German Workers' Party – Nazi Party (*Nationalsozialistische Partei Deutschlands*).

Nationalism
Essentially, believing that a nation should be independent. In Germany it originally grew out of the national spirit to unify Germany in the nineteenth century. However, more extreme nationalists supported an expansionist policy towards eastern Europe.

Table 1.1: NSDAP results in the *Reichstag* elections 1928–32

	May 1928	September 1930	July 1932	November 1932
No. of *Reichstag* seats	12	107	230	196
Percentage	2.6	18.3	37.3	33.1

The Nazi message

It is really questionable whether Hitler would have become a national political figure without the severity of that economic downturn. However, his mixture of racist, **nationalist** and anti-democratic ideas was readily received by a broad spectrum of German people, and especially by the disgruntled middle classes. (For a detailed analysis of Nazi ideology see pages 51–2.)

Nazi organisation and methods

Other extreme right-wing groups with similar ideas and conditions to the Nazis did not enjoy similar success. This is partially explained by the impressive manner in which the Nazi message was communicated through:

- the use of modern propaganda techniques
- the violent exploitation of scapegoats – especially the Jews and Communists
- the development of the Party's well-organised structure.

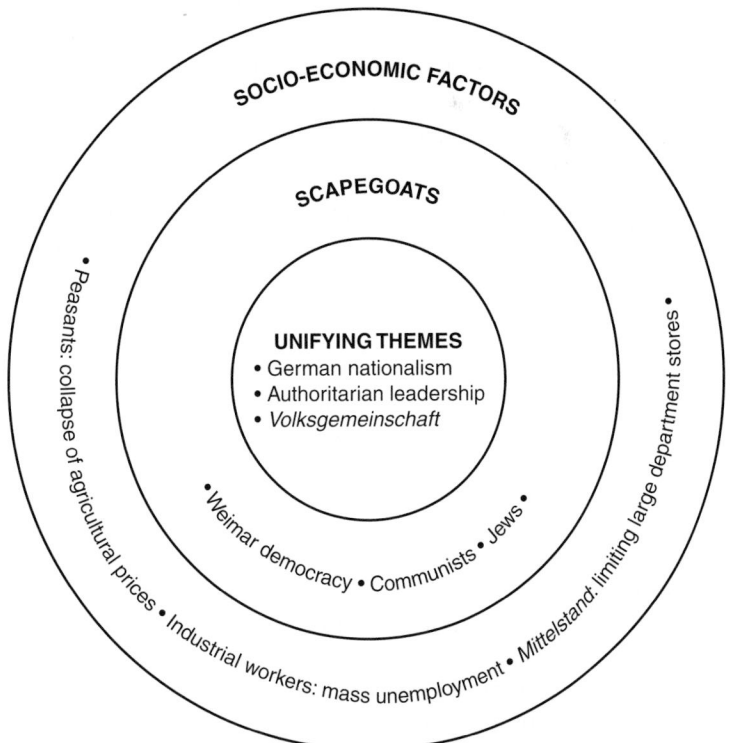

Figure 1.1: Nazi propaganda

Profile: Franz von Papen 1879–1969

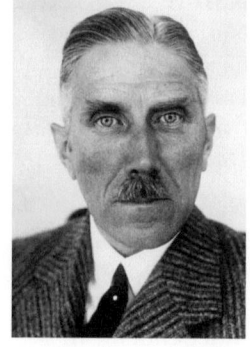

1879		– Born into a Catholic aristocratic family
1913–18		– Having been trained as a cavalry officer, he embarked on his diplomatic career and served in the USA, Mexico and Turkey
1921		– Elected to the Prussian regional state as a member of the Centre Party
1932	May	– Appointed as chancellor by Hindenburg to head the so-called **Cabinet of Barons**, which did not include any member of the *Reichstag*
		– Decided to call for the *Reichstag* election of July 1932 with serious consequences
	July	– Removed the state regional government of Prussia and appointed himself as Reich Commissioner of Prussia
	November	– Dismissed by Hindenburg, but schemed to replace Schleicher and to recover his power
1933	January	– Organised the formation of a Nazi–Nationalist coalition government with the élites and approved by Hindenburg
		– Appointed as vice-chancellor in Hitler's Nazi–Nationalist coalition
1934	July	– Resigned after the Night of Long Knives (see page 19)
1934–44		– Ambassador for Germany in Austria and then Turkey
1946		– Charged with war crimes in the Nuremberg trials, but found not guilty
1947		– Sentenced by a German court to eight years in a labour camp (released after two years)
1969		– Lived privately until his death

Key term

Cabinet of Barons
A derogatory name given by opponents to the government created by Franz von Papen because it was dominated by aristocrats and businessmen.

Franz von Papen had limited political experience and was out of his depth. His advance was mainly due to his connections with the aristocracy, the Catholic Church and big business (his wife was the daughter of a very rich industrialist).

He was always a monarchist and a nationalist (although he remained nominally a member of the Centre Party). When he was chancellor briefly, he aspired to undo the Weimar Constitution and so he was quite happy to rule by presidential decrees.

Despite his forced resignation in November 1932, Papen pursued his personal ambitions and played a crucial role in the events culminating in the appointment of Hitler. He organised the formation of a Nazi–Nationalist coalition government with himself as vice-chancellor along with the backing of the élites in the delusion that he could control Hitler. Finally, he exploited his friendship with President Hindenburg to endorse the appointment of Hitler. However, Papen was quickly outmanoeuvred by Hitler during 1933. Despite his doubts about the Nazi regime he accepted various diplomatic posts.

Hitler's character and leadership

All these factors undoubtedly helped but, in terms of electoral appeal, it is impossible to ignore the powerful impact of Hitler himself as a **charismatic** leader with a cult following. Furthermore, he exhibited a quite extraordinary political skill and ruthlessness when he was involved in the detail of political infighting.

The appointment of Hitler as chancellor

Nevertheless, the large popular following of the Nazis that helped to undermine the continued operation of democracy was insufficient on its own to give Hitler power. In the final analysis, it was the mutual recognition by Hitler and the élites that they needed each other which led to Hitler's appointment as chancellor.

From September 1930 every government (see Table 1.2) had been forced to resort almost continuously to the use of presidential emergency decrees because they lacked popular support. In the chaos of 1932 the only other realistic alternative to including the Nazis in the government was some kind of military regime – a presidential dictatorship backed by the army, perhaps. However, that, too, would have faced similar difficulties. Indeed, by failing to satisfy the extreme left and the extreme right there would have been a very real possibility of civil war.

Key term

Charismatic
Suggests a personality that has the ability to influence and to inspire people.

Key date

Hitler appointed Chancellor:
30 January 1933

Table 1.2: Germany's governments 1930–3

Chancellors	Dates in office	Type of government
Heinrich Brüning (Centre Party)	March 1930–May 1932	Presidential government dependent on emergency decrees. A coalition cabinet from political centre and right
Franz von Papen (Centre Party but very right wing)	May 1932–December 1932	Presidential government dependent on emergency decrees. Many non-party cabinet members
General Kurt von Schleicher (Non-party)	December 1932–January 1933	Presidential government dependent on emergency decrees. Many non-party cabinet members
Adolf Hitler (NSDAP)	1933–45	Coalition cabinet of NSDAP and Nationalists but gave way to Nazi dictatorship

Therefore, between December 1932 and January 1933, back-stage intrigue took over to unseat Chancellor Schleicher. On January 1933, secret contacts were made culminating in a meeting between Papen and Hitler and there it was agreed in essence that Hitler should head a Nazi–Nationalist coalition government with Papen as vice-chancellor. Papen then looked for support for his plan from the élites who saw an escape from the threat of communism and a solution to the political chaos. Even then, it was only possible if Papen could convince President Hindenburg to back the plan. Eventually, Hindenburg agreed, on 30 January 1933, to sanction the creation of a Nazi–Nationalist coalition government. Although it can be seen that it was a decisive day the dictatorship did not start technically until the completion of the 'legal revolution' in the period February–March 1933 (see the next section).

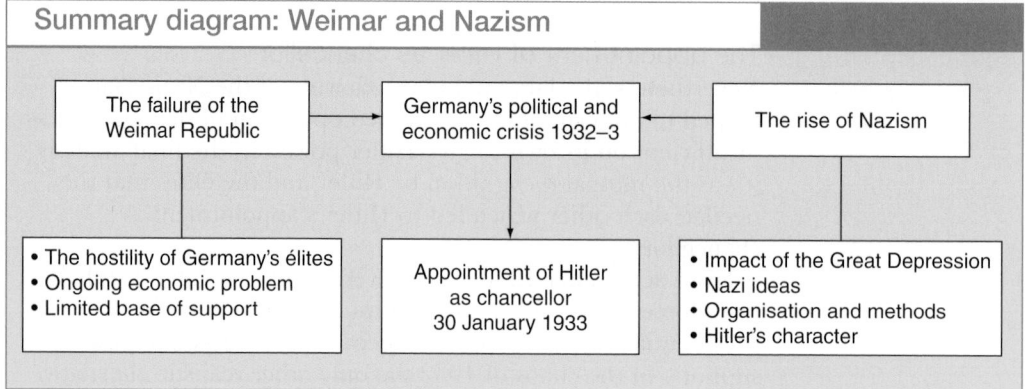

Summary diagram: Weimar and Nazism

```
The failure of the          Germany's political and          The rise of Nazism
Weimar Republic      →      economic crisis 1932–3      ←

• The hostility of Germany's élites                              • Impact of the Great Depression
• Ongoing economic problem        Appointment of Hitler         • Nazi ideas
• Limited base of support              as chancellor            • Organisation and methods
                                      30 January 1933           • Hitler's character
```

2 | The 'Legal Revolution'

Although Hitler had been appointed chancellor, his power was by no means absolute. Hindenburg had not been prepared to support Hitler's appointment until he had been satisfied that the chancellor's power would remain limited. Such was Papen's confidence about Hitler's restricted room for manoeuvre that he boasted to a friend, 'In two months we'll have pushed Hitler into a corner so hard that he'll be squeaking'.

At first sight, the confidence of the **conservatives** seemed to be justified, since Hitler's position was weak in purely constitutional terms:

- There were only two other Nazis in the cabinet of 12 – Wilhelm Frick as Minister of the Interior, and Hermann Göring as a Minister without Portfolio (a minister with no specific responsibility) (see profile, page 39). There were, therefore, nine other non-Nazi members of the cabinet, all from conservative–nationalist backgrounds, such as the army, industry and landowners.
- Hitler's coalition government did not have a majority in the *Reichstag*, which suggested that it would be difficult for the Nazis to introduce any dramatic legislation.
- The chancellor's post, as the previous 12 months had clearly shown, was dependent on the whim of President Hindenburg, and he openly resented Hitler. Hindenburg had made Hitler chancellor but he could as easily sack him.

Hitler was very much aware of the potential power of the army and the trade unions. He could not alienate these forces, which could break his government. The army could arrange a military *coup*, while the trade unions could organise a general strike, as they had done in 1920.

Key question
What were the political constraints on Hitler?

Key term

Conservative Opposing fundamental change and maintaining the traditional political order. During Weimar Germany conservatives were unsympathetic to democracy and the Republic.

Key question
What were Hitler's main political strengths?

Key term

Policy of legality
Hitler's political strategy after his failed armed *coup* in the Beer Hall *putsch* of 1923. He felt that the only sure way to succeed was to work within the Weimar Constitution and to gain power by legal means.

Hitler's strengths

Within two months, these constraints were shown not to be real limitations when Hitler became a dictator. Moreover, power was to be achieved by carrying on with the **policy of legality** that the Party had pursued since 1925. Hitler already possessed several key strengths when he became chancellor:

- He was the leader of the largest political party in Germany, which was why the policy of ignoring him had not worked. During 1932 it had only led to the ineffectual governments of Papen and Schleicher. Therefore, political realism forced the conservatives to work with him. They probably needed him more than he needed them. The alternative to Hitler was civil war or a Communist *coup* – or so it seemed to many people at the time.

- More importantly, the Nazi Party had now gained access to the resources of the state. For example, Göring not only had a place in the cabinet but was also Minister of the Interior in

'Not the most comfortable seat'. A US cartoon drawn soon after Hitler's appointment as chancellor. What does it suggest about Hitler's political position at that time?

Prussia, with responsibility for the police. It was a responsibility that he used blatantly to harass opponents, while ignoring Nazi crimes. Goebbels (see pages 128–9), likewise, exploited the propaganda opportunities on behalf of the Nazis. 'The struggle is a light one now', he confided in his diary, '... since we are able to employ all the means of the State. Radio and Press are at our disposal'.

- Above all, however, Hitler was a masterly political tactician. He was determined to achieve absolute power for himself whereas Papen was really politically naive. It soon became clear that 'Papen's political puppet' was too clever to be strung along by a motley collection of ageing conservatives.

The *Reichstag* election, 5 March 1933

Hitler lost no time in removing his strings. Within 24 hours of his appointment as chancellor, new *Reichstag* elections had been called. He felt new elections would not only increase the Nazi vote, but also enhance his own status.

The campaign for the last *Reichstag* elections held according to the Weimar Constitution had few of the characteristics expected of a democracy: violence and terror dominated with meetings of the Socialists and Communists being regularly broken up by the Nazis. In Prussia, Göring used his authority to enrol an extra 50,000 into the police – nearly all were members of the **SA** and **SS**. Altogether 69 people died during the five-week campaign.

The Nazis also used the atmosphere of hate and fear to great effect in their election propaganda. Hitler set the tone in his 'Appeal to the German People' of 31 January 1933. He blamed the prevailing bad economic conditions on democratic government and the terrorist activities of the Communists. He cultivated the idea of the government as a 'National Uprising' determined to restore Germany's pride and unity. In this way he played on the deepest desires of many Germans, but never committed himself to the details of a political and economic programme.

Another key difference in this election campaign was the improved Nazi financial situation. At a meeting on 20 February with 20 leading industrialists, Hitler was promised three million **Reichsmarks**. With such financial backing and Goebbels's exploitation of the media, the Nazis were confident of securing a parliamentary majority.

The *Reichstag* fire

As the campaign moved towards its climax, one further bizarre episode strengthened the Nazi hand. On 27 February the *Reichstag* building was set on fire, and a young Dutch Communist, van der Lubbe, was arrested in incriminating circumstances. At the time, it was believed by many that the incident was a Nazi plot to support the claims of a Communist *coup*, and thereby to justify Nazi repression. However, to this day the episode has defied satisfactory explanation.

Key question
How did Hitler create a dictatorship in two months?

Key terms

SA
Sturm Abteilung – Stormtroopers. Also referred to as the Brownshirts after the colour of the uniform (see page 2).

SS
Schutz Staffel (protection squad). Became known as the Blackshirts, after the colour of the uniform. Formed in 1925 as an élite bodyguard for Hitler. Himmler became its leader in 1929. By 1933 the SS numbered 52,000, establishing a reputation for blind obedience and total commitment to the Nazi cause.

Reichsmark
New German currency. Introduced after 1923 inflation, initially called *Rentenmark*.

Key dates

The Nazis blame the Communists for the *Reichstag* fire: 27 February 1933

Last elections according to the Weimar Constitution: 5 March 1933

Potsdam ceremony: 21 March 1933

Enabling Act passed: 23 March 1933

A major investigation in 1962 concluded that van der Lubbe had acted alone; a further 18 years later the West Berlin authorities posthumously acquitted him, whereas the recent biography of Hitler by Ian Kershaw remains convinced that van der Lubbe acted on his own in a series of three attempted arsons within a few weeks.

So, it is probable that the true explanation will never be known. The real significance of the *Reichstag* fire is the cynical way it was exploited by the Nazis to their advantage.

On the next day, 28 February, Frick drew up, and Hindenburg signed, the 'Decree for the Protection of the People and the State'. In a few short clauses most civil and political liberties were suspended and the power of central government was strengthened. The justification for the Decree was the threat posed by the Communists. Following this, in the last week of the election campaign, hundreds of anti-Nazis were arrested, and the violence reached new heights.

Election result

In this atmosphere of fear, Germany went to the polls on 5 March. The election had a very high turnout of 88 per cent – a figure so high suggests the influence and intimidation of the SA, corruption by officials and an increased government control of the radio.

Somewhat surprisingly, the Nazis increased their vote from 33.1 per cent to only 43.9 per cent, thereby securing 288 seats. Hitler could claim a majority in the new *Reichstag* only with the help of the 52 seats won by the Nationalists. It was not only disappointing; it was also a political blow, since any change in the existing Weimar Constitution required a two-thirds majority in the *Reichstag*.

The Enabling Act, March 1933

Despite this constitutional hurdle, Hitler decided to propose to the new *Reichstag* an Enabling Bill which would effectively do away with parliamentary procedure and legislation and which would instead transfer full powers to the chancellor and his government for four years. In this way the dictatorship would be grounded in legality. However, the successful passage of the Enabling Bill depended on gaining the support or abstention of some of the other major political parties in order to get a two-thirds majority.

Key term

DNVP German National People's Party (*Deutschenationale Volkspartei*). A right-wing party formed in 1919 from the old conservative parties and some of the racist, anti-Semitic groups. It was monarchist and anti-republican and had close ties to heavy industry and agriculture, including landowners and small farmers.

A further problem was that the momentum built up within the lower ranks of the Nazi Party was proving increasingly difficult for Hitler to contain in the regional areas. Members were impatiently taking the law into their own hands and this gave the impression of a 'revolution from below'. It threatened to destroy Hitler's image of legality, and antagonise the conservative vested interests and his **DNVP** coalition partners. Such was his concern that a grandiose act of reassurance was arranged. On 21 March, at Potsdam Garrison Church, Goebbels orchestrated the ceremony to celebrate the opening of the *Reichstag*. In the presence of

Hindenburg, the Crown Prince (the son of Kaiser Wilhelm II), and many of the army's leading generals, Hitler symbolically aligned National Socialism with the forces of the old Germany.

Two days later the new *Reichstag* met in the Kroll Opera House to consider the Enabling Bill, and on this occasion the Nazis revealed a very different image. The Communists (those not already in prison) were refused admittance, whilst the deputies in attendance faced a barrage of intimidation from the ranks of the SA who surrounded the building.

However, the Nazis still required a two-thirds majority to pass the bill and, on the assumption that the Social Democrats would vote against, they needed the backing of the Centre Party. Hitler thus promised in his speech of 23 March to respect the rights of the Catholic Church and to uphold religious and moral values. These were false promises, which the Centre Policy deputies deceived themselves into believing. In the end only the Social Democrats voted against, and the Enabling Bill was passed by 444 to 94 votes.

Germany had succumbed to what Karl Bracher, a leading German scholar, has called 'legal revolution'. Within the space of a few weeks Hitler had legally dismantled the Weimar Constitution. The way was now open for him to create a one-party totalitarian dictatorship.

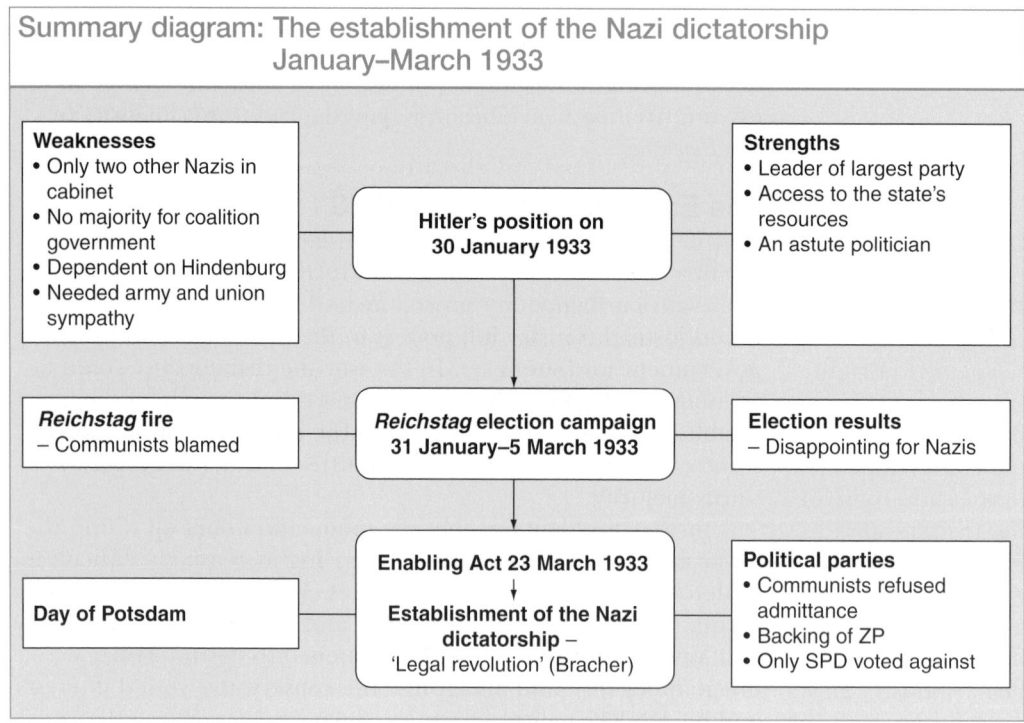

Summary diagram: The establishment of the Nazi dictatorship January–March 1933

Weaknesses
- Only two other Nazis in cabinet
- No majority for coalition government
- Dependent on Hindenburg
- Needed army and union sympathy

Hitler's position on 30 January 1933

Strengths
- Leader of largest party
- Access to the state's resources
- An astute politician

Reichstag **fire**
– Communists blamed

Reichstag **election campaign 31 January–5 March 1933**

Election results
– Disappointing for Nazis

Day of Potsdam

Enabling Act 23 March 1933
↓
Establishment of the Nazi dictatorship –
'Legal revolution' (Bracher)

Political parties
- Communists refused admittance
- Backing of ZP
- Only SPD voted against

3 | Co-ordination: *Gleichschaltung*

Key question
What was
Gleichschaltung?

The Enabling Act was the constitutional foundation stone of the Third Reich. In purely legal terms the Weimar Constitution was not dissolved until 1945, but, in practice, the Enabling Act provided the basis for the dictatorship that evolved from 1933. In this legal way, the intolerance and violence used by the Nazis to gain power could now be used as tools of government by the dictatorship of Hitler and the Party.

The degeneration of Weimar's democracy into the Nazi state system is usually referred to as *Gleichschaltung* or co-ordination. In practice, it applied to the Nazifying of German society and structures and refers specifically to the establishment of the dictatorship, 1933–4. To some extent it was generated by the power and freedom exploited by the SA at the local level – in effect a 'revolution from below'. But it was also directed by the Nazi leadership from the political centre in Berlin – a 'revolution from above'. Together, these two political forces attempted to 'co-ordinate' as many aspects of German life as possible along Nazi lines, although differences over the exact long-term goals of National Socialism laid the basis for future conflict within the Party (see pages 16–21).

Co-ordination has been viewed rather neatly as the 'merging' of German society with Party associations and institutions in an attempt to Nazify the life of Germany. At first many of these Nazi creations had to live alongside existing bodies, but over the years they gradually replaced them. In this way, much of Germany's cultural, educational and social life became increasingly controlled (see Chapter 3). However, in the spring and summer of 1933 the priority of the Nazi leadership was to secure its political supremacy. So its real focus of attention was the 'co-ordination' of the **federal states**, the political parties and the independent trade unions – which were at odds with Nazi political aspirations.

Key terms

Gleichschaltung
'Bringing into line' or 'co-ordination'.

Federal states
In a federal system of government, power and responsibilities are shared between national and regional governments. Weimar Germany had a federal structure with 17 *Länder* (regional states), e.g. Prussia, Bavaria, Saxony.

Main features of co-ordination

The federal states

Key question
In what ways did Nazism achieve co-ordination?

The regions had a very strong tradition in Germany history. Even after the creation of the German Empire in 1871, the previously independent states carried on as largely self-governing federal states. Yet, this stood in marked contrast to Nazi desires to create a fully unified country.

Nazi activists had already exploited the climate of February–March 1933 to intimidate opponents and to infiltrate federal governments. Indeed, their 'political success' rapidly degenerated into terror and violence that seemed even beyond the control of Hitler, who called for restraint because he was afraid of losing the support of the conservatives. Consequently, the situation was resolved in three legal stages:

- First, by a law of 31 March 1933, the regional parliaments (*Landtage*) were dissolved and then reformed with acceptable majorities, which allowed the Nazis to dominate regional state governments.

- Secondly, a law of 7 April 1933 created Reich Governors (*Reichstatthalter*) who more often than not were the local party **Gauleiters** with full powers.
- The process of centralisation was finally completed in January 1934 when the regional parliaments were abolished. Federal governments and governors were subordinated to the authorities of the Ministry of the Interior in the central government.

By early 1934 the federal principle of government was as good as dead. Even the Nazi Reich governors existed simply 'to execute the will of the supreme leadership of the Reich'.

The trade unions

Germany's trade union movement was powerful because of its mass membership and its strong connections with socialism and Catholicism. Back in 1920 it had clearly shown its industrial muscle when it had successfully ended a right-wing **putsch** against the Weimar government by calling a general strike. On the whole, German organised labour was hostile to Nazism and so posed a major threat to the stability of the Nazi state.

Yet, by May 1933 it was shown to be a spent force. Admittedly, the Great Depression had already severely weakened it by reducing membership and lessening the will to resist. However, the trade union leaders deceived themselves into believing that they could work with the Nazis and thereby preserve a degree of independence and at least the structure of trade unionism. Their hope was that:

- In the short term, trade unionism would continue to serve its social role to help members.
- In the long term, it could provide the framework for development in the post-Nazi era.

However, the labour movement was deceived by the Nazis.

The Nazis surprisingly declared 1 May (the traditional day of celebration for international socialist labour) a national holiday, which gave the impression to the trade unions that perhaps there was some scope for co-operation. This proved to be the briefest of illusions. The following day, trade union premises were occupied by the SA and SS, union funds were confiscated and many of the leaders were arrested and sent to the early concentration camps, e.g. Dachau.

Independent trade unions were then banned and in their place all German workers' organisations were absorbed into the German Labour Front, DAF (*Deutscher Arbeitsfront*), led by Robert Ley. DAF became the largest organisation in Nazi Germany with 22 million members, but it acted more as an instrument of control than as a genuine representative body of workers' interests and concerns (see pages 53–5). Also, it lost the most fundamental right to negotiate wages and conditions of work. So, by the end of 1933, the power of the German labour movement had been decisively broken.

Key terms

Gauleiters
Regional leaders of the Nazi Party.

Putsch
An uprising, although often the French phrase, *coup d'état*, is used.

Political parties

It was inconceivable that *Gleichschaltung* could allow the existence of other political parties. Nazism openly rejected democracy and any concessions to alternative opinions. Instead, it aspired to establish authoritarian rule within a one-party state. This was not difficult to achieve:

- The Communists had been outlawed since the *Reichstag* fire (see pages 10–11).
- Soon after the destruction of the trade unions the assets of the Social Democrats were seized and they were then officially banned on 22 June.
- Most of the major remaining parties willingly agreed to dissolve themselves in the course of late June 1933 – even the Nationalists (previously coalition partners to the Nazis) obligingly accepted.
- Finally, the Catholic Centre Party decided to give up the struggle and followed suit on 5 July 1933.

Thus, there was no opposition to the decree of 14 July that formally proclaimed the Nazi Party as the only legal political party in Germany.

Key date

All political opposition to NSDAP declared illegal: 14 July 1933

Key question

How advanced was the process of Nazi co-ordination by the end of 1933?

Success of *Gleichschaltung* in 1933

By the end of 1933 the process of *Gleichschaltung* was well advanced in many areas of public life in Germany. However, it was certainly far from complete. In particular, it had failed to

A photograph of Prussian policemen in Berlin in 1933. Although they wore the traditional helmet with the insignia, they are 'brought into line' by carrying Nazi flags and give the Nazi salute.

make any impression on the role and influence of the Church, the army and big business. Also, the civil service and education had only been partially co-ordinated. This was mainly due to Hitler's determination to shape events through the 'revolution from above' and to avoid antagonising such powerful vested interests. Yet, there were many in the lower ranks of the Party who had contributed to the 'revolution from below' and who now wanted to extend the process of *Gleichschaltung*. It was this internal party conflict that laid the basis for the bloody events of June 1934 (see pages 19–22).

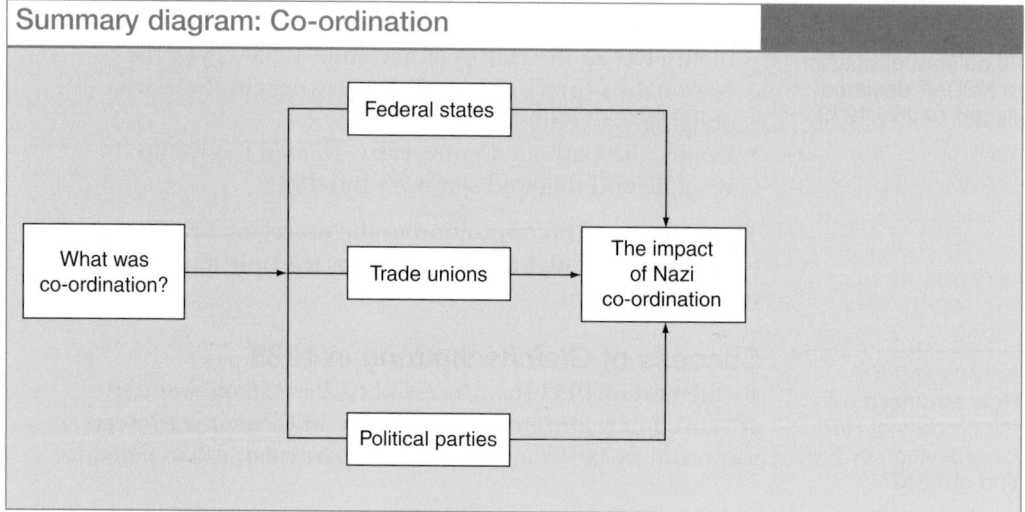

Summary diagram: Co-ordination

4 | From Chancellor to *Führer*

Key question
What exactly was the political dilemma faced by Hitler in 1933?

Within just six months of coming to power Hitler had indeed managed to turn Germany into a one-party dictatorship. However, in a speech on 6 July 1933 to the Reich Governors, Hitler warned of the dangers posed by a permanent state of revolution. He therefore formally declared an end to the revolution and demanded that 'the stream of revolution must be guided into the safe channel of evolution'.

Hitler was caught in a political dilemma. He was increasingly concerned that the behaviour of Party activists was running beyond his control. This was likely to create embarrassment in his relations with the more conservative forces whose support he still depended on, e.g. big business, civil service and, above all, the army. Hitler's speech amounted to a clear-cut demand for the Party to accept the realities of political compromise and also the necessity of change from above.

The position of the SA

However, Hitler's appeal failed to have the desired effect. If anything, it reinforced the fears of many Party members that the Nazi leadership was prepared to dilute the ideology of National

Second revolution
Refers to the aims of the SA, led by Ernst Röhm, which wanted social and economic reforms and the creation of a 'people's army' – merging the German army and the SA. The aims of a second revolution were more attractive to the 'left-wing socialist Nazis' or 'radical Nazis', who did not sympathise with the conservative forces in Germany.

Socialism. Such concerns came in particular from within the ranks of the SA giving rise to calls for a **second revolution**.

The SA represented the radical, left wing of the Nazi Party and to a large extent it reflected a more working-class membership – which in the depression was often young and unemployed. It placed far more emphasis on the socialist elements of the Party programme than Hitler ever did and, therefore, saw no need to hold back simply for the sake of satisfying the élites. It had played a vital role in the years of struggle by winning the political battle on the streets, and many of its members were embittered and frustrated over the limited nature of the Nazi revolution. They were also disappointed by their own lack of personal gain from this acquisition of power.

Such views were epitomised by the leader of the SA, Ernst Röhm (see Profile, page 18), who openly called for a genuine 'National Socialist Revolution'. Röhm was increasingly disillusioned by the politics of his old friend Hitler and he recognised that the developing confrontation would decide the future role of the SA in the Nazi state. In a private interview in early 1934 with a local Party boss, Rauschning, Röhm gave vent to his feelings and his ideas:

> Adolf is a swine. He will give us all away. He only associates with the reactionaries now ... Getting matey with the East Prussian generals. They're his cronies now ... Adolf knows exactly what I want. I've told him often enough. Not a second edition of the old imperial army.

Röhm, therefore, had no desire to see the SA marches and rallies degenerating into a mere propaganda show now that the street-fighting was over. He wanted to amalgamate the army and the SA into a people's militia – of which he would be the commander.

The power struggle between the SA and the army
However, Röhm's plan was anathema to the German army, which saw its traditional role and status being directly threatened. Hitler was therefore caught between two powerful, but rival, forces – both of which could create considerable political difficulties for him.

On the one hand, the SA consisted of three million committed Nazis with his oldest political friend leading it. Also, it had fought for Hitler in the 1923 Munich *putsch* and in the battle of the streets, 1930–3. The SA was also far larger than the army.

Table 1.3: SA membership 1931–4

	1931	1932	1933	1934
Membership figures	100,000	291,000	425,000	3,000,000

SA membership grew at first because of the large number of unemployed young men, but from 1933 many joined as a way to advance themselves.

Profile: Ernst Röhm 1887–1934

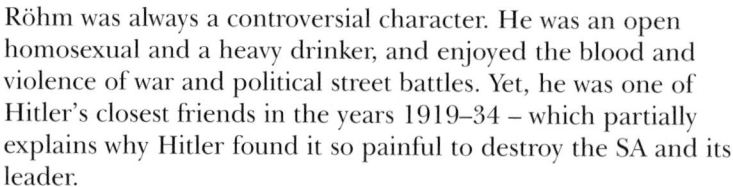

1887		– Born in Munich
1914–18		– Served in the First World War and reached the level of captain
1919		– Joined the *Freikorps*
		– Met Hitler and joined the Nazi Party
1921		– Helped to form the SA and became its leader in the years 1921–3
1923	November	– Participated in the Munich Beer Hall *putsch*
1924		– Initially jailed, but soon released on probation
1925–30		– Left for Bolivia in South America
1930		– Returned to Germany at Hitler's request
1930–4		– SA leader
1933	December	– Invited to join the cabinet
1934	June	– Arrested and then murdered in the Night of the Long Knives

Röhm was always a controversial character. He was an open homosexual and a heavy drinker, and enjoyed the blood and violence of war and political street battles. Yet, he was one of Hitler's closest friends in the years 1919–34 – which partially explains why Hitler found it so painful to destroy the SA and its leader.

He played a key role in the earliest years, when he introduced Hitler to the Nazi Party in 1919. He formed the SA in 1921 but he left Germany after the Beer Hall *Putsch*. Most significantly, in the years 1930–3 Röhm was given the responsibility by Hitler of reorganising the SA and restoring its discipline. By intimidation and street violence Röhm's SA had turned itself into a powerful force by 1931 – though conflict between the Party leadership and the SA grew increasingly serious.

After the Nazi consolidation of power Röhm was committed to pursue 'a second revolution' which reflected the reforms of the 'left-wing socialist Nazis' or 'radical Nazis'. He did not sympathise with the conservative forces in Germany and, above all, aimed to create a 'people's army' by merging the German army and the SA. This fundamental difference culminated in the 'Night of the Long Knives' and his own death.

On the other hand, the army was the one organisation that could unseat Hitler from his position of power. The officer class was suspicious of Hitler and it had close social ties with many of the powerful interests, e.g. civil service and **Junkers**. Moreover, the army alone possessed the military skills that were essential to the success of his foreign policy aims. Also, however large the SA was, it could never hope to challenge the discipline and professional expertise possessed by the army.

Junkers
The landowning aristocracy, especially those from eastern Germany.

Key term

So, political realities dictated that Hitler had to retain the backing of the army but, in the winter of 1933–4, he was still loath to engineer a showdown with his old friend, Röhm.

Hitler tried to make concessions to Röhm by bringing him into the cabinet. He also called a meeting in February between the leaders of the army, the SA and the SS in an attempt to reach an agreement about the role of each organisation within the Nazi state. However, the tension did not ease. Röhm and the SA resented Hitler's apparent acceptance of the privileged position of the army. Moreover, the unrestrained actions and ill discipline of the SA only increased the feelings of dissatisfaction amongst the generals.

The Night of the Long Knives

Key question
When and why did the political conflict come to a head?

The developing crisis came to a head in April 1934 when it became apparent that President Hindenburg did not have much longer to live. The implications of his imminent death were profound, for Hitler wanted to assume the presidency without opposition. He certainly did not want a contested election, nor did he have any sympathy for those who wanted the restoration of the monarchy. It seems that Hitler's hand was forced by the need to secure the army's backing for his succession to Hindenburg.

The support of the army had become the key to the survival of Hitler's regime in the short term, while in the long term it offered the means to fulfil his ambitions in the field of foreign affairs. Whatever personal loyalty Hitler felt for Röhm and the SA was finally put to one side. The army desired their elimination and an end to the talk of 'a second revolution' and 'a people's army'. By agreeing to this, Hitler could gain the favour of the army generals, secure his personal position and remove an increasingly embarrassing millstone from around his neck.

Without primary written evidence it is difficult to establish the exact details of the events in June 1934. However, it seems highly probable that, at a meeting on the battleship *Deutschland* in April 1934, Hitler and the two leading generals, Blomberg and Fritsch, came to an agreed position against Röhm and the SA. Furthermore, influential figures within the Nazi Party, in particular Göring and Himmler, were also manoeuvring behind the scenes. They were aiming for a similar outcome in order to further their own ambitions by removing a powerful rival. Given all that, Hitler probably did not decide to make his crucial move to solve the problem of the SA until mid-June when Vice-Chancellor Papen gave a speech calling for an end to SA excesses and criticised the policy of co-ordination. Not surprisingly, these words caused a real stir and were seen as a clear challenge. Hitler now recognised that he had to satisfy the conservative forces – and that meant he had to destroy the power of the SA immediately.

Key term
Night of the Long Knives
The events of the night 29–30 June 1934 when Hitler ordered the murder of about 200 SA leaders.

On 30 June 1934, the '**Night of the Long Knives**', Hitler eliminated the SA as a political and military force once and for all. Röhm and the main leaders of the SA were shot by members of the SS – although the weapons and transport were actually provided by the army. There was no resistance of any substance.

In addition, various old scores were settled: Schleicher, the former Chancellor, and Strasser, the leader of the radical socialist wing of the Nazi Party, were both killed. Altogether it is estimated that 200 people were murdered.

From a very different perspective, on 5 July 1934 the *Völkischer Beobachter* (*The People's Observer*), the Nazi newspaper, reported on the Reich cabinet meeting held two days earlier:

> Defence Minister General Blomberg thanked the *Führer* in the name of the Cabinet and the Army for his determined and courageous action, by which he had saved the German people from civil war…

> The Reich Cabinet then approved a law on measures for the self-defence of the State. Its single paragraph reads: 'The measures taken on 30 June and 1 and 2 July to suppress the acts of high treason are legal, being necessary for the self-defence of the State.'

Profile: Paul von Hindenburg 1847–1934

1847		– Born in Posen, East Prussia
1859–1911		– Joined the Prussian army and served until his retirement with the rank of General in 1911
1914		– Recalled at start of First World War
		– Won the victory of the Battle of Tannenberg on Eastern front
1916		– Promoted to Field Marshal and war supremo
1918		– Accepted the defeat of Germany and retired again
1925		– Elected President of Germany
1930–2		– Appointed Brüning, Papen and Schleicher as chancellors, who ruled by presidential decree
1932		– Re-elected president
1933	January	– Persuaded by Papen to appoint Hitler as chancellor
1934	August	– Death. Granted a national funeral

Hindenburg was born into a Prussian noble family that could trace its military tradition back over many centuries. He was regularly promoted in his military career although he was described as 'steady rather than exceptional'. In 1914, he was recalled from retirement and by 1916 he worked with General Ludendorff to become the military dictators of Germany.

After the war, Hindenburg briefly retired but in 1925 he was elected President of Germany, a position he accepted reluctantly. He was not a democrat and looked forward to the return of the monarchy, although he performed his duties correctly. Very old by the time of the 1932–4 crisis, Hindenburg was easily influenced by the intrigues of Papen and Schleicher which led him to appoint Hitler. He had no respect for Hitler at all, but in the final months of his life he did not have the will and the determination to make a stand against Nazism.

The significance of the Night of Long Knives

It would be difficult to overestimate the significance of the Night of the Long Knives. In one bloody action Hitler overcame the radical left in his own party, and the conservative right of traditional Germany. By the summer of 1934, the effects of the purge could be seen clearly:

- The German army had clearly aligned itself behind the Nazi regime, as was shown by Blomberg's public vote of thanks to Hitler on 1 July. Perhaps even more surprisingly, German soldiers agreed to take a personal oath of loyalty to Hitler.
- The SA was rendered almost unarmed and it played no significant role in the political development of the Nazi state. Thereafter its major role was to attend propaganda rallies as a showpiece force.
- More ominously for the future, the incident marked the emergence of the SS. German generals had feared the SA, but

Key question
How significant was the Night of the Long Knives?

Key date
Night of the Long Knives – destruction of SA by SS: 29–30 June 1934

A cartoon/photomontage published by the German communist John Heartfield in July 1934. The image is of a Stormtrooper who has been murdered on Hitler's order in the Night of the Long Knives. What is ironic about his Heil Hitler salute?

they failed to recognise the SS as the Party's élite institution of terror.

- Above all, Hitler had secured his own personal political supremacy. His decisions and actions were accepted, so in effect he had managed to legalise murder. From that moment, it was clear that the Nazi regime was not a traditional authoritarian one, like Imperial Germany 1871–1918; it was a personal dictatorship with frightening power.

Consequently, when Hindenburg died on 2 August, there was no political crisis. Hitler was simply able to merge the offices of Chancellor and President, and also to take on the new official title of **Führer**. The Nazi regime had been stabilised and the threat of a 'second revolution' had been completely removed.

Key date

Death of Hindenburg – Hitler combined the offices of Chancellor and President: 2 August 1934

Key term

Führer
(Leader) Hitler was declared leader of the Party in 1921. In 1934 he became leader of the country after the death of Hindenburg.

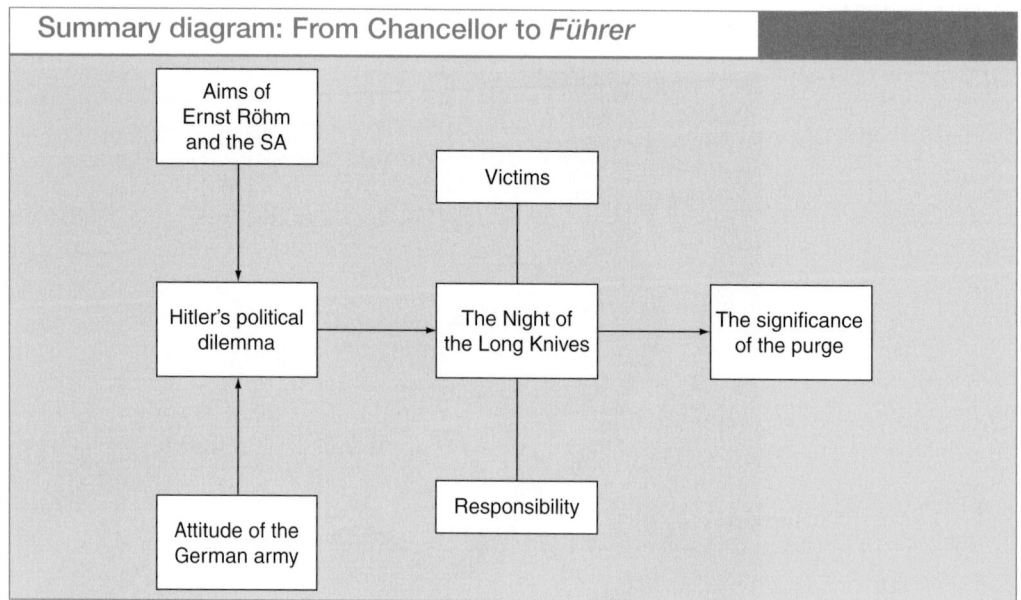

Summary diagram: From Chancellor to *Führer*

5 | Conclusion: Consolidation

With hindsight it may seem as if the consolidation of the Nazi dictatorship unfolded quite naturally in the years 1933–4. However, as both Papen's boast in January 1933 (see page 8) and the American cartoon (see page 9) suggest, the events were not inevitable. So it is important to bear in mind the key factors that can help to explain the establishment of the dictatorship:

Key question
How was Hitler able to consolidate Nazi power between 1933 and 1934?

- Terror. The Nazis used violence – and increasingly so without legal restriction, e.g. the Night of the Long Knives and the arrest of the Communists. The Nazis' organisations also employed violence at the local level to intimidate opposition.
- Legality. The use of law by the Nazis gave a legal justification for the development of the regime, e.g. the Enabling Act, the Emergency Decree of 28 February 1933, the dissolution of the parties.

- Deception. Hitler misled powerful groups in order to destroy them, e.g. the trade unions and the SA.
- Propaganda. The Nazis successfully cultivated powerful images – especially when Goebbels took on responsibility for the Propaganda Ministry. Myths were developed about Hitler as a respectable statesman, e.g. the Day of Potsdam (see page 11).
- Weaknesses of the opposition. In the early Weimar years the left had considerable potential power, but it became divided between the Social Democrats and the Communists – and was marred by the economic problems of the depression.
- Sympathy of the conservative right. Many of the traditional vested interests, e.g. the army, civil service, were not wholly committed to Weimar and they really sympathised with a more right-wing authoritarian regime. They accepted the Night of the Long Knives.

The Nazi revolution

Key question
Did Germany undergo a political revolution in the years 1933–4?

At the Nuremberg Party Rally of September 1934 Hitler declared triumphantly and with exultant optimism:

> Just as the world cannot live on wars, so people cannot live on revolutions … Revolutions have always been rare in Germany … In the next thousand years there will be no other revolution in Germany.

The word 'revolution' has figured prominently throughout this chapter. Hitler spoke of a 'national revolution', whilst Röhm demanded a 'second revolution'. Likewise, political and historical analysts have written of 'the legal revolution' and the 'revolution from above and below'. How appropriate is such terminology to describe the events of 1933–4? To what extent had Germany undergone a political revolution?

It is important to recognise that the term 'revolution' cannot just be claimed by the political left. It simply means a fundamental change – an overturning of existing conditions. All too often, the term is used for effect and with scant regard for its real meaning. If Germany did undergo a 'political revolution' in the course of 1933–4, the evidence must support the idea that there was a decisive break in the country's course of political development.

Arguments for

At first sight the regime created by the Nazis by the end of 1934 seems to be the very opposite of the Weimar Republic. However, it should be remembered that the Weimar democracy had ceased to function effectively well before Hitler became chancellor. Moreover, the strength of the anti-democratic forces had threatened the young democracy from the very start, so that it was never able to establish strong roots. Yet, even by comparison with pre-1918 Germany, the Nazi regime had wrought fundamental changes:

- the destruction of the **autonomy** of the federal states
- the intolerance shown towards any kind of political opposition
- the reduction of the *Reichstag* to complete impotence.

In all these ways the process of *Gleichschaltung* decisively affected political traditions that had been key features of Imperial Germany 1871–1918. In this sense it is reasonable to view the events of 1933–4 as a 'political revolution', since the Nazis had turned their backs quite categorically on the federal and constitutional values which had even influenced an authoritarian regime like that of Imperial Germany.

Arguments against

However, support for the idea of a Nazi political revolution must also take into account elements of continuity. At the time of Hindenburg's death, major forces within Germany continued to operate independent of the Nazi regime; namely, the army, big business and the civil service. One might even include the Protestant and Catholic Churches, although they did not carry the same degree of political weight.

It was Hitler's willingness to enter into political partnership with these representatives of the old Germany that had encouraged Röhm and the SA to demand a 'second revolution'. The elimination of the power of the SA in the Night of the Long Knives suggests that Hitler's claim for a 'national revolution' had just been an attractive slogan.

In reality this 'revolution' was strictly limited in scope; it involved political compromise and it had not introduced any fundamental social or economic change. In this sense, one could take the view that the early years of the Nazi regime were merely a continuation of the socio-economic forces that had dominated Germany since 1871.

Certainly, such an interpretation would seem to be a fair assessment of the situation up until late 1934. However, the true revolutionary extent of the regime can only be fully assessed by considering the political, social and economic developments that took place in Germany throughout the entire period of the Third Reich. These will be the key points of the next few chapters.

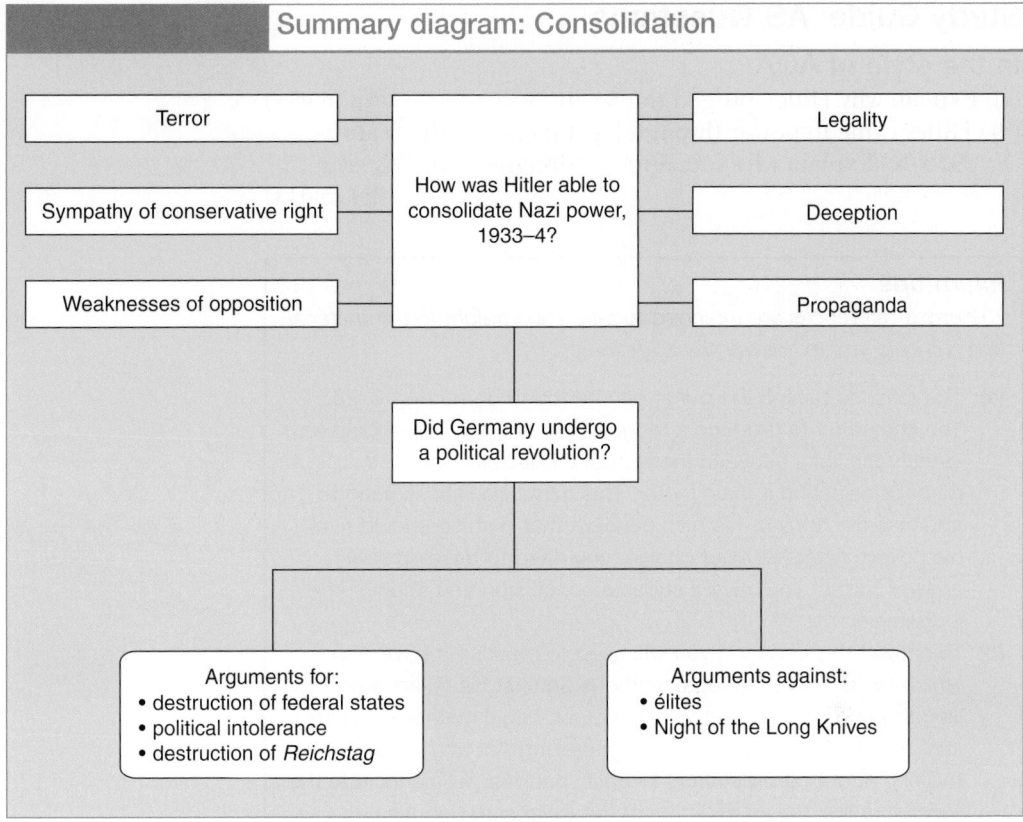

Summary diagram: Consolidation

Terror

Legality

Sympathy of conservative right

How was Hitler able to consolidate Nazi power, 1933–4?

Deception

Weaknesses of opposition

Propaganda

Did Germany undergo a political revolution?

Arguments for:
• destruction of federal states
• political intolerance
• destruction of *Reichstag*

Arguments against:
• élites
• Night of the Long Knives

Study Guide: AS Questions

In the style of AQA

(a) Explain why Hitler purged the SA in 1934.   (12 marks)

(b) 'Hitler came to power through legal means in the years 1933–4.' Explain why you agree or disagree with this view.

(24 marks)

Exam tips

The cross-references are intended to take you straight to the material that will help you to answer the questions.

(a) The reasons behind the purge can be found on pages 16–20. You should try to produce a range of factors, but you should also identify the links between these and, if possible, prioritise, perhaps selecting a main factor. This might be Hitler's need to appease the army or his own concern that nothing should rival his power. Whatever your choice, you need to develop your answer so that you have a suitable conclusion and show some judgement.

(b) To answer this question you will need to balance the ways in which Hitler employed legal methods against his reliance on illegality and fear to establish his power. Legal methods included standing in elections, passing the Enabling Act and passing laws to bring about co-ordination. Illegality and fear would include the *Reichstag* fire, the intimidation of the *Reichstag* deputies, the activities of the SA and that force's own suppression. Decide which way you will argue and then present a balanced case that leads to a well-substantiated conclusion.

2 The Nazi Economy

POINTS TO CONSIDER
The purpose of this chapter is to consider Nazi economic policies and their effects on the performance of the Nazi economy over the years of the Third Reich. The economy went through various stages and to appreciate the significance of these, it is important to consider the following main themes:

- The economic background to the establishment of the Nazi regime
- The economic recovery of Germany 1933–6
- The introduction of the Four-Year Plan 1936–9
- The economy at war 1939–45

Key dates

1933	March	Appointment of Schacht as President of the Reichsbank
1934	July	Appointment of Schacht as Minister of Economics
	September	New Plan introduced
1936	October	Four-Year Plan established under Göring
1937	November	Resignation of Schacht as Minister of Economics
1939	December	War Economy decrees
1941	December	Rationalisation Decree issued by Hitler
1942	February	Appointment of Albert Speer as Minister of Armaments
1944	August	Peak of German munitions production

1 | The Economic Background

Key question
Did the Nazis have an economic policy?

In the years before 1933, Hitler had been careful not to become tied down to the details of an economic policy. Hitler even told his cabinet in February 1933 to 'avoid all detailed statements concerning an economic programme of the government'.

However, Hitler was also politically astute enough to realise that his position depended on bringing Germany out of depression and so during 1932 the Nazi leadership had begun to consider a number of *possible* approaches to the management of the economy.

- First were the socio-economic aspects of the Nazi Party's original aims, as outlined in the anti-capitalist sentiments of the **25-points programme** of the Nazi Party of 1920 such as:
  - profit sharing in large industrial enterprises
  - the extensive development of insurance for old age
  - the **nationalisation** of all businesses.

  Hitler accepted these points in the early years because he recognised their popular appeal but he himself never showed any real commitment to such ideas. As a result, they created important differences within the Party, as a faction within it still demanded these.

- Secondly, attention was given to the emerging idea of deficit financing. This found its most obvious expression in the theories of the British economist J.M. Keynes and the new President of the USA, F.D. Roosevelt, from 1933. By spending money on public works, deficit financing was intended to create jobs, which would then act as an artificial stimulus to demand within the economy. Indeed, work schemes were actually started in Germany in 1932 by Chancellors Papen and Schleicher.

- Finally, there was the idea of the *Wehrwirtschaft* (defence economy), whereby Germany's peacetime economy was geared to the demands of **total war**. This was to avoid a repetition of the problems faced during the First World War when a long, drawn-out conflict on two fronts eventually caused economic collapse. Related to this was the policy of **autarky**. This envisaged a scheme for the creation of a large trading area in Europe under the dominating influence of Germany, which could be developed to rival the other great economic powers. It played upon the idea of German power and harked back to the expansionist views of some First World War nationalists (see page 5).

(see page 5)

Of these three economic approaches, Hitler himself identified his long-term political and military aims most clearly with the defence economy. However, there were important differences within the Party over economic planning so, despite the consideration given to such policies by the Nazi leaders, no coherent plan had emerged by January 1933. Hitler himself had no real understanding of economics and to a large extent the implementation of economic policy was initially left to bankers and civil servants.

From the start then, there was a lack of real direction and elements of all three approaches can be detected in the economic history of the Third Reich. This suggests that economic policy tended to be pragmatic. It evolved out of the demands of the situation rather than being the result of careful planning. As the leading historian A. Schweitzer stated, 'no single unified economic system prevailed throughout the entire period of the Nazi regime'.

Key question
How serious were
Germany's economic
problems in the Great
Depression 1929–33?

Germany's economic condition in 1933

Germany had faced ongoing economic problems since the end of the First World War. However, the sheer scale of the world economic depression that began in 1929 meant that Germany undoubtedly suffered in a particularly savage way.

Trade

Germany depended heavily on its capacity to sell manufactured goods. In the slump of world trade, the demand for German exports declined rapidly and its sale of manufactured goods, e.g. steel, machinery and chemicals, collapsed. As a result, the value of exports dropped from 13.5 billion *Reichsmarks* in 1929 to 4.9 billion in 1933, which amounted to a fall of 62 per cent.

Industry

Despite its post-war problems Germany was an industrial power. However, when it began to lose economic confidence from 1929, demand fell and businesses cut production – or worse, collapsed. An index of industrial production shows that it fell from 100 in 1929 to 58 to 1932. In practical terms, it resulted in 50,000 businesses going bankrupt.

Employment

The most obvious feature of the industrial contraction was mass long-term unemployment. Even before the onset of the Great Depression, workers were being laid off and in 1929 the annual average of registered unemployed was 1.9 million. However, the length and severity of the economic recession greatly increased the number of unemployed with all the associated social problems. In 1932 the figure rose to 5.6 million. If the number of unregistered unemployed is added, the total without work was about eight million in 1932.

Agriculture

The situation in the countryside was no better than in the towns. The agricultural depression deepened, leading to widespread rural poverty. As world demand fell, agricultural prices, according to an index of 100 in 1913, collapsed from 138 in 1927 to 77 in 1932. As a result farmers' wages and incomes fell sharply, which forced some to sell off farms that had been owned for generations.

Finance

As a result of war debts, reparations and inflation, German banking had faced serious financial problems in the years before the Great Depression. The onset of the Great Depression undermined the confidence of the financial sector even further. Foreign investment disappeared and German share prices collapsed. In 1931 five major banks collapsed.

Summary diagram: The economic background

```
                    ┌─────────────────────────┐
                    │ The economic background │
                    └────────────┬────────────┘
            ┌────────────────────┴────────────────────┐
┌───────────────────────────┐        ┌─────────────────────────────────┐
│ Nazi economic ideas:      │        │ Germany's economic condition:   │
│ • Socio-economic aspects  │        │ • Trade                         │
│ • Deficit financing       │        │ • Industry                      │
│ • Defence economy         │        │ • Agriculture                   │
│                           │        │ • Employment                    │
│                           │        │ • Finance                       │
├───────────────────────────┤        ├─────────────────────────────────┤
│ Was there a Nazi economic │        │ How serious was Germany's       │
│         policy?           │        │      economic condition?        │
└───────────────────────────┘        └─────────────────────────────────┘
```

2 | Economic Recovery 1933–6

Schacht's economic strategy

In the early years Nazi economic policy was under the control of
Hjalmar Schacht, President of the *Reichsbank* (1933–9), and
Minister of Economics (1934–7). This reflected the need of the
Nazi leadership to work with the powerful forces of big business.
Schacht was already a respected international financier because of
his leading role in the creation of the new currency in the wake of
the 1923 hyperinflation.

It is certainly true that the economic depression reached its
low-point in the winter of 1932–3 and that afterwards the trade
cycle began to improve. This undoubtedly worked to the political
and economic advantage of the Nazis. Nevertheless, there was no
single, easy 'quick fix' solution.

The heart of economic recovery lay in the major revival of
public investment led, for the most part, by the state itself, which
embarked on a large-scale increase in its own spending in an
effort to stimulate demand and raise national income. So, under
Schacht's guidance and influence, deficit financing was adopted
through a range of economic measures.

Banking and the control of capital

Initially, because the German banking system had been so
fundamentally weakened, the state increasingly assumed greater
responsibility for the control of capital within the economy. It
then proceeded to set interest rates at a lower level and to
reschedule the large-scale debts of local authorities.

Assistance for farming and small businesses

Particular financial benefits were given to groups, such as farmers
and small businesses. This not only stimulated economic growth,
it also rewarded some of the most sympathetic supporters of the

Key question
How did Schacht's
policies stimulate
economic recovery?

Appointment of
Schacht as President
of the *Reichsbank*:
March 1933

Key date

Nazis in the 1930–3 elections. Some of the measures included (see also pages 55–7):

Tariffs
Taxes levied by an
importing nation
on foreign goods
coming in, and paid
by the importers.

Key term

- maintaining **tariffs** on imported produce in order to protect German farmers
- the Reich Food Estate giving subsidies as part of a nationally planned agricultural system (see page 57)
- the Reich Entailed Farm Law reducing debts by tax concessions and lower interest rates in an attempt to offer more security of land ownership to small farmers
- giving allowances to encourage the re-hiring of domestic servants
- allocating grants for house repairs.

State investment – public works

However, of the greatest significance was the direct spending by the state on a range of investment projects. In June 1933 the Law to Reduce Unemployment was renewed and expanded (from a scheme which had originally been started by Papen in 1932) and the RAD (*Reichsarbeitsdienst*, Reich Labour Service) was expanded to employ 19–25 year olds. For a long time most historians assumed that rearmament was the main focus of investment, but the figures for public expenditure show that this was initially spread among rearmament, construction and transportation. So the investment in the first three years was directed towards work creation schemes such as:

- reforestation
- land reclamation
- motorisation – the policy of developing the vehicle industry and the building of improved roads, e.g. the autobahns (motorways)
- building – especially the expansion of the housing sector and public buildings.

The cumulative effect of these policies was to triple public investment between 1933 and 1936 and to increase government expenditure by nearly 70 per cent over the same period. By early 1936 the economic recovery was well advanced and then emphasis began to turn even more towards rearmament.

Table 2.1: Public investment and expenditure by billion *Reichsmarks* (RM)

	1928	1932	1933	1934	1935	1936
Total public investment	6.6	2.2	2.5	4.6	6.4	8.1
Total government expenditure	11.7	8.6	9.4	12.8	13.9	15.8

Table 2.2: Public expenditure by category by billion *Reichsmarks* (RM)

	1928	1932	1933	1934	1935	1936
Construction	2.7	0.9	1.7	3.5	4.9	5.4
Rearmament	0.7	0.7	1.8	3.0	5.4	10.2
Transportation	2.6	0.8	1.3	1.8	2.1	2.4

Table 2.3: Unemployment and production in Germany 1928–36

	1928	1929	1930	1931	1932	1933	1934	1935	1936
Unemployment (millions)	1.4	1.8	3.1	4.5	5.6	4.8	2.7	2.2	1.6
Industrial production (1928 = 100)	100	100	87	70	58	66	83	96	107

As a result of these strategies, there was a dramatic growth in jobs. From the registered peak of 5.6 million unemployed in 1932, the official figure of 1936 showed that it had declined to 1.6 million. For those many Germans who had been desperately out of work, it seemed as if the Nazi economic policy was to be welcomed. Even in other democratic countries scarred by mass unemployment, observers abroad admired Germany's achievement of job creation.

Yet, even in 1936, the government public deficit certainly did not run out of control, since Schacht maintained taxes at a relatively high level and encouraged private savings in state savings banks. Of course, it must be remembered that all this took place as the world economy began to recover and Schacht was aided by the natural upturn in the business cycle after its low-point in winter 1932. Nevertheless, it is difficult to believe that such a marked turnaround in investment and employment could have been achieved without Nazi economic policy.

The balance of payments problem

Germany made an impressive economic recovery between 1933 and 1936, but two underlying worries remained:

- the fear that a rapid increase in demand would rekindle inflation
- the fear that a rapid increase in demand would lead to the emergence of a **balance of trade** deficit.

In fact, the problem of inflation never actually materialised – partly because there was a lack of demand in the economy, but also because the regime established strict controls over prices and wages. This had been helped by the abolition of the trade unions in May 1933 (see page 14). On the other hand, what was to be a recurring balance of payments problem emerged for the first time in the summer of 1934. This was a consequence of Germany's importing more raw materials while failing to increase its exports. Its gold and foreign currency reserves were also low.

Key question
Why was Germany's balance of trade problem so significant?

Key term

Balance of trade
Difference in value between exports and imports. If the value of the imports is above that of the exports, the balance of the payments has a deficit that is often said to be 'in the red'.

Unemployed men (with shovels) enrol for work on one of the autobahns in September 1933.

Adolf Hitler opens the first stretch of the Autobahn between Frankfurt am Main and Darmstadt on 19 May 1935. The first autobahn was not initiated by the Nazis, but was prompted by the mayor of Cologne, Adenauer; the stretch from Cologne to Bonn was opened in 1932. Nevertheless, 3000 km of motorway roads were developed before the onset of the war. They served as an economic stimulus, but were also used politically as a propagandist tool. Their military value has been doubted.

The balance of payments problem was not merely an economic issue, for it carried with it large-scale political implications. If Germany was so short of foreign currency, which sector of the economy was to have priority in spending the money? The early Economics Minister, Schmitt, wanted to try to reduce unemployment further by manufacturing more consumer goods for public consumption, e.g. textiles. However, powerful voices in the armed forces and big business were already demanding more resources for major programmes, e.g. rearmament.

Hitler could not ignore such pressure – especially as this economic problem coincided with the political dilemma over the SA. Consequently, Schmitt's policy was rejected and he was removed, thereby allowing Schacht to combine the offices of Minister of Economics and President of the Reichsbank.

Appointment of Schacht as Minister of Economics: July 1934

New Plan introduced: September 1934

Key dates

Schacht's 'New Plan'

By the law of 3 July, Schacht was given dictatorial powers over the economy, which he then used to introduce the 'New Plan' of September 1934. This provided for a comprehensive control by the government of all aspects of trade, tariffs, capital and currency exchange in an attempt to prevent excessive imports. From that time the government decided which imports were to be allowed or disapproved. For example, imports of raw cotton and wool were substantially cut, whereas metals were permitted in order to satisfy the demands of heavy industry.

Key question
How did Schacht try to resolve the balance of payments problem?

The economic priorities were set by a series of measures:

- *Bilateral trade treaties*
  Schacht tried to promote trade and save foreign exchange by signing bilateral trade treaties, especially with the countries of south-east Europe, e.g. Romania and Yugoslavia. These often took the form of straightforward barter agreements (thus avoiding the necessity of formal currency exchange). In this way Germany began to exert a powerful economic influence over the Balkans long before it obtained military and political control.

- *The* Reichsmark *currency*
  Germany agreed to purchase raw materials from all countries it traded with on the condition that *Reichsmarks* could only be used to buy back German goods (at one time it is estimated that the German *Reichsmark* had 237 different values depending on the country and the circumstances).

- *Mefo bills*
  Mefo were special government money bills (like a credit note) designed by Schacht. They were issued by the *Reichsbank* and guaranteed by the government as payment for goods, and were then held for up to five years earning four per cent interest per annum. The main purpose of Mefo bills was that they successfully disguised government spending.

Schacht was never a member of the Nazi Party, but he was drawn into the Nazi movement and the regime. His proven economic

Profile: Hjalmar Schacht 1877–1970

1877		– Born in North Schleswig, Germany
1899		– Graduated in political economy
1916		– Appointed as Director of the National Bank
1923	November	– Appointed as Reich currency commissioner to set up the new currency, *Rentenmark*
	December	– Appointed President of the *Reichsbank*
1930	March	– Resigned in protest at the Young Plan
1931		– Became increasingly sympathetic to Nazism. Agreed to raise money for the Nazi Party through his contacts in banking and industry, e.g. Gustav and Alfred Krupp
1932	November	– Played a leading role in organising the letter from the petition of German industrialists who pressed Hindenburg to support Hitler's appointment
1933	March	– Re-appointed as President of the *Reichsbank*
1934	July	– Appointed as Minister of Economics
	September	– Drew up and oversaw the New Plan
1937	November	– Resigned as Minister of Economics
1939	January	– Resigned as President of the *Reichsbank* in protest at Nazi economic policy
1939–43		– Remained in the government as Minister without Portfolio, but became increasingly at odds with the Nazi regime
1944–5		– In contact with the anti-Nazi resistance and arrested after the 20 July Bomb Plot. Held in Ravensbrück concentration camp until the end of war
1945–6		– Charged at the Nuremberg War Crimes Trials, but acquitted
1950–63		– Private financial consultant to the government of many countries
1970	June	– Died in Munich

Schacht was undoubtedly an economic genius. He built his reputation on the way he stabilised the German economy by the creation of the new currency, the *Rentenmark*, in 1923. He served as President of the *Reichsbank* to all the Weimar governments 1923–30, but he was a strong nationalist and eventually resigned over the Young Plan.

Schacht was increasingly taken in by Hitler's political programme. From 1930, his influence went through three clear stages.

- In 1930–3 he played an essential role in encouraging big business to finance the rise of the Nazis and he backed Hitler's appointment as chancellor.
- In the years 1933–6 Schacht was in effect economic dictator of Germany and it was he who shaped Germany's economic recovery by deficit financing and the New Plan of 1934.
- However, he fundamentally disagreed with the emphasis on rearmament in the Four-Year Plan and after 1936 his influence was gradually eclipsed.

skills earned him respect both in and outside the Party and it was he who laid the foundations for economic recovery. By mid-1936:

- unemployment had fallen to 1.5 million
- industrial production had increased by 60 per cent since 1933
- **GNP** had grown over the same period by 40 per cent.

However, such successes disguised fundamental structural weaknesses that came to a head in the second half of 1936 over the future direction of the German economy.

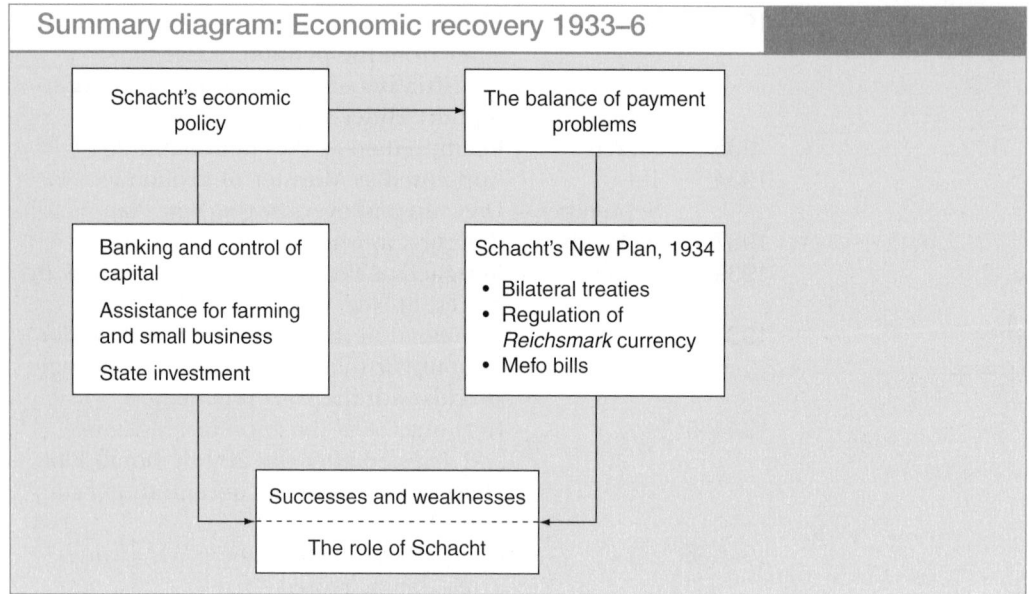

Summary diagram: Economic recovery 1933–6

- Schacht's economic policy → The balance of payment problems
- Banking and control of capital

  Assistance for farming and small business

  State investment
- Schacht's New Plan, 1934
  - Bilateral treaties
  - Regulation of *Reichsmark* currency
  - Mefo bills
- Successes and weaknesses

  The role of Schacht

3 | Implementation of the Four-Year Plan 1936

In many respects, as Schacht himself was only too aware, he had merely hidden the balance of payments problem by a series of clever financial tricks. And, despite his apparent sympathy for deficit financing, Schacht believed that a combination of a budget deficit and a balance of payments deficit could not be maintained indefinitely. In early 1936 it became clear to him that, as the demands for rearmament and consumption of goods increased, the German balance of payments would go deeply into the red. He therefore suggested a reduction in arms expenditure in order to increase the production of industrial goods that at least could be exported so as to earn foreign exchange. Such a solution had its supporters, especially among industries geared to exporting, e.g. electrics, tools. However, it was unacceptable to the armed forces and to the Nazi leadership. By the mid-1930s, then, this debate was popularly summed up by the question: should the economy concentrate on producing '**Guns or Butter?**'

Guns or butter? A cartoon published by the German magazine *Simplicissimus* in 1933. Critics of the new Nazi regime felt that it was more interested in rearmament than encouraging trade and peace.

The aims and objectives of the Plan

Most significantly, Hitler himself expressed his position in a secret memorandum in August 1936. This has been seen as one of the most important documents of Nazi history, as it provides a clear insight into Hitler's war aims and the development of the Nazi economy. He concluded by writing:

> There has been time enough in four years to find out what we cannot do. Now we have to carry out what we can do. I thus set the following tasks.
>
> (i) The German armed forces must be operational within four years
> (ii) The German economy must be fit for war within four years.

The politico-economic crisis of 1936 was resolved by the introduction of the Four-Year Plan under the control of Hermann Göring who, in October of that year, was appointed 'Plenipotentiary of the Four-Year Plan'. Its aims were clearly to expand rearmament and autarky to make Germany as self-sufficient as possible in food and industrial production. In order to achieve this, the Plan highlighted a number of objectives:

Key date

Four-Year Plan established under Göring: October 1936

- To regulate imports and exports, so as to prioritise strategic sectors, e.g. chemicals and metals at the expense of agricultural imports.
- To control the key sectors of the labour force, so as to prevent price inflation, e.g. the creation of a Reich Price Commissioner and increased work direction by DAF (see pages 53–5).
- To increase the production of raw materials, so as to reduce the financial cost of importing vital goods, e.g. steel, iron and aluminium.
- To develop *ersatz* (substitute) products, e.g. oil (from coal), artificial rubber (buna).
- To increase agricultural production, so as to avoid imported foodstuffs, e.g. grants for fertilisers and machinery.

The effects of the Four-Year Plan

The decision to implement the Four-Year Plan marked an important turning point in the Nazi regime. Nazi control over the German economy became much tighter, as Schacht described in his own book written in 1949:

Key question
Why was the creation of the Four-Year Plan so significant?

> … On December 17th 1936, Göring informed a meeting of big industrialists that it was no longer a question of producing economically, but simply of producing. And as far as getting hold of foreign exchange was concerned it was quite immaterial whether the provisions of the law were complied with or not … Göring's policy of recklessly exploiting Germany's economic substance necessarily brought me into more and more acute conflict with him, and for his part he exploited his powers, with Hitler and the Party behind him, to counter my activity as Minister of Economics to an ever-increasing extent.

Profile: Hermann Göring 1893–1946

1893		– Born in Bavaria, the son of the governor of German Southwest Africa
1914–18		– Served in the First World War and became a pilot officer of the Richthofen Squadron
1922		– Dropped out of university and joined the Party as an SA commander
1923	November	– Took part in the Munich *putsch* and was seriously injured
1928	May	– Elected to the *Reichstag*
1933	January	– Appointed to the cabinet of Hitler's government as Minister without Portfolio
	February	– Exploited the *Reichstag* fire to discredit the Communists
	March	– Organised the terror to impose the dictatorship and to uphold co-ordination
1934	June	– Helped to organise the Night of the Long Knives
1935		– Commander-in-Chief of the new *Luftwaffe* (airforce)
1936	October	– Appointed Plenipotentiary of the Four-Year Plan by Hitler
1939		– Named as Hitler's successor, and at the height of his power and influence
1940–1		– After the failures of the *Luftwaffe* to win the Battle of Britain, his influence declined
1941–5		– He retained most of his offices, but he was increasingly isolated within the Nazi leadership
1946		– Committed suicide two hours before he was due to be executed at the Nuremberg trials

Göring played a crucial role in the rise of Nazism and during the consolidation of its power 1933–40. He came from a well-to-do family and with this status and the contacts provided by his aristocratic first wife, he was able to give Nazism a more respectable image in high society.

Göring's approach was uncompromising and brutal. During 1933–4 he organised the infiltration of the German police with the SA and SS – and willingly used violence and murder in the terror to secure Nazi power. He was deeply involved in the *Reichstag* fire (see page 10) and the Night of the Long Knives (see page 19).

At first, he was popular because of his witty and charming conversation, but he became increasingly resented for his ambition and greed – he was given a whole host of titles and posts. From 1936 he became in effect economic dictator, though after the failures of the *Luftwaffe* to win the Battle of Britain, his influence sharply declined.

Schacht had no real respect for Göring, who had no economic expertise and deliberately and increasingly ignored Schacht's advice. Schacht recognised that his influence was on the wane and eventually in November 1937 he resigned. He was replaced by the weak Walther Funk, although from this time Göring himself became the real economic dictator.

The success of the Plan was mixed over the years (see Table 2.4). On the one hand, production of a number of key materials, such as aluminium and explosives, had expanded greatly, or at least at a reasonable rate. On the other hand, it fell a long way short of the targets in the essential commodities of rubber and oil, while arms production never reached the levels desired by the armed forces and Hitler. All in all, the Four-Year Plan had succeeded in the sense that Germany's reliance on imports had not increased. However, this still meant that when war did break out Germany was dependent on foreign supplies for one-third of its raw materials.

Resignation of Schacht as Minister of Economics: November 1937

Key date

Table 2.4: The Four-Year Plan; launched in 1936

Commodity (in thousands of tons)	Four-Year Plan target	Actual output 1936	Actual output 1938	Actual output 1942
Oil	13,830	1,790	2,340	6,260
Aluminium	273	98	166	260
Rubber (buna)	120	0.7	5	96
Explosives	223	18	45	300
Steel	24,000	19,216	22,656	20,480
Hard coal	213,000	158,400	186,186	166,059

Key debate

From the very start, the Nazi economy was the focus of historical controversy because it was closely linked with the Nazi dictatorship and the onset of war from 1939. Among historians, at the heart of the economic analysis there lies one important question:

Did Germany have a war economy in peacetime?

Klein

The research of B.H. Klein in the 1950s led him to argue that Germany's economic mobilisation was actually limited in the early years of the war. He claimed that Nazi economic policy was deliberately connected with the military strategy of **Blitzkrieg**. In his view, Hitler and the armed forces recognised Germany's precarious position over the production of raw materials, and consequently developed the strategy of short wars. This would avoid the economic strain of 'total war' and also it had the political advantage of not reducing the production of consumer goods excessively. In that way, Germany seemed to have both 'Guns and Butter'. Klein argued that pre-1939 civilian consumption remained comfortable and not limited, and that

Blitzkrieg
Literally 'lightning war'. It was the name given to the military strategy developed to avoid static war. It was based on the use of dive-bombers, paratroopers and motorised infantry.

Key term

'the scale of Germany's economic mobilisation for war was quite modest'. Indeed, he claimed, it was not until after the defeat at Stalingrad in the winter of 1942–3 (see page 177) that a 'total war economy' began in earnest.

Milward

Klein's basic thesis proved to be very influential, although it was somewhat modified in the mid-1960s by A. Milward. He accepted that *Blitzkrieg* was meant to avoid total war, but he also pointed out that 'no nation had ever previously spent so vast a sum on preparations for war'. Moreover, he suggested that it was the German failure to take Moscow at the end of 1941 (see page 176) that was the real economic turning point. By spring 1942 the German economic machine was ready for the **war of attrition** (see pages 176–8).

Mason

In contrast, the **Marxist historian** Tim Mason from the 1970s has argued that the Nazi economy was in fact under increasing strain from 1937. He believes that Hitler's war aims were clearly driving the pace of rearmament to such an extent that the economy was put under tremendous pressures and it was in danger of expanding too quickly and overheating. He particularly points out economic indicators that:

- there were growing shortages, in such areas as raw materials, food and consumer goods
- there were labour shortages, especially among skilled workers, which tended to increase wages
- the balance of trade was going further into the red and becoming increasingly difficult to finance
- the government expenditure and deficit were expanding and becoming increasingly difficult to finance.

Most significantly, Mason argues that all these pressures were contributing to significant social discontent amongst the working class. He goes so far as to suggest that by 1939 the situation was so serious that Hitler embarked on the war as the only way out of Germany's domestic economic dilemma.

Overy

However, Richard Overy has rejected the traditional opinions. This is because Overy, although still an economic historian, has come to be influenced by the work of diplomatic historians, who see Hitler stumbling unintentionally into a major European war in September 1939. Overy has argued forcefully that Hitler had always envisaged a great conflict for world power and that this necessitated the transformation of the economy to the demands of total war. However, his preparations for this kind of war were not intended to be finished until 1943. The war with Poland in 1939 was meant to be a local war that Hitler wrongly believed would not involve Britain and France. The premature outbreak of continental conflict inevitably found the German economy only partially mobilised.

Overy, therefore, believes that the underlying principles of Nazi economic policy were abundantly clear from 1936. The German economy had been unashamedly directed towards war preparation, so that two-thirds of all German investment went into war-related projects:

- Full employment was achieved, but over a quarter of the workforce was involved in rearmament.
- Levels of government expenditure more than doubled in the same period with the result that the government debt increased accordingly.
- In the last full year of peace 17 per cent of Germany's GNP went on military expenditure (compared to eight per cent in Britain and one per cent in the USA).

According to such a view then, the German economy by 1939 was already an economy dominated by the preparations for war, though this did not yet amount to the full-scale mobilisation required of total war, since total war was not envisaged until about 1943. In a thought-provoking conclusion Overy suggested:

> ... If war had been postponed until 1943–5 as Hitler had hoped, then Germany would have been much better prepared, and would also have had rockets, jet aircraft, inter-continental bombers, perhaps even atomic weapons. Though Britain and France did not know it, declaring war in 1939 prevented Germany from becoming the super-power Hitler wanted. The drive for total war became instead *Blitzkrieg* by default.

Germany therefore found itself at war in September 1939 really because of diplomatic miscalculation. The German economy in 1939 was still a long way short of being fully mobilised, but it was certainly on more of a war footing than Britain or France. The question now was whether Germany could complete the economic mobilisation and thereby bring about military victory.

Some key books in the debate

B.H. Klein, *Germany's Economic Preparations for War* (Harvard, 1959).

T. W. Mason, *Social Policy in the Third Reich* (Oxford, 1992).

A.S. Milward, *The German Economy at War* (London, 1965).

R.J. Overy, *The Nazi Economic Recovery*, 1932–38, 2nd ed. (Cambridge, 1996).

R.J. Overy, 'Did Hitler Want Total War?' in *History Sixth*, No. 4, 1989, p. 30.

R.J. Overy, *Göring: The Iron Man* (London, 1984).

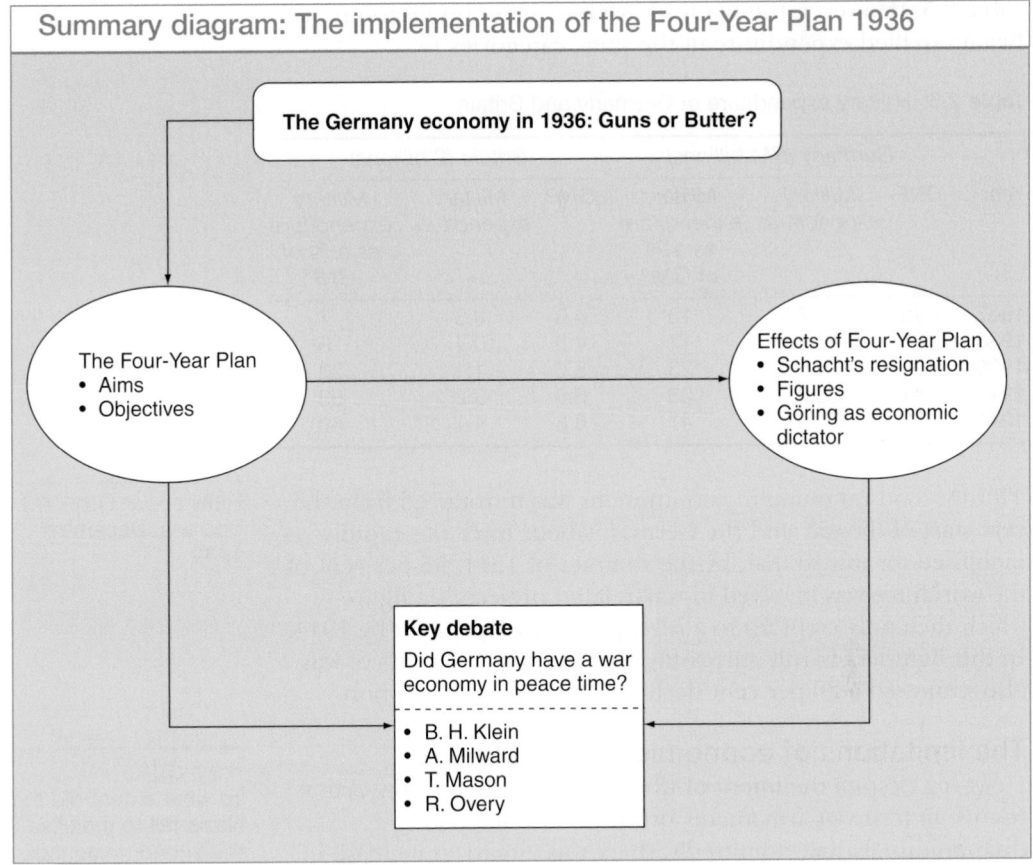

Summary diagram: The implementation of the Four-Year Plan 1936

The Germany economy in 1936: Guns or Butter?

The Four-Year Plan
• Aims
• Objectives

Effects of Four-Year Plan
• Schacht's resignation
• Figures
• Göring as economic dictator

Key debate
Did Germany have a war economy in peace time?
- -
• B. H. Klein
• A. Milward
• T. Mason
• R. Overy

4 | The Nazi Economy at War 1939–45

The string of military successes achieved by the German armed forces with their use of *Blitzkrieg* strategy up to December 1941 won Hitler and the regime valuable popular support. Moreover, it gave the impression of an economy that had not been over-strained by the demands of war. This has been used to substantiate the claims of the historians Klein and Milward that there was only a partial economic mobilisation until 1942 or 1943. Such a view, however attractive, does not actually square with either Nazi intentions or the economic statistics.

The expansion of the Nazi economy

First, Hitler himself was determined to avoid the problems faced by Germany in the First World War and to fight the coming war with an economy thoroughly prepared for a major and perhaps extended conflict. To this end, a series of war economy decrees was issued by Hitler in December 1939 outlining vast programmes for every possible aspect of war production, e.g. submarines and aircraft. These plans suggest that the Nazis went well beyond the demands of *Blitzkrieg* and a limited war.

Secondly, in real and percentage terms, German military expenditure doubled between 1939 and 1941, as shown by

Key question
How did the German economy expand?

Table 2.5. (However, the figures have important implications, as Britain trebled expenditure in the same categories.)

Table 2.5: Military expenditure of Germany and Britain

Year	Germany (RM billions)			Britain (£ billions)		
	GNP	Military expenditure	Military expenditure as a % of GNP	GNP	Military expenditure	Military expenditure as a % of GNP
1937	93	11.7	13	4.6	0.3	7
1938	105	17.2	17	4.8	0.4	8
1939	130	30.0	23	5.0	1.1	22
1940	141	53.0	38	6.0	3.2	53
1941	152	71.0	47	6.8	4.1	60

Thirdly, food rationing in certain items was introduced from the very start of the war and the German labour force was rapidly mobilised for war so that, by the summer of 1941, 55 per cent of the workforce was involved in war-related projects – a figure which then only crept up to a high-point of 61 per cent by 1944. In this light it is hardly surprising that the first two years of war also witnessed a 20 per cent decline in civilian consumption.

Key date

Hitler's War Economy decrees: December 1939

The limitations of economic mobilisation

However, despite the intent of wholesale mobilisation the actual results, in terms of armaments production, remained disappointingly low. Admittedly, there was a marked increase in the number of submarines, but amazingly, Germany's airforce had only increased from 8290 aircraft in 1939 to 10,780 in 1941 while in Britain over the same period the number of aircraft had trebled to 20,100. Likewise, Hitler was astonished to learn when drawing up plans for the invasion of the USSR that the Germans' armoured strength totalled only 3500 tanks, which was just 800 more than for the invasion of the West.

Key question

To what extent did the Nazis fail to mobilise the economy during the war?

It seems that despite the Nazi image of German order and purposefulness, the actual mobilisation of the German economy was marred by inefficiency and poor co-ordination. The pressures resulting from the premature outbreak of war created problems, since many of the major projects were not due to be ready until 1942–3. So, at first, there was undoubtedly confusion between the short-term needs and long-term plans of the Nazi leadership.

Nevertheless, this should not have been an impossible barrier if only a clear and authoritative central control had been established over the economy. Instead, a host of different agencies all continued to function in their own way and often in a fashion which put them at odds with each other. So, although there was a Ministry of Armaments, it existed alongside three other interested governmental ministries, those of Economics, Finance and Labour. In addition, there was political infighting between the leading Nazi figures – for example, the *Gauleiters* tried to control their local areas at the expense of the plans of the state and the Party (see pages 114–17) – and also considerable financial corruption.

There were a number of groups responsible for armaments: the Office of the Four-Year Plan, the SS bodies and the different branches of the armed forces, *Wehrmacht*, *Luftwaffe* and navy. The armed forces, in particular, were determined to have their way over the development of munitions with the very best specifications possible and as a result the drive for quality was pursued at the expense of quantity. The consequence of all this was that after two years of war, and with the armed forces advancing into the USSR, Germany's economic mobilisation for total war had not achieved the expected levels of armaments production.

Total war 1942–5

By the end of 1941, Germany was at war with Britain, the USSR and the USA and yet its armaments production remained inferior to that of Britain. Preparations for a new approach had begun in the autumn of 1941 and Hitler himself had issued a '**Rationalisation Decree**' in December of that year.

However, it was the appointment of Albert Speer as Minister of Armaments in February 1942 that marked the real turning point. Speer had previously been the *Führer*'s personal architect and he enjoyed excellent relations with Hitler. He now used the *Führer*'s authority to cut through the mass of interests and to implement his programme of 'industrial self-responsibility' to provide mass production. The controls and constraints previously placed upon business, in order to fit in with Nazi wishes, were relaxed. In their place a Central Planning Board was established in April 1942, which was in turn supported by a number of committees, each representing one vital sector of the economy. This gave the industrialists a considerable degree of freedom, while ensuring that Speer as the director of Central Planning was able to maintain overall control of the war economy. Speer also encouraged industrialists and engineers to join his ministerial team. At the same time, wherever possible, he excluded military personnel from the production process.

Speer was what would now be called a 'technocrat'. He simply co-ordinated and rationalised the process of war production and more effectively exploited the potential of Germany's resources and labour force. Speer was able to exert influence because of his friendship with Hitler and he used his personal skills to charm or blackmail other authorities. In his way, he took a whole range of other personal initiatives to improve production, such as:

- employing more women in the arms factories
- making effective use of concentration camp prisoners as workers
- preventing skilled workers being lost to military conscription.

The successes and limitations of Speer's economic rationalisation

In a famous speech in February 1943, after the German army surrender at Stalingrad, Joseph Goebbels invited the crowd to support 'total war'. However, the transformation of the Nazi economy really pre-dated Goebbels's propagandist appeal to 'total war' and was down to the work of Speer. As a result of Speer's first six months in power:

- ammunition production increased by 97 per cent
- tank production rose by 25 per cent
- total arms production increased by 59 per cent.

By the second half of 1944, when German war production peaked, it can be noted that there had been more than a three-fold increase since early 1942.

Table 2.6: Number of German, British, US and Soviet tanks produced 1940–5

	Germany	Britain	USA	USSR
1940	1,600	1,400	300	2,800
1941	3,800	4,800	4,100	6,400
1942	6,300	8,600	25,000	24,700
1943	12,100	7,500	29,500	24,000
1944	19,000	4,600	17,600	29,000
1945	3,900	N/A	12,000	15,400

Table 2.7: Number of German, British, US and Soviet aircraft produced 1940–5

	Germany	Britain	USA	USSR
1940	10,200	15,000	6,100	7,000
1941	11,000	20,100	19,400	12,500
1942	14,200	23,600	47,800	26,000
1943	25,200	26,200	85,900	37,000
1944	39,600	26,500	96,300	40,000
1945	N/A	12,100	46,000	35,000

Despite Speer's economic successes, Germany probably had the capacity to produce even more and could have achieved a level of output close to that of the USSR or the USA. He was not always able to counter the power of the Party *Gauleiters* at a local level and the SS remained a law unto themselves, especially in the conquered lands. Indeed, although the occupied territories of the Third Reich were well and truly plundered, they were not exploited with real economic efficiency. Above all, though, from 1943 Speer could not reverse the detrimental effects of Anglo-American bombing.

After the war 'blanket bombing' by the Allies was condemned by some on moral grounds and its effectiveness denied – indeed, critics pointed to Speer's production figures as proof that the strategy had failed to break the German war economy. However, it is probably more accurate to say that the effects of bombing prevented Germany from increasing its levels of arms production even further. The results of Allied bombing caused industrial destruction and breakdown in communications. Also, Germany was forced to divert available resources towards the construction of anti-aircraft installations and underground industrial sites. Because of this Germany was unable to achieve a total war economy. As it was, German arms production peaked in August 1944 at a level well below its full potential.

In the end, the Nazi economy had proved incapable of rising to the demands of total war and the cost of that failure was all too clearly to be seen in the ruins and economic collapse of 1945.

Key date

Peak of German munitions production: August 1944

Profile: Albert Speer 1905–81

1905		– Born in Mannheim
1924–8		– Trained as an architect at Karlsruhe, Munich and Berlin
1931	January	– Joined the Nazi Party
1934		– Became Hitler's personal architect
1942		– Minister of Armaments
1946	October	– Sentenced to 20 years as a result of the Nuremberg trials
1966		– Released from Spandau prison
1969		– Publication of his books, *Inside the Third Reich* and *Spandau: The Secret Diaries*
1981		– Died in London while on a visit

Speer remains an interesting, and significant figure on several counts:

- He was a talented and able architect who was commissioned for the design of the German pavilion at the Paris Exhibition in 1937, the Reich Chancellery in Berlin and the Party Palace in Nuremberg. His close friendship with Hitler and their common interest in architecture allowed him to exert increasing political influence.
- He quickly proved himself a skilful manager of the war economy, which resulted in a fundamental increase in armaments production, 1942–4.
- Despite his friendship with Hitler he clashed with leading Nazis, particularly Himmler.
- He always claimed after the war that he opposed forced labour in the occupied countries. Yet his opponents maintained that this policy had more to do with efficiency than morality, and even claimed that he was aware of the treatment of the Jews.

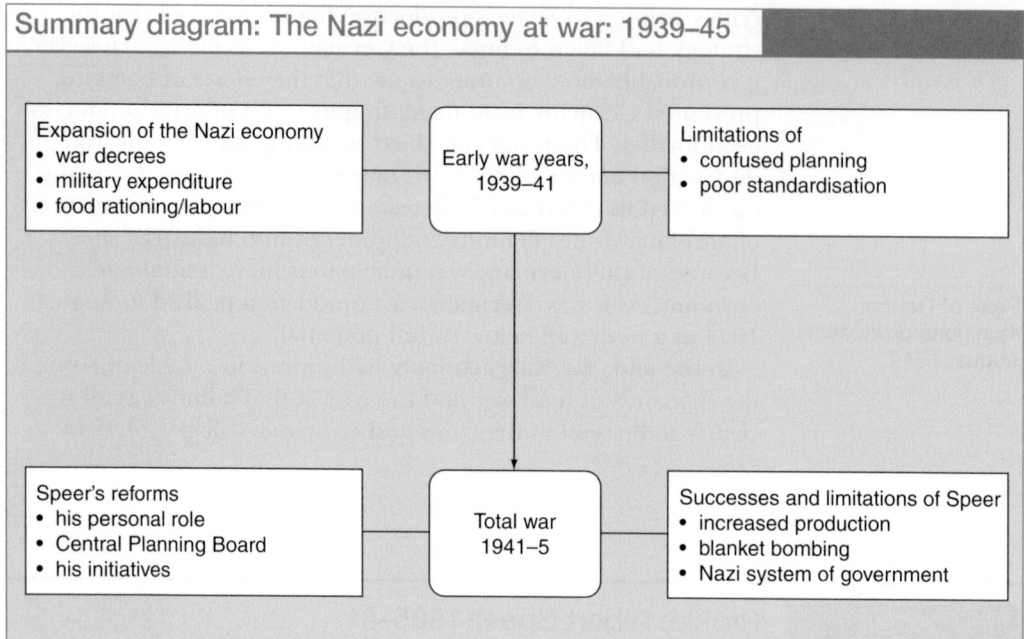

Summary diagram: The Nazi economy at war: 1939–45

Expansion of the Nazi economy
- war decrees
- military expenditure
- food rationing/labour

Early war years, 1939–41

Limitations of
- confused planning
- poor standardisation

Speer's reforms
- his personal role
- Central Planning Board
- his initiatives

Total war 1941–5

Successes and limitations of Speer
- increased production
- blanket bombing
- Nazi system of government

Study Guide: AS Questions

In the style of AQA

(a) Explain why Germany faced major economic problems in 1933. (12 marks)

(b) 'Göring and Speer were both equally important to the development of the Nazi economy.' Explain why you agree or disagree with this view. (24 marks)

Exam tips

The cross-references are intended to take you straight to the material that will help you to answer the questions.

(a) You will need to consider a range of factors and should look again at page 29 to remind yourself of some of these. Try to distinguish between long-term factors, stemming from the dislocation of Germany's economy in the inter-war years and short-term ones linked to the Great Depression and the subsequent trade depression. Remember you are looking for reasons and you will need to show how these reasons link together and whether any one or two are more important than the others and why.

(b) Avoid the temptation of being drawn into just writing a couple of potted biographies of Göring and Speer. You must show a good understanding of the detail of their roles, but you must also work towards making an assessment of their significance in the development of the Nazi economy.

It is important that you compare the two ministers and provide some comparative comment on their contributions. One good way is to choose a number of relevant key questions for each character. In that way, you are more likely to assess and compare their significance throughout the essay:

- What were the main economic problems faced by each man at the start of his period of power and influence (pages 38 and 44–5)?
- What were their main policies (pages 38 and 45–6)?
- What were the benefits and losses of their main policies, both short and long term (pages 38–9, 46–8, 78 and 134–5)?
- What problems emerged over time in each character's specific case (pages 39 and 47)?
- Why did their positions in office come to an end (pages 39, 40 and 134–5)?

3 Nazi Society

POINTS TO CONSIDER

The purpose of this chapter is to consider Nazi social aims and policies and their effects on the Third Reich. However, this chapter will introduce the concept of *Volksgemeinschaft*, which is essential to an understanding of German society in the period. It will examine the following themes of German social history and should help you to answer the historical question of whether *Volksgemeinschaft* fundamentally changed German society during the Third Reich:

- Nazi ideology and the *Volksgemeinschaft*
- Social groups
- Youth and education
- Religion
- Women and the family
- Culture
- Outsiders
- The Nazi social revolution

The major issue of anti-Semitism will be covered in Chapter 4, The Racial State.

Key dates

1933	May	The burning of the books
		Creation of German Labour Front
	July	Concordat signed with the Papacy
1934		Reich Ministry of Education created: control of education was taken away from *Länder*
		Creation of the Confessional Church
1937	March	Papal encyclical, *Mit Brennender Sorge*, issued

1 | Nazi Ideology and the *Volksgemeinschaft*

When Nazi ideology developed in the 1920s it was based on three key elements: race, nationalism and authoritarianism.

Race

Race was at the centre of Nazi thinking. Consequently, it was only those viewed as 'racially pure' who could be members of the *Volk*. Nazism advocated that humanity consisted of a hierarchy of races and that life was no more than 'the survival of the fittest'. It taught that **Social Darwinism** necessitated a struggle between races, just as animals fought for food and territory in the wild. Furthermore, Nazism considered it vital to maintain racial purity, so that the blood of the weak could not undermine the strong. This was a crude philosophy, which appears even more simplistic when the Nazi analysis of the races is considered. The *Herrenvolk* (master-race) was the **Aryan** race and was exemplified by the Germans. It was the task of the Aryan to remain pure and to dominate the inferior races. At the lower end of this racial pyramid Nazism placed Negroes, Slavs, Gypsies and, the particular focus of Hitler's hatred, Jews.

Nationalism

Nazi racism came out as an aggressive form of German nationalism. It aimed to create an empire (*Reich*) that would include all those members of the German *Volk* who lived beyond the frontiers of Germany: the Austrian Germans; the Germans in Poland and the Sudetenland; the German communities along the Baltic coast.

Yet, Nazi nationalists' aims did not end there. They dreamed of a 'Greater Germany', a superpower, based on territorial expansion on a grand scale. This was the basis of Hitler's demand for *Lebensraum* for Germany. Only by the conquest of Poland, Ukraine and Russia could Germany obtain the raw materials, cheap labour and food supplies so necessary for continental supremacy.

Authoritarianism

Nazism not only excluded racial groups, like Jews and Gypsies, but also those who were politically unacceptable, e.g. Communists. Nazism therefore rejected alternative concepts such as democracy and socialism. As a result, the Nazi state was open only to those who were prepared to accept the constraints of Nazi authoritarianism and to surrender their individual freedoms. In place of democracy and its liberal values, Hitler wanted an all-embracing one-party state that would be run on the *Führerprinzip*. Thus, the masses in society were expected to fulfil their role and to be submissive for the common good.

Key terms

Volk
Often translated as 'people', although it tends to suggest a nation with the same ethnic and cultural identities and a collective sense of belonging.

Social Darwinism
A philosophy that portrayed the world as a 'struggle' between people, races and nations. Influenced by Darwin's theories, it viewed life as 'the survival of the fittest'. Distorted into a political and social philosophy by racist thinkers.

Aryan
Refers broadly to all the peoples of the Indo-European family. Defined by the Nazis as the non-Jewish people of northern Europe.

Lebensraum
'Living space'. Hitler's aim to create an empire and to make Germany into a great power by establishing German supremacy over the eastern lands in Europe, e.g. Poland and Russia.

Führerprinzip
The leadership principle. Hitler upheld the idea of a one-party state, controlled by an all-powerful leader.

The Nazi *Volksgemeinschaft*

Hitler always claimed that National Socialism was more than just a political ideology. It was a movement that aimed to transform German society. It rejected the values of socialism, liberalism and Christianity and in their place it upheld the concept of *Volksgemeinschaft*.

Volksgemeinschaft was probably the vaguest element of Nazi ideology and it is therefore difficult to define precisely. Indeed, historians are divided between those who see it as 'a pseudo-ideology' built on image alone and those who see it as a more concrete movement with genuine support.

The essential purpose of the Nazi *Volksgemeinschaft* was to overcome the old German divisions of class, religion and politics and to bring about a new collective national identity by encouraging people to work together. This new Nazi social mentality aimed to bring together the disparate elements and to create a German society built on the Nazi ideas of race and struggle.

Very closely associated with Nazi racism was the aim of *Volksgemeinschaft* to get people working together for the benefit of the nation by promoting traditional German values. The ideal German image was that of the classic peasant working on the soil in the rural community; this was exemplified in the concept of 'Blood and Soil' (*Blut und Boden*) (see pages 55–7) and the upholding of traditional roles by the two sexes.

Key question
What was the purpose of the Nazis in creating the idea of *Volksgemeinschaft*?

Key term

Volksgemeinschaft
A people's community. Nazism stressed the development of a harmonious, socially unified and racially pure community. It did not support Marxism and communism.

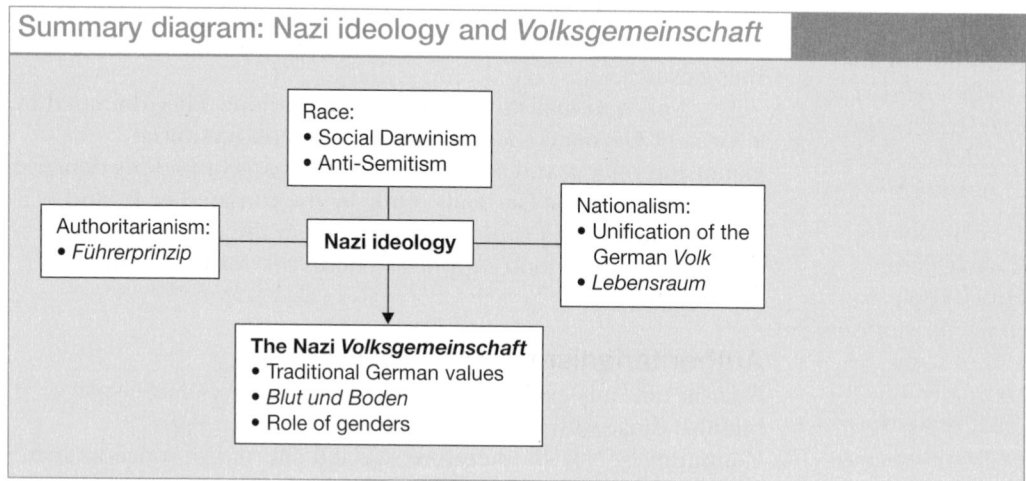

Summary diagram: Nazi ideology and *Volksgemeinschaft*

Race:
• Social Darwinism
• Anti-Semitism

Authoritarianism:
• *Führerprinzip*

Nazi ideology

Nationalism:
• Unification of the German *Volk*
• *Lebensraum*

The Nazi *Volksgemeinschaft*
• Traditional German values
• *Blut und Boden*
• Role of genders

2 | Social Groups

The revival of the economy (see pages 30–2) in conjunction with Hitler's diplomatic successes (see pages 160–71) contributed greatly to the German people's acceptance, or at least tolerance, of the regime. In the pre-war years it really did seem to many Germans as if the Nazis had pulled their country out of the economic quagmire. However, in material terms the effects varied considerably from one class to another.

Key question
Did the workers benefit under the Third Reich?

Industrial workers

The working class was by far the largest social group in German society (see Table 3.1). The Nazi regime definitely could not assume that that the workers could be won over to the promised ideas of the *Volksgemeinschaft*. Under Weimar, many workers had belonged to independent trade unions and politically they had generally voted for the left-wing parties – the Social Democrats and Communists.

At first, the Nazi regime simply wanted to establish its authority and so it closed down all the established trade unions (see page 14). As a result, workers completely lost the right of industrial bargaining. Consequently management and the government controlled pay increases and were able to limit workers' freedom of movement.

Table 3.1: German society

	Working class	Middle classes			Peasants	Others
		White-collar workers	Self-employed	Government officials/ employees		
As a % of German society (1933)	46.3	12.4	9.6	4.8	20.7	6.2

Key date
Creation of German Labour Front: May 1933

In the place of the unions, from May 1933, the only available option to workers was to join the German Labour Front (DAF, *Deutsche Arbeitsfront*). Led by Robert Ley, DAF became the largest Nazi organisation in the Third Reich with a membership that increased from five million in 1933 to 22 million in 1939. It became responsible for virtually all areas of work such as:

- setting working hours and wages
- dealing harshly with any sign of disobedience, strikes or absenteeism
- running training schemes for apprenticeships
- setting stable rents for housing
- supervising working conditions through the DAF sub-section called the Beauty of Labour (SdA, *Schönheit der Arbeit*). The SdA aimed to provide cleaning, meals, exercise, etc.
- organising recreational facilities through the Strength through Joy (KdF, *Kraft durch Freude*). It provided very real opportunities to millions of workers: cultural visits, sports facilities and holiday travel – although such benefits were only available to the loyal workers.

However, assessing the material effects of the Nazi regime on the workers is a highly complicated issue mainly because there are so many variables, such as age, occupation and geographical location. The obvious and most significant benefit for industrial workers was the creation of employment. For the many millions

A Nazi propaganda poster advertising the benefits of saving for 'Your own KdF car'. Workers enthusiastically paid millions of marks to the scheme but the Volkswagen was never actually produced until after the war.

who had suffered from the distress of mass unemployment, the creation of jobs was accepted gratefully (see pages 31–2). Indeed, by the late 1930s Germany had achieved full employment and there was a growing shortage of workers.

Yet, to put that major benefit into context, it is important to bear in mind a number of key factors:

- Average workers' **real wages** only rose above 1929 levels in 1938. Also, workers were forced to pay extensive contributions for DAF and insurance/tax.
- The generalised picture disguises the fact that the biggest gains were clearly made by the workers associated with the boom in the rearmament industries, whereas those in consumer goods struggled to maintain their real incomes.

Real wages
The actual purchasing power of income taking into account inflation/deflation and also the effect of deductions, e.g. taxes.

Key term

Profile: Robert Ley 1890–1945

1890 – Born in the Rhineland, the son of a farmer
1914 – Graduated with a degree in chemistry
1914–17 – First World War pilot
1920–8 – Worked with the major chemicals company IG Farben, but sacked for drunkenness
1924 – Joined the NSDAP
1930 – Elected to the *Reichstag*
1933–45 – Leader of the German Labour Front. Used the money to fund KdF (the Volkswagen scheme, see the poster on page 54) and the élite training schools, *Ordensburgen* (see page 62)
1939–45 – Lost influence to Fritz Todt and Albert Speer
1945 – Captured by US forces, but committed suicide before trial

Ley enjoyed a very significant power-base as the leader of DAF, which was the largest Nazi organisation in the Third Reich. However, he personally failed to develop the institution to its political potential and simply exploited the position for his own self-advancement. He became an alcoholic and although he retained his position, he lost the support of other leading Nazis.

- Working hours increased over time. The average working week was officially increased from 43 hours in 1933 to 47 hours in 1939 – and as military demands grew, there was pressure on many workers to do more overtime.

So, there is considerable evidence to suggest there was workers' discontent even before 1939. Once the war set in, pressures increased further – especially from 1942 when bombing began to hit German industrial urban sectors. By 1944 the working week had grown to 60 hours.

Peasants and small farmers

Key question
Did the peasantry and small farmers benefit under the Third Reich?

The farming community had been attracted to the Nazi cause by the promise of financial aid, as they had suffered from a series of economic problems from the mid-1920s. Moreover, peasants felt increasingly that they were losing out to the growing urban society of industrial Germany. The Nazi ideology of 'Blood and Soil' outlined by Richard Darré (see page 56) expressed a real sympathy for the role of peasants in society. It portrayed the peasantry as racially the purest element of the *Volk*, the providers of Germany's food and as the symbol of traditional German values.

Profile: Richard Darré 1895–1953

1895		– Born in Buenos Aires, Argentina of German and Swedish parents
1914–18		– Served in the First World War and reached the rank of lieutenant
1920–5		– Studied at Halle and gained a doctorate in agriculture specialising in animal breeding
1928–30		– Published three books on Nazi views of race; the most significant was *The Peasantry as the Life-source of the Nordic Race*
1930	June	– Created a Nazi agrarian political organisation
	July	– Joined the Nazi Party
1933	May 28	– Appointed Reich Peasant Leader
	June 29	– Appointed Minister of Agriculture and Food
	September	– Responsible for introducing the Reich Entitled Law and the Reich Food Estate (see page 57)
1938	September	– Made leader of the Central Office for Race and Settlement (RuSHA)
1940		– Delivered his infamous speech outlining the fate of the British people in his plans for race and settlement
1942		– Forced to resign from all his positions
1945		– Arrested and held by Allied forces
1949		– Sentenced to seven years in prison for confiscating Jewish and Polish property
1953		– Died in Munich

Darré was more intellectual than many Nazi leaders. He was well travelled, fluent in four languages and eventually was awarded a doctoral degree for his studies. In 1930 he was drawn into the NSDAP and played an important role in the rise of the Nazis by creating an agrarian political organisation. He effectively exploited the rural unrest winning electoral support in the countryside.

There were two elements to Darré's thinking:

- To restore the role and values of the countryside, so reversing the drive towards urbanisation by promoting the concept of 'Blood and Soil'.
- To support the expansionist policy of *Lebensraum* and to create a German racial aristocracy based on selective breeding.

Initially, his agricultural reforms were well received by the Nazi regime and certainly helped to enable many farmers to recover in the mid-1930s. In particular, his ideas were supported by Himmler and they worked closely together in RuSHA. The extent of Darré's racism is shown in his speech of 1940:

As soon as we beat England we shall make an end of you Englishmen once and for all. Able-bodied men and women between the ages of 16 and 45 will be exported as slaves to the Continent. The old and weak will be exterminated.

All men remaining in Britain as slaves will be sterilised; a million or two of the young women of the Nordic type will be segregated in a number of stud farms where, with the assistance of picked German sires, during a period of ten or twelve years, they will produce annually a series of Nordic infants to be brought up in every way as Germans.

However, Darré increasingly fell out with the leadership. His idealistic vision of a rural utopia was at odds with the economic demands of war production and in 1942 he was forced to resign by Hitler.

The Nazi regime certainly took initiatives on agriculture:

- A substantial number of farm debts and mortgages were written off and small farmers were given low interest rates and a range of tax allowances.
- The government maintained extensive tariffs to reduce imports.
- The introduction of the Reich Entailed Farm Law of 1933 gave security of tenure to the occupiers of medium-sized farms between 7.5 and 125 hectares and forbade the division of farms.
- The Reich Food Estate, established in 1933, supervised every aspect of agricultural production and distribution – especially food prices and working wages (although its bureaucratic meddling became the focus of much resentment, when, for example, it stipulated that each hen had to lay 65 eggs per year).

The economic realities meant that in practice the impact of Nazi agricultural policy was rather mixed. At first, all farmers benefited from an increase in prices between 1933 and 1936 and so farmers' incomes did improve markedly – though they only recovered to 1928 levels in 1938. However, it seems that by 1936–7 any benefits were giving way to a growing peasant disillusionment. This was for several reasons:

- Although the regime succeeded in increasing agricultural production by 20 per cent from 1928 to 1938, there continued to be a significant drift of workers to the towns where wages were higher. German agriculture just did not have the economic power to compete with other sectors of the economy. As a result, three per cent of the German population drifted from the countryside to the town.
- Of course, the positive aspects of the Reich Food Estate were accepted, but the regulation became increasingly resented.

- The Reich Entailed Farm Law also caused resentment and family discontent. In trying to solve one problem by passing on farms to just one child, farmers faced the very real dilemma of not being able to provide a future for their remaining children.

With the onset of the war in 1939 the peasantry's pressures developed in all sorts of ways. Men were increasingly conscripted to the military fronts – so the problem of the shortage of agricultural labour was exacerbated. This resulted in the transportation to Germany of cheap forced labour of peasants from eastern Europe, e.g. Poles and Czechs. This also conflicted with Nazi thinking since the labourers were not even viewed as racially acceptable.

Landowners

The landed classes had been initially suspicious of the idea of radical social change. They resented the political interference of the Party, but above all they feared the Nazis would redistribute the large landed estates. However, they soon learned to live quite comfortably with the Nazi regime and in the years before 1939 their economic interests were not really threatened. Indeed, German victories in the early years of the war offered the chance of acquiring more cheap land.

The real blow for the landowners actually came in 1945 when the occupation of eastern Germany by the USSR resulted in the reform of land. The traditional social and economic supremacy of the German landowners was broken.

Mittelstand

Another social class that expected to benefit from the Nazi regime was the **Mittelstand**. The problems confronting the *Mittelstand* were in many ways comparable to the problems faced by the peasantry. It had suffered from the decline in commerce in Germany since the First World War and it found it difficult to compete with the increasing power of big business and trade unions.

Research has shown that in the elections 1930–3 the *Mittelstand* had voted for Nazism in greater proportion than the rest of German society and the Nazi regime was keen to take sympathetic measures to maintain that support:

- The government used the money available from the confiscation of Jewish businesses to offer low interest rate loans.
- It introduced the Law to Protect Retail Trade (1933) against large department stores, of which many were Jewish. This banned the opening of new department stores and taxed the existing ones.
- It imposed a host of new trading regulations to protect small craftsmen.

Key question
Did the landowners lose out?

Key question
Did the *Mittelstand* benefit under the Third Reich?

Mittelstand
Can be translated as 'the middle class', but in German society it tends to represent the lower middle classes, e.g. shopkeepers, craft workers and clerks. It was traditionally independent and self-reliant but increasingly it felt squeezed out between the power and influence of big business and industrial labour.

Key term

However, despite the Nazis' attempt to implement their electoral promises before 1933 and the economic recovery, the position of the *Mittelstand* continued the decline that had started with Germany's industrialisation. The costs of small businesses meant that they could not compete with the lower costs of the large department stores. Moreover the problem was made worse because of the Nazi preference for big business, whose support was required for rearmament.

In 1933, 20 per cent of the owners of small businesses were under 30 years old and 14 per cent over 60. By 1939 the corresponding figures were 10 per cent under 30 and 19 per cent over 60, which highlighted the ageing trend of the *Mittelstand*. And in the years 1936–9 it is reckoned that the number of traditional skilled craftsmen declined by 10 per cent. The truth is that the *Mittelstand* found itself being significantly squeezed out.

Key question
Why did big business benefit?

Big business

The influence of big business will be considered in more depth in Chapter 5. At this stage, it is sufficient to say that it generally benefited from the Nazis' economic programme. Despite an increasing range of government controls, the financial gains were impressive. The value of German industry steadily increased, as shown by the following:

- The share price index increased from 41 points in 1932 to 106 in 1940, while annual dividends to investors grew from an average 2.83 per cent to 6.6 per cent over the same period.
- The improvement of salaries of management from an average 3700RM in 1934 to 5420RM in 1938 also reflected the economic growth.

Moreover, from 1939 the onset of the war provided enormous opportunities for taking over foreign property, land and companies. For example, Oskar Schindler (1908–74), a German businessman, set up business in Krakow in 1939 and drew much of his workforce from the Jewish labour camp. After initially exploiting these workers he eventually saved thousands from extermination.

Summary diagram: Social groups

Mittelstand
• Problems
• Nazi initiatives
• Decline

Did it benefit?

Peasants and small farmers
• Darré's ideas
• Nazi initiatives
• Benefits and disillusion

Did the peasantry benefit?

Nazi social groups

Industrial workers
• Loss of rights
• Robert Ley and DAF
• Material effects

Did they benefit in the Third Reich?

Landowners
• Comfortable survival
• Post-1945 losses

Did the landowners lose out?

Big business
• Financial gains
• Initial advantages of war

Why did big business benefit?

3 | Education and Youth

Key question
What were the aims of Nazi education?

In Nazi Germany, education became merely a tool for the consolidation of the Nazi system. Hitler expressed his views chillingly in 1933:

> When an opponent declares, 'I will not come over to your side', I calmly say, 'Your child belongs to us already … What are you? You will pass on. Your descendants, however, now stand in the new camp. In a short time they will know nothing else but this new community.'

Education in the Third Reich was therefore intended to **indoctrinate** its youth so completely in the principles and ethos of National Socialism that the long-term survival of the 'New Order' would never be brought into question. A National Socialist Teachers' League official wrote pompously in 1937:

Indoctrination
Inculcating and imposing a set of ideas.

Key term

> German youth must no longer – as in the Liberal era in the cause of so-called objectivity – be confronted with the choice of whether it wishes to grow up in a spirit of materialism or idealism, of racism or internationalism, of religion or godlessness, but it must be consciously shaped according to the principles which are

recognised as correct and which have shown themselves to be correct: according to the principles of the ideology of National Socialism.

This was to be achieved not only through the traditional structure of the educational system, but also by the development of various Nazi youth movements.

Key question
How did German schools change under the Nazis?

Key date
Reich Ministry of Education created – control of education was taken away from *Länder*: 1934

Schools

The actual organisation of the state educational system was not fundamentally altered, although by a law of 1934 control was taken from the regional states and centralised under the Reich Ministry of Education, Culture and Science led by Reich Minister Bernhard Rust. The Ministry was then able to adapt the existing system to suit Nazi purposes.

First, the teaching profession itself was 'reconditioned'. Politically unreliable individuals were removed and Jewish teachers were banned – and of course many women were encouraged to conform to Nazi values by returning to the home (see pages 71–4). Special training courses were arranged for those teachers who remained unconvinced by the new requirements. In addition, the National Socialist Teachers' League (NSLB, *Nationalsozialistische Lehrerbund*) was established and its influence and interference continued to grow. By 1937, it included 97 per cent of all teachers and two-thirds of the profession had been on special month-long courses on Nazi ideology and the changes to the curriculum.

Secondly, the curricula and syllabuses were adapted. To fit in with the Nazi Aryan ideal, a much greater emphasis was placed on physical education, so that 15 per cent of school time was given over to it, and games teachers assumed an increased status and importance in the school hierarchy. On the academic front, Religious Studies were dropped to downgrade the importance of Christianity, whereas German, Biology and History became the focus of special attention:

- German language and literature were studied to create 'a consciousness of being German', and to inculcate a martial and nationalistic spirit. Among the list of suggested reading for 14-year-old pupils was a book entitled *The Battle of Tannenberg*, which included the following extract: 'A Russian soldier tried to bar the infiltrator's way, but Otto's bayonet slid gratingly between the Russian's ribs, so that he collapsed groaning. There it lay before him, simple and distinguished, his dream's desire, the Iron Cross.'

Key term
Population policy
In 1933–45 the Nazi government aimed to increase the birth rate.

- Biology became the means by which to deliver Nazi racial theory: ethnic classification, **population policy** and racial genetics were all integrated into the syllabus.
- History, not surprisingly, was also given a special place in the Nazi curriculum, so that the glories of German nationalism could be emphasised.

One final innovation was the creation of various types of élite schools. They were intended to prepare the best of Germany's youth for future political leadership, were modelled on the principles of the Hitler Youth, and focused on physical training, paramilitary activities and political education. The 21 *Napolas* (National Political Educational Institutions) and the ten Adolf Hitler Schools were both for boys of secondary school age, and the three *Ordensburgen* for boys of college age.

Hitler Youth

The responsibility for developing a new outlook lay with the youth movements. There was already a long and well-established tradition of youth organisation in Germany before 1933, but at that time the Hitler Youth (HJ, *Hitler Jugend*) represented only one per cent of the total.

The term 'Hitler Youth' in fact embraced a range of youth groups under the control of its leader Baldur von Schirach and in the next six years the structure and membership of the HJ grew remarkably – although this was partly because parents were pressurised to enrol the children and by 1939 membership became compulsory.

Key question
How did the Hitler Youth try to indoctrinate Germany's young people?

Profile: Baldur von Schirach 1907–74

1907	– Born in Berlin, the son of an aristocratic German father and an American mother
1924	– Joined the NSDAP as a student of art history at Munich
1928	– Leader of National Socialist German Students' League
1933–9	– Youth Leader of the German Reich
1939–40	– Joined the German army and won the Iron Cross
1940–5	– *Gauleiter* of Vienna
1945	– Arrested by the Allies
1946–66	– Sentenced to 20 years' imprisonment at the Nuremberg War Crimes Trials
1967	– Publication of his book, *I believed in Hitler*
1974	– Lived privately in West Germany until his death

Schirach's only real significant role was as 'Youth Leader of the German Reich', which gave him the responsibility to supervise all the youth organisations, 1933–9. He became obsessed with Hitler from the mid-1920s – he even wrote poetry to the *Führer*! He was not greatly respected by other leading Nazis, partly because of his effeminate nature. However, his loyalty and charm allowed him to remain influential with Hitler and he was appointed *Gauleiter* of Vienna.

Schirach denied responsibility for war crimes, but the Nuremberg Trials found him guilty of having deported the Jews from Austria.

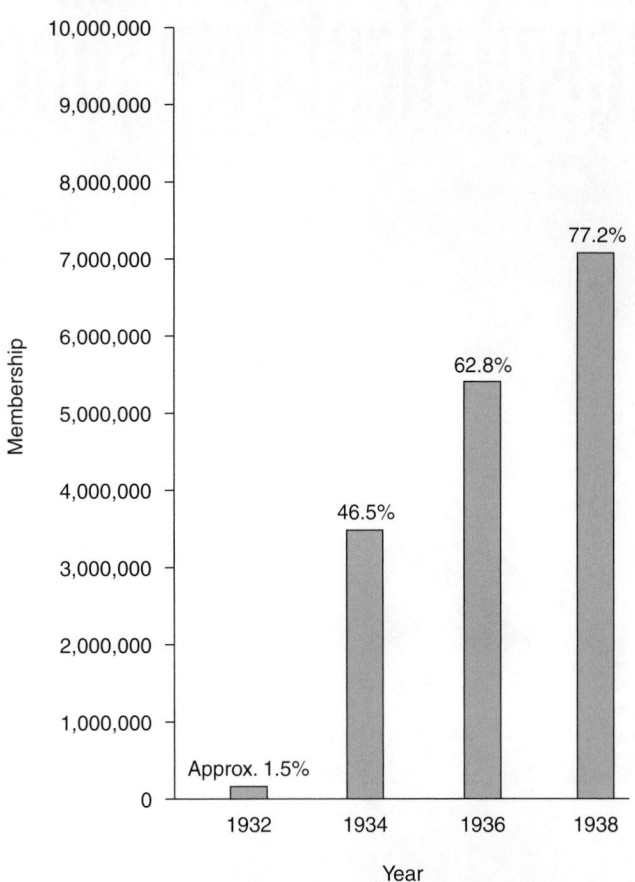

Figure 3.1: Hitler Youth movements. The percentages indicate the percentage of total youth population aged 10–18 years who were members

Table 3.2: Youth groups

Boys 10–14 years old	German Young People (DJ, *Deutsche Jungvolk*)
Boys 14–18 years old	Hitler Youth (HJ, *Hitler Jugend*)
Girls 10–14 years old	League of Young Girls (JM, *Jungmädel*)
Girls 14–18 years old	League of German Girls (BDM, *Bund Deutscher Mädel*)

In all four groups shown in Table 3.2 there was a great stress on political indoctrination, emphasising the life and achievements of the *Führer*, German patriotism, athletics and camping. In addition, the sexes were moulded for their future roles in Nazi society. Boys engaged in endless physical and military-type activities, e.g. target shooting, and girls were prepared for their domestic and maternal tasks, e.g. cooking.

Jugend dient dem Führer

ALLE ZEHNJÄHRIGEN IN DIE HJ.

'Youth serves the *Führer*. Every ten year old into the Hitler Youth'. The Nazi propaganda poster cleverly plays on the combined images of the young boy and Hitler sharing a common vision. It was produced in 1940, by which time war had started and membership was compulsory.

Successes and failures

It is difficult to assess the success of any educational system. It depends on the criteria chosen and the 'evidence' is open to conflicting interpretations. Therefore, conclusions must be tentative.

The teaching profession certainly felt its status to be under threat, despite its initial sympathy for the regime. Thirty-two per cent were members of the Party in 1936 – a figure markedly higher than the figure of 17 per cent of the Reich Civil Service as a whole. The anti-academic ethos and the crude indoctrination alienated many, while the Party's backing of the HJ and its activities caused much resentment. Not surprisingly, standards in traditional academic subjects had fallen by the early years of the war. This was particularly the case in the various élite schools,

Key question
Did Nazi education succeed?

where physical development predominated. By 1938 recruitment of teachers had declined and there were 8000 vacancies – and only 2500 were coming out of the teacher training colleges. In higher education, the number of students had halved even before the onset of the war. The overall effect of these changes was described in 1937 in a report from the teachers' organisation in Bavaria:

> Many pupils believe that they can simply drift through for eight years and secure their school leaving certificate with minimal intellectual performance. The schools receive no support whatsoever from the Hitler Youth units; on the contrary, it is those pupils who are in positions of leadership there who often display unmannerly behaviour and laziness at school. School discipline has declined to an alarming extent.

The impact of the HJ seems to have been very mixed. In some respects the emphasis on teamwork and extracurricular activities was to be commended – especially when compared to the limited provision available in many European countries. So, the provision for sports, camping and music genuinely excited many youngsters – and for those from poorer backgrounds, the Hitler Youth really offered opportunities. However, the organisation suffered from its over-rapid expansion and the leadership was inadequate. When the war started it became even more difficult to run the movement effectively and, as a result, the increasing Nazi emphasis on military drill and discipline was certainly resented by many adolescents. This point was made by a BDM leader in her memoirs:

> Apart from its beginnings during the 'years of struggle', the Hitler Youth was not a youth movement at all: it became more and more the 'state youth organisation', that is to say, it became more and more institutionalised, and finally became the instrument used by the National Socialist regime to run its ideological training of young people and the war work for certain age groups.

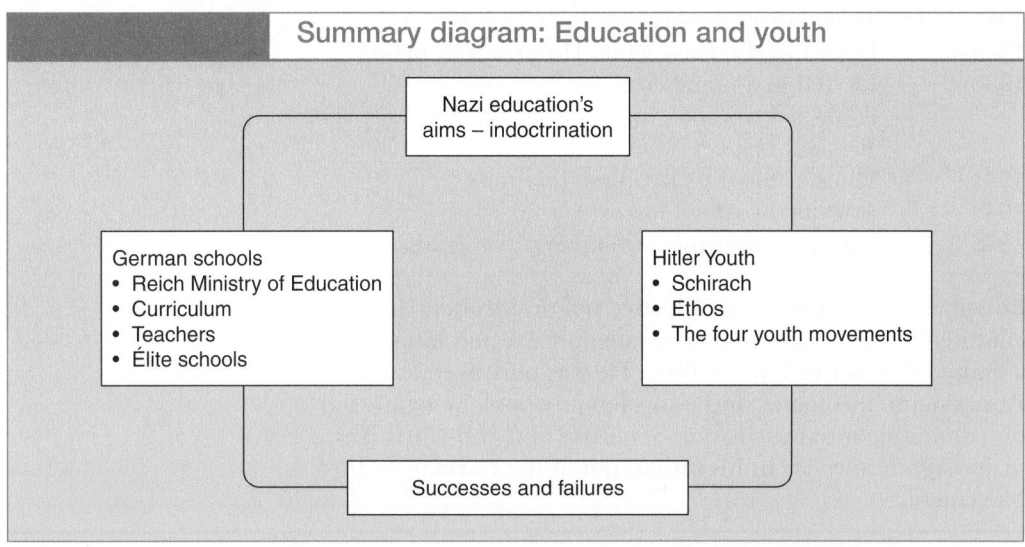

Summary diagram: Education and youth

Nazi education's aims – indoctrination

German schools
- Reich Ministry of Education
- Curriculum
- Teachers
- Élite schools

Hitler Youth
- Schirach
- Ethos
- The four youth movements

Successes and failures

4 | Religion

In the 1930s the majority of German people were Christian, two-thirds of whom were **Protestant** and the remaining one-third Catholic. The rise of Nazism posed fundamental political and ethical problems for the Christian Churches, while Nazism could not ignore those Churches, which were well-established and powerful institutions.

In his rise to power Hitler avoided direct attacks on the Churches and number 24 of the Party's 25-points programme spoke in favour of 'positive Christianity' which was closely linked to racial and national views (see page 28). However, there can be little doubt that Nazism was based on a fundamentally anti-Christian philosophy. Where Nazism glorified strength, violence and war, Christianity taught love, forgiveness and neighbourly respect. Moreover, Christianity was regarded as the product of an inferior race – Jesus was a Hebrew – and therefore, it could not be reconciled with Nazi *völkisch* thought. Some leading Nazis, such as Himmler and his deputy, Heydrich, openly revealed their contempt for Christianity. Hitler himself was more cautious, although what were probably his true feelings were revealed in a private conversation in 1933:

> Neither of the denominations – Catholic or Protestant, they are both the same – has any future left … That won't stop me stamping out Christianity in Germany root and branch. One is either a Christian or a German. You can't be both.

Key question
How did the Nazis regard religion?

Key terms

Protestant
General name for the reformed Churches created in sixteenth-century Europe that split from the Roman Catholic Church. There were 28 different Protestant Churches in Germany, of which the largest was the Lutheran (the German state Church, like the Church of England).

Völkisch
Nationalist views associated with racism (especially anti-Semitism).

Profile: Alfred Rosenberg 1893–1946

1893	– Born in Russian Estonia, but of German parents
1919	– Joined the Party as one of its earlier members
1923	– Took part in the Munich Beer Hall *Putsch*
1924–5	– Leader of the Party while Hitler was in prison
1930	– Elected as a member of the *Reichstag*
	– Published his book on racial theory, *The Myth of the Twentieth Century*
1941	– Minister for the Occupied Territories
1945	– Arrested by Allied forces
1946	– Executed after the Nuremberg War Trials

Rosenberg was not really an effective political leader. He was an educated and scholarly figure, but he only exerted influence with a limited number within the Party. He was portrayed as the Party's main 'ideologue' and in his lengthy book he expressed his commitment to racism, anti-Semitism and anti-Christianity. His major significance lay in his promotion of the German Faith Movement.

Teutonic paganism
The non-Christian beliefs of the Germans in ancient history (heathens).

Cult of personality
Using the power and charisma of a political leader to dominate the nation.

The German Faith Movement

In place of Christianity, the Nazis aimed to cultivate a **teutonic paganism**, which became known as the German Faith Movement. Although a clear Nazi religious ideology was never fully outlined, the development of the German Faith Movement, promoted by the Nazi thinker Alfred Rosenberg, revolved around four main themes:

- the propagation of the 'Blood and Soil' ideology (see pages 55–7)
- the replacement of Christian ceremonies – marriage and baptism – by pagan equivalents
- the wholesale rejection of Christian ethics – closely linked to racial and nationalist views
- the **cult of** Hitler's **personality**.

However, the Nazi government knew that religion was a very delicate issue and it initially adopted a cautious conciliatory stance towards both the Churches.

Why did conciliation lead to conflict?

Concordat signed with the Papacy: July 1933

Kulturkampf
'Cultural struggle'. Refers to the tension in the 1870s between the Catholic Church and the German state, when Bismarck was chancellor.

Concordat
An agreement between Church and state.

Conciliation and conflict 1933–5

In his very first speech as Chancellor, Hitler paid tribute to the Churches as being integral to the well-being of the nation. Members of the SA were even encouraged to attend Protestant Church services. This was done to give weight to the idea that the Nazi state could accommodate Protestantism. The 'Day of Potsdam' (see page 11) further gave the impression of a unity between the Protestant Church and the state.

Likewise, the Catholic Church responded sympathetically to the overtures of the Nazis. Catholic bishops, in particular, were frightened of the possibility of a repeat of the so-called *Kulturkampf* in the late nineteenth century. So, Catholic bishops were concerned to safeguard the position of the Church under the Nazis and in July 1933 a **Concordat** was signed between the Papacy and the regime (represented by Vice-Chancellor Papen who was a Catholic). In the agreement it was decided that:

- the Nazis would guarantee the Catholic Church religious freedom
- the Nazis would not interfere with the Catholic Church's property and legal rights
- the Nazis would accept the Catholic Church's control over its own education
- in return, the Catholic Church would not interfere in politics and would give diplomatic recognition to the Nazi government.

In the short term the Concordat seemed to be a significant success. However, the courting of both of the Churches by the Nazis was totally insincere. They were merely being lulled into a false sense of security while the dictatorship was being established. By the end of 1933 Nazi interference in religious affairs was already causing resentment and disillusionment in both Catholic and Protestant Churches.

The Nazi regime hoped that the Protestant Churches would gradually be 'co-ordinated' through the influence of the group known as the German Christians (*Deutsche Christen*). This group hoped to reconcile their Protestant ideas with Nazi nationalist and racial thinking by finding common ground. So, a new Church constitution was formulated in July 1933 with the Nazi sympathiser Ludwig Müller as the first Reich Bishop – an interesting application of the *Führerprinzip*.

However, such Nazi policies alienated many Protestant pastors, and there soon developed an opposition group, the Confessional Church (*Bekennende Kirche*), which upheld orthodox Protestantism and rejected Nazi distortions. Led by Pastor Niemöller, by 1934 the Confessional Church gained the support of about 7000 pastors out of 17,000. They claimed to represent the true Protestant Churches of Germany.

Churches and state 1935–45

By 1935 it was clear that the Nazi leadership had achieved only limited success in its control over the Churches. It was torn between a policy of total suppression, which would alienate large numbers of Germans, and a policy of limited persecution, which would allow the Churches an unacceptable degree of independence outside state control. In fact, although the ultimate objective was never in doubt, Nazi tactics degenerated into a kind of war of attrition against the Churches.

Key question
How did the relationship between the Churches and state change over time?

In order to destabilise the Churches, the Ministry of Church Affairs, led by Hanns Kerrl, was established. He adopted a policy of undermining both the Protestant and Catholic Churches by a series of anti-religious measures, including:

- closure of Church schools
- undermining of Catholic youth groups
- personal campaigns to discredit and harass the clergy, e.g. monasteries were accused of sexual and financial malpractices
- confiscation of Church funds
- campaign to remove crucifixes from schools
- arrest of more and more pastors and priests.

The standing of the Churches was undoubtedly weakened by this approach, but it also stimulated individual declarations of opposition from both Protestants and Catholics:

- Niemöller delivered a sermon in which he said that 'we must obey God rather than man'; he was interned in 1937 and for the next eight years he was held in various concentration camps.
- The Pope, Pius XI, himself eventually vehemently attacked the Nazi system in his encyclical, or public letter, of 1937 entitled *With Burning Concern* (*Mit Brennender Sorge*).

Papal encyclical, *Mit Brennender Sorge*, issued: 1937

Key date

Clearly, the conflict between the Churches and the state was set to continue.

The outbreak of war initially brought about a more cautious policy, as the regime wished to avoid unnecessary tensions.

Profile: Pastor Martin Niemöller 1892–1984

1892	– Born in Lippstadt
1914–18	– U-boat commander and won the Iron Cross
1920–4	– Studied theology and ordained as a Protestant pastor in Berlin
1934	– Co-founder of the Confessional Church
1937	– A critical sermon resulted in his arrest
1937–45	– Held in the concentration camps of Sachsenhausen and Dachau
1946	– President of the Protestant Church in Hessen
1946–84	– A strong supporter of the World Peace Movement
1984	– Died in Wiesbaden, Germany

In the 1920s Niemöller was a nationalist, anti-communist and against the Weimar Republic – he even sympathised with Hitler in the rise of Nazism. However, during 1933 his doubts emerged because of Nazism's racism and its attempt to control the Churches. Therefore, he played a crucial role in the formation of the Confessional Church in 1934 and after a highly critical sermon he was imprisoned from 1937 to 1945. Although his actions in the Third Reich were limited, his words have resonated through the years:

> When the Nazis came for the Communists
> I stayed quiet:
> I was not a Communist.
>
> When they came for the Social Democrats
> I stayed quiet:
> I was not a Social Democrat.
>
> When they came for the Trade Unionists
> I stayed quiet:
> I was not a Trade Unionist.
>
> When they came for the Jews
> I stayed quiet:
> I was not a Jew.
>
> Then they came for me
> And there was no-one left to protest.

However, following the easy military victories against Poland and France (1939–40), and then the invasion of atheistic Soviet Union (1941), the persecution intensified. This was the result of pressure applied by anti-Christian enthusiasts, such as Bormann and Heydrich (see profiles on pages 116 and 98) and the SS hierarchy.

So, once again, monasteries were closed, Church property was attacked and Church activities were severely restricted. Even so, religion was such a politically sensitive issue that Hitler did not allow subordination of the Churches to give way to wholesale suppression within Germany. It was only in the occupied territory of Poland – the area designated as an experimental example of the 'New Order' – that events were allowed to run their full course. Here, many of the Catholic clergy were executed and churches were closed down. In the end the Nazi persecution of the Churches failed, but only because the war itself was lost.

Conclusion

The Nazis achieved only limited success in their religious policy. The German Faith Movement was a clearly a failure. Neo-paganism never achieved support on any large scale. The 1939 official census recorded only five per cent of the population as members – though it shows the direction that might have been taken, if the likes of Himmler and Rosenberg had won the war.

Key question
Did Nazi religious policy succeed in its aims?

There were numerous individual Christians who made brave stands against the Nazis. This made the dictatorship wary of launching a fundamental assault on religion. As a result, German loyalty to the Christian faith in the Protestant and Catholic Churches survived in the long term despite Nazism. The historian J.R.C. Wright says: 'The Churches were severely handicapped but not destroyed. Hitler's programme needed time: he was himself destroyed before it had taken root'.

However, as will be discussed in Chapter 6 on the issue of resistance, it could also be argued that the Christian Churches failed. The Catholic and Protestant Churches were prepared to compromise with the Nazi regime to preserve their religious institutions and also, they both had a degree of sympathy for Nazism because of their traditional values and their hostility to communism.

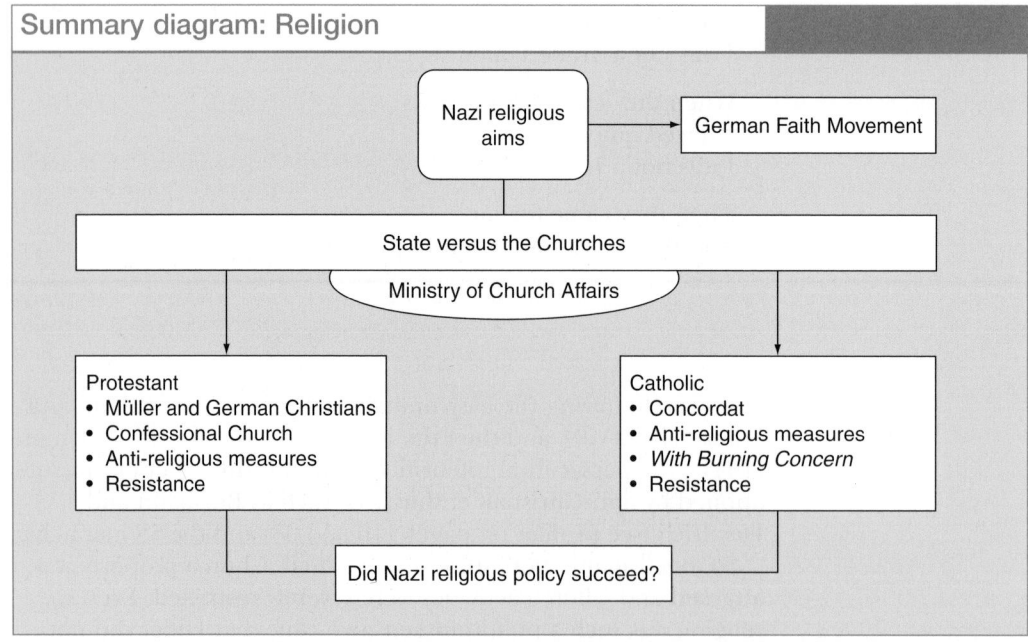

Summary diagram: Religion

Nazi religious aims → German Faith Movement

State versus the Churches

Ministry of Church Affairs

Protestant
• Müller and German Christians
• Confessional Church
• Anti-religious measures
• Resistance

Catholic
• Concordat
• Anti-religious measures
• *With Burning Concern*
• Resistance

Did Nazi religious policy succeed?

Key question
How and why was German society changed in the twentieth century?

5 | Women and the Family

The first quarter of the twentieth century witnessed two important social changes in German family life:

- Germany's population growth had decelerated markedly – which is *not* to say that the actual population had declined. In 1900 there had been over two million live births per annum, whereas by 1933 the figure was below one million.
- Over the same period female employment expanded by at least a third, far outstripping the percentage increase in population.

Both of these trends had been partially brought about by long-term changes in social behaviour common to many industrialised countries. It was recognised that the use of contraception to limit family size would improve the standard of living and give the better-educated female population the opportunity to have a vocation as well as children. However, Germany's recent past history exaggerated these developments. Economic mobilisation during the First World War had driven women into the factories, while the post-war difficulties caused by the inflation had encouraged them to stay on working out of economic necessity. In addition, the war had left a surplus of 1.8 million marriageable women, as well as many wives with invalided husbands. Finally, the changing balance of the economy in the 1920s had led to an increased demand for non-manual labour and the growth of mass-production techniques requiring more unskilled workers. These factors tended to favour the employment of women, who could be paid less than men.

Key question
What was the ideal role of women in Nazi society?

The Nazi view towards women

The ideology of National Socialism was in stark contrast to the above social trends. Nazism fundamentally opposed social and economic female emancipation and had the following aims for women:

- To have more children and to take responsibility for bringing them up.
- To care for the house and their husbands.
- To stop paid employment except for very specialist vocations such as midwifery.

In the view of the Nazis, nature had ordained that the two sexes should fulfil entirely different roles, and it was simply the task of the state to maintain this distinction. What this amounted to was that 'a woman's place was to be in the home'. Or, as the Nazi slogan presented it, they were to be devoted to the three German Ks – '*Kinder, Küche, Kirche*' ('children, kitchen and Church' – see the 'Nazi Ten commandments' for choosing a spouse, on page 72). Such dogma was upheld by the Party, even before 1933 – there was not a single female Nazi deputy in the *Reichstag*, and a Party regulation of 1921 excluded women from all senior positions within its structure.

Nazi Ten Commandments for the choice of a spouse

1. Remember that you are German!
2. If you are genetically healthy, do not stay single.
3. Keep your body pure.
4. Keep your mind and spirit pure.
5. Marry only for love.
6. As a German, choose only a spouse of similar or related blood.
7. In choosing a spouse, ask about his forebears.
8. Health is essential to physical beauty.
9. Don't look for a playmate but for a companion in marriage.
10. You should want to have as many children as possible.

Nazis' views on women tied in with their concern about the demographic trends. A growing population was viewed as a sign of national strength and status – a reflection of Germany's aspiration to the status of an international power. How could they demand nationalist expansionism in eastern Europe, if the number of Germans was in fact levelling out? It was therefore considered essential to increase the population substantially and, to this end, women were portrayed as primarily the mothers of the next generation – an image that suited Nazi anti-feminism.

Female employment

Initially, attempts to reduce the number of women in work seem to have been quite successful. Between 1933 and 1936 married women were in turn debarred from jobs in medicine, law and the higher ranks of the civil service. Moreover, the number of female teachers and university students was reduced considerably – only 10 per cent of university students could be female. Such laws had a profound effect on professional middle-class women, although their actual number was small.

Nazi incentives

In other sectors of the economy a mixture of Party pressure and financial inducements was employed to cajole women out of the workplace and back into the home. From June 1933 interest-free loans of 600RM were made available to young women who withdrew from the labour market in order to get married. The effects of the Depression also worked in favour of Nazi objectives. They not only drastically reduced the number of female workers (although proportionately far less than male workers), but also enabled the government to justify its campaign for women to give up work for the benefit of unemployed men. On these grounds, **labour exchanges** and employers were advised to discriminate positively in favour of men. As a result of all this, the percentage of women in employment fell from 37 per cent to 31 per cent of the total from 1932 to 1937.

Key question
Did the Nazis reduce the number of women in employment?

Labour exchanges Local offices created by the state for finding employment. Many industrialised countries had labour exchanges to counter mass unemployment.

Key term

Nazi women's organisations

Women were quite specifically excluded from the Nazi machinery of government. The only employment opportunities available to them were within the various Nazi women's organisations, such as the National Socialist Womanhood (NSF, *National Sozialistische Frauenschaft*) and the German Women's Enterprise (DFW, *Deutsches Frauenwerk*), led by Gertrud Scholtz-Klink. Yet, the NSF and DFW were regarded by the Party as mere tools for the propagation of the **anti-feminist** ideology by means of cultural, educational and social programmes. And so, when a campaign started in the NSF for enhanced opportunities for women within the Party, its organisers were officially discredited.

Key term

Anti-feminist Opposing female advancement.

Effects

However, by 1937 Nazi ideological convictions were already threatened by the pressures of economic necessity. The introduction of conscription and the rearmament boom from the mid-1930s soon led to an increasing shortage of labour, as the Nazi economy continued to grow. The anti-feminist ideology could only be upheld if economic growth was slowed down and that, in turn, would restrict the rearmament programme. Of course, Hitler was not prepared to sanction this. Consequently, market forces inevitably began to exploit this readily available pool of labour, and the relative decline in female employment was reversed. Between 1937 and 1939 it rose from 5.7 million to 7.1 million, and the percentage of women increased from 31 per cent to 33 per cent of the total workforce (see Table 3.3) At this point the government decided to end the marriage loan scheme (see page 72) for women who withdrew from the labour market.

Table 3.3: Women in regular manual and non-manual employment

	1932	1937	1939
Millions of women	4.8	5.7	7.1
Women as a percentage of the total	37	31	33

Note: the comparative figure for 1928 was 7.4 million.

The contradictions between theory and practice of female employment were exacerbated further with the onset of war. So, although the trend of female employment continued to increase, the Nazi regime did not fully exploit the valuable resource of women as munitions workers – and the figures show that women remained underemployed right to the end of the war. This was due to:

- Germany's poor economic mobilisation. At first it was badly organised and (see pages 43–5) there was no general conscription of female labour. When in 1943 Speer did try to mobilise the economy on a total war footing by suggesting the conscription of women workers, he encountered opposition from Bormann, Sauckel (the Plenipotentiary for Labour) and indeed from Hitler himself, who was always concerned about civilian morale.

- The appeal for women to do war work was not convincing. Long hours in an arms factory made life very arduous, especially if there were the added responsibilities of maintaining a household and raising children. In addition, the Nazi government had also given all sorts of financial incentives to have more children with welfare benefits (see page 74).
- Farming responsibilities. One reason that distorts the picture of female employment was that women had traditionally played an important part in German farming. The shortage of agricultural labour had created major problems from the 1930s (see page 58–9), but once the young men were sent away for the war it got worse. As a result many German women experienced considerable hardship meeting the continuous demands of running a farm. By 1944 it is estimated that 65 per cent of the agricultural workforce were women.

The Nazis were caught in the contradictions of their own ideology. They were motivated by military expansionism which needed to employ women effectively, so, in the final two years of the Nazi state, more and more women ended up at work. Yet, the government could not bring itself to renounce fully its anti-feminist stance. As an official in the NSF wrote, 'It has always been our chief article of faith that a woman's place is in the home – but since the whole of Germany is our home we must serve wherever we can best do so'.

Marriage and family

The Nazi state was obsessed with a desire to increase Germany's population and a series of measures were promptly introduced:

Key question
What were the effects of Nazi population policy?

- Marriage loans. The loan was worth just over half a year's earnings and a quarter of it was converted into a straight gift for each child that was born. (The scheme was introduced in June 1933, but progressively reduced from 1937.)
- Family allowances were improved dramatically, particularly for low-income families.
- Income tax was reduced in proportion to the number of children and those families with six or more did not pay any.
- Maternity benefits were improved.
- The anti-abortion law introduced under the Weimar Republic was enforced much more strictly.
- Contraceptive advice and facilities were restricted.

Inevitably, these incentives and laws were backed up by an extensive propaganda campaign, which glorified motherhood and the large family. There were also rewards: the Honour Cross of the German Mother in bronze, silver and gold, awarded for four, six and eight children, respectively. Such glorification reached its climax in the coining of the Nazi slogan 'I have donated a child to the *Führer*' (as contemporary humorists soon pointed out, this was presumably because of Hitler's personal unwillingness or inability to father children of his own).

Table 3.4: Social trends in Nazi Germany 1933–9

	Marriages per 1000 inhabitants	Divorces per 10,000 existing marriages	Births per 1000 inhabitants
1933	9.7	29.7	14.7
1936	9.1	32.6	19.0
1939	11.1	38.3	20.3

The statistics in Table 3.4 show several trends:

- From 1933 the birth rate increased significantly, reaching a peak in 1939 (although thereafter it again slowly declined).
- The divorce rate continued to increase.
- The figure of marriages was fairly consistent (apart from the blips in 1934 and 1939 – probably connected to the improving economy and the onset of the war).

The real problem for the historian is deciding whether Nazi population policy was actually *responsible* for the demographic trends. Interpreting population statistics is difficult because it involves so many different factors – social, economic and even psychological factors. Also, it is extremely hard to assess the *relative* significance of Nazi population policy when it is set against the importance of events such as the Depression and later on the Second World War.

Lebensborn

Key term

Lebensborn
Literally, the 'spring' or 'fountain' of life. Founded by Himmler and overseen by the SS to promote doctrines of racial purity.

Nazi population policy not only aimed to increase the number of children being born, but also tried to improve 'racial standards'. It led to the establishment of one of the most extraordinary features of Nazi social engineering, **Lebensborn**, set up by Himmler and the SS. Initially, the programme provided homes for unmarried mothers of the increasing number of illegitimate children who were seen as racially correct. However, later the institution also made the necessary arrangements for girls to be 'impregnated' by members of the SS in organised brothels. It is reckoned that by the end of the regime about 11,000 children were born under these circumstances.

Conclusion

Key question
How successful was Nazi policy on women and family?

Feminist historians have been highly critical of Nazi population and family policy that had reduced the status of women. One historian, Gisela Bock, in the 1980s has viewed Nazi thinking on women as a kind of secondary racism in which women were the victims of a sexist–racist male regime that reduced women to the status of mere objects. Such an interpretation would, of course, have been denied by the Nazis who claimed to regard women as different rather than inferior. But some modern-day non-feminist historians have tried to explain the positive features of Nazi policy on women. Improved welfare services made life easier for women, especially in more isolated rural areas. Also, with so many husbands away during the war, women were protected from having to combine paid work with bringing up a family and running the household.

Yet, despite these different perspectives, Nazi policy objectives for women and the family could not really be squared with the social realities of twentieth-century Germany. With the changing population trend and the increasing employment of women, Nazi views on women and the family were idealistic but impractical. Consequently, Nazi policy towards women and the family was contradictory and incoherent.

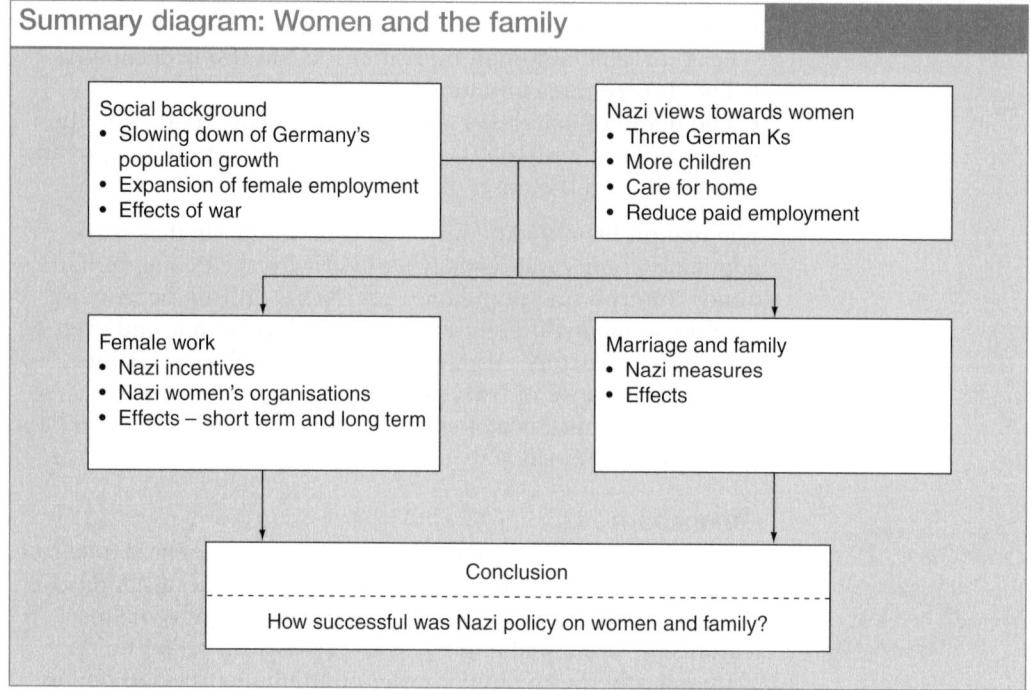

Summary diagram: Women and the family

Social background
- Slowing down of Germany's population growth
- Expansion of female employment
- Effects of war

Nazi views towards women
- Three German Ks
- More children
- Care for home
- Reduce paid employment

Female work
- Nazi incentives
- Nazi women's organisations
- Effects – short term and long term

Marriage and family
- Nazi measures
- Effects

Conclusion
How successful was Nazi policy on women and family?

6 | Culture

During the evening of 10 May 1933, in the middle of a square just off the centre of Berlin, there took place an event that soon became known as 'the burning of the books'. Thousands of volumes seized from private and public libraries were hurled into the flames by Nazi activists and university students because they were considered undesirable on account of their Jewish, socialist or pacifist tendencies. For a nation whose literary heritage was one of the greatest in Europe, it was seen by many as an act of mindless barbarism. It also rather aptly set the tone for the cultural life of Nazi Germany.

Nazi culture was no longer to be promoted merely as 'art for art's sake'. Rather, it was to serve the purpose of moulding public opinion, and, with this in mind, the Reich Chamber of Culture was supervised by the Propaganda Ministry. Germany's cultural life during the Third Reich was simply to be another means of

Key question
What was the purpose of Nazi culture?

The burning of the books: 10 May 1933

Key date

achieving censorship and indoctrination, although Goebbels expressed it in more pompous language:

> What we are aiming for is more than a revolt. Our historic mission is to transform the very spirit itself to the extent that people and things are brought into a new relationship with one another.

Culture was therefore 'co-ordinated' by means of the Reich Chamber of Culture, established in 1933, which made provision for seven sub-chambers: fine arts, music, the theatre, the press, radio, literature and films. In this way, just as anyone in the media had no option but to toe the Party line (see page 123–7), so all those involved in cultural activities had to be accountable for their creativity. Nazi culture was dominated by a number of key themes reflecting the usual ideological prejudices:

- **anti-Semitism**
- militarism and the glorification of war
- nationalism and the supremacy of the Aryan race
- the cult of the *Führer* and the power of absolutism
- **anti-modernism** and the theme of 'Blood and Soil'
- neo-paganism and a rejection of traditional Christian values.

Major cultural themes

Music

The world of music managed to cope reasonably well in the Nazi environment, partly because of its less obvious political overtones. Also, Germany's rich classical tradition from the works of Bach to Beethoven was proudly exploited by the regime. However, Mahler and Mendelssohn, both great Jewish composers, were banned, as were most modern musical trends. The new wave of modern classical composers, Schoenberg and Hindemith, were disparaged for their atonal music. Also the new 'genres' of jazz and dance-band were respectively labelled 'Negroid' and 'decadent'.

Literature

Over 2500 of Germany's writers left their homeland during the years 1933–45. This fact alone is a reflection of how sadly German writers and dramatists viewed the new cultural atmosphere. Among those who departed were:

- Thomas Mann, the author and Nobel Prize winner, who was a democrat and an old-fashioned liberal.
- Bertolt Brecht, the prestigious modern playwright, who was a communist.
- Erich Maria Remarque, the author of *All Quiet on the Western Front*, who was a pacifist.

Their place was taken by a lesser literary group, who either sympathised with the regime or accepted the limitations. It is difficult to identify a single book, play or poem written during the Third Reich, and officially blessed by the regime, which has stood the test of time.

Key question

In what ways did the Nazis shape German culture?

Key terms

Anti-Semitism
Hatred of Jews. It became the most significant part of Nazi racist thinking. For Hitler, the 'master race' was the pure Aryan (the people of northern Europe) and the Germans represented the highest caste. The lowest race for Hitler was the Jews.

Anti-modernism
Strand of opinion that rejects, objects to or is highly critical of changes to society and culture brought about by technological advancement.

Actors, like the musicians, tended to content themselves with
productions of the classics – Schiller, Goethe (and Shakespeare) –
in the knowledge that such plays were politically acceptable and
in the best traditions of German theatre.

Visual arts

The visual arts were also effectively limited by the Nazi
constraints. Modern schools of art were held in total contempt
and Weimar's rich cultural awakening was rejected as degenerate
and symbolic of the moral and political decline of Germany
under a system of parliamentary democracy. Thus, the following
were severely censored:

- **'New objectivity'** artists, like Georg Grosz and Otto Dix,
  wanted to depict ordinary people in everyday life – and by their
  art they aimed to comment on the state of society. Their
  paintings had strong political and social messages and in their
  artistic approach they showed a seedy, ugly and aggressive style.
- The Bauhaus style started by Walter Gropius influenced all
  aspects of design. e.g. furniture and architecture. Its approach
  was functional and it used materials such as steel, cement and
  plastic, and geometric shapes. It emphasised the close
  relationship between art and technology, which is underlined
  by its motto 'Art and Technology – a new unity'.

> **Key term**
>
> **New objectivity**
> Artists in favour of
> the 'new objectivity'
> broke away from the
> traditional romantic
> nostalgia of the
> nineteenth century.

The modern style of art was resented by Nazism so much that in
July 1937 two contrasting art exhibitions were launched entitled
'Degenerate Art' and 'Great German Art'. The first one was
deliberately held up to be mocked and many of the pieces were
destroyed; the second one glorified all the major Nazi themes of
Volksgemeinschaft and celebrated classic styles and traditional
nineteenth-century romanticism. Most admired were:

- the sculptor Arno Breker (see the image on page 79)
- the architect Albert Speer, who drew up many of the great plans
  for rebuilding the German cities and oversaw the 1936 Berlin
  Olympics stadium
- the artists Adolf Ziegler and Hermann Hoyer.

Cinema

Only in the field of film can it be said that the Nazi regime made
a genuine cultural contribution. Germany's cinematic reputation
had been established in the 1920s and a degree of continuity was
maintained, as many of the major film studios were in the hands
of nationalist sympathisers. However, Jewish film actors and
directors such as Fritz Lang were removed – and then decided to
leave Germany. Perhaps the most famous German émigrée was
Marlene Dietrich, who swiftly established a new career in
Hollywood.

Goebbels recognised the importance of expanding the film
industry, not only as a means of propaganda, but also as an
entertainment form – this explains why, out of 1097 feature films
produced between 1933 and 1945, only 96 were specifically at the

Arno Breker, *Comrades*. Breker was sculptor-in-chief to the Third Reich. By collaborating closely with Albert Speer he undertook numerous government commissions. His statue celebrated Aryan physical perfection and the importance of comradeship.

request of the Propaganda Ministry. The films can be divided into three types:

- Overt propaganda, e.g. *The Eternal Jew* (*Ewige Jude*), a tasteless, racist film that portrayed the Jews like rats, and *Hitlerjunge Queux*, based on the story of a Nazi murdered by the communists.
- Pure escapism, e.g. *The Adventures of Baron von Münchhausen*, a comedy based on an old German legend which gives the baron the powers of immortality.
- Emotive nationalism, e.g. *Olympia*, Leni Riefenstahl's docu-drama of the Berlin Olympics, *Triumph of the Will*, Riefenstahl's film about the 1934 Nuremberg Rally, and *Kolberg*, an epic produced in the final year of the war, which played on the national opposition to Napoleon. These last two films are still held in high regard by film critics for their use of subtle cinematic techniques despite the clear underlying political messages.

Conclusion

In the play *Schlageter* (1934) by Hanns Johst there is the line, 'Whenever I hear the word culture, I reach for my gun'. It is a phrase that is often, and incorrectly, attributed to Göring, but it still neatly underlines the anti-culture approach of the Nazis. Cultural life during the Third Reich was effectively silenced – it could only operate within the Nazi strait-jacket and to that extent Goebbels succeeded in censoring it.

However, the regime most certainly failed in its attempts to create a new Nazi cultural identity firmly rooted in the minds of the *Volk*. Some might suggest that it was simply a matter of time, and that the regime's success in building new theatres and libraries and attracting more people to cultural events would have eventually brought about the desired result. On the other hand, the very powerful cultural resurgence in Germany since 1945 suggests that the traditions and spirit of Germany's cultural identity were not destroyed by the essentially brutal and negative force of Nazism.

Key question
Did the Third Reich manage to create a cultural identity of its own?

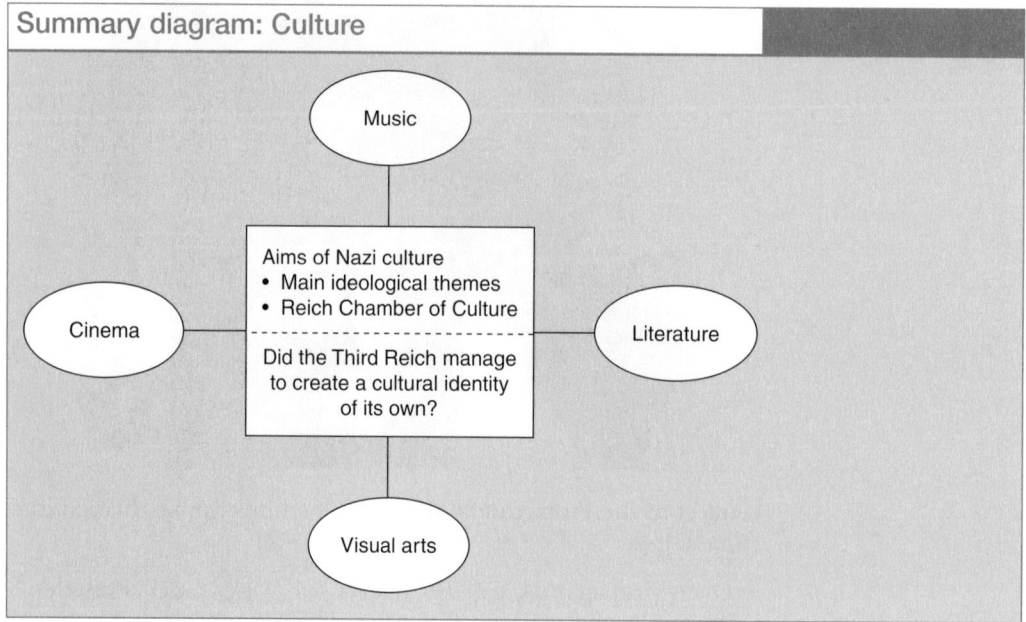

Summary diagram: Culture

- Music
- Cinema
- Aims of Nazi culture
  - Main ideological themes
  - Reich Chamber of Culture
  - Did the Third Reich manage to create a cultural identity of its own?
- Literature
- Visual arts

7 | Outsiders

Despite all its claims to create a *Volksgemeinschaft*, Nazism believed that certain people were not allowed to join the Third Reich – and they were to be discriminated against and persecuted. Nazism was an all-embracing society, but only of those who conformed to their criteria – and there were certain groups who were definitely 'outsiders'.

Key question
Who were the outsiders in the *Volksgemeinschaft*?

Ideological opponents

This term could most obviously be applied to the Communists, so many of whom were sent to the early concentration camps in 1933 (see page 10). However, it increasingly became a term to cover anyone who did not politically accept the regime and, as the years went on, a broader range of political and ideological opponents was imprisoned or worse, e.g. Pastor Niemöller (see page 69) and General Stauffenberg (see page 147).

The 'biologically inferior'

This covered all the races that, according to the Nazis, were 'inferior' or sub-human, such as the Gypsies, Slavs and Jews (see Chapter 4).

It also included those who were mentally and physically disabled. As early as July 1933 the Nazis proclaimed 'The Law for the Prevention of Hereditarily Diseased Offspring', which allowed for the compulsory sterilisation of those with hereditary conditions – examples included schizophrenia, Huntington's chorea, hereditary blindness or deafness. Over the 12 years of the Nazi period, 350,000 people were sterilised under this law.

However, the policy went much further from 1939, when Hitler himself initiated the idea of using euthanasia for children with severe disabilities (such as Down's syndrome and cerebral palsy) by using the phrase 'mercy death'. No specific law permitted this, but patients were killed in asylums under the name of 'Operation T4'. About 70,000 were gassed in 1940–1 but, following public rumours and Catholic opposition, the operation was stopped (see pages 148–9).

Asocials

The term was used very broadly to cover anyone whose behaviour was not viewed as acceptable.

These social outcasts included alcoholics, prostitutes, criminals, tramps and the workshy. Those asocials who were 'orderly', but avoided work were rounded up and organised into a compulsory labour force; and those who were judged as 'disorderly' were imprisoned and sometimes sterilised or experimented on.

Homosexuals were also classed as asocials. They were seen as breaking the laws of nature and undermining traditional Nazi family values. In 1936 the Reich Central Office for the Combating of Homosexuality and Abortion was established. Between 10,000 and 15,000 homosexuals were imprisoned and those sent to camps were forced to wear pink triangles (it is worth noting that lesbians were not persecuted).

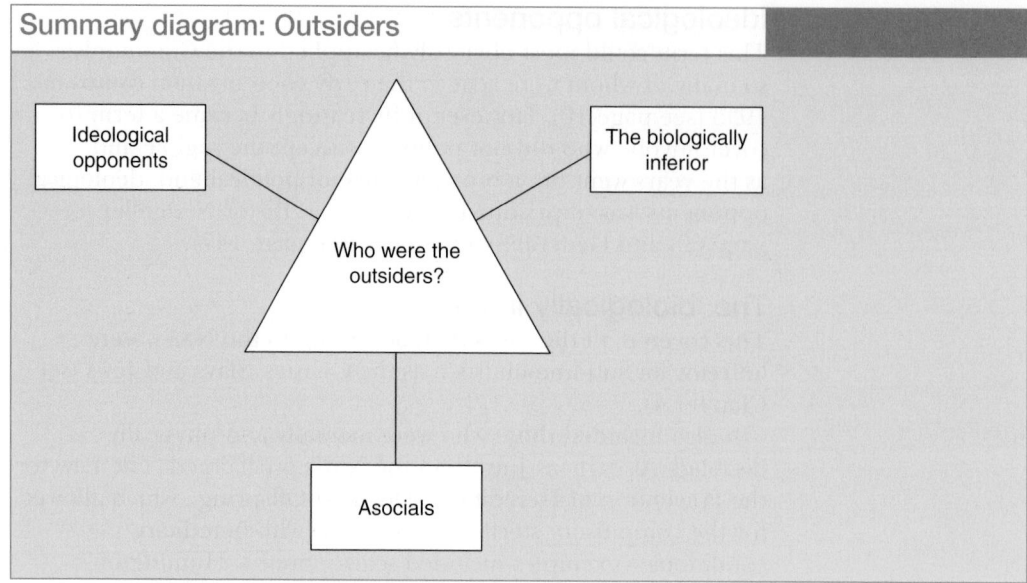

Summary diagram: Outsiders

- Ideological opponents
- The biologically inferior
- Who were the outsiders?
- Asocials

8 | The Key Debate

In a very obvious sense the effects of the 12 years of the Third Reich had a dramatic impact on the German people. Yet, historians have found it difficult to define and interpret the exact nature of the social changes. So we are left with the question:

Did Nazism's *Volksgemeinschaft* create a social revolution in the Third Reich?

Marxist historians: Nazism as reaction

After the Second World War Marxist historians in East Germany argued that Nazism failed to bring about revolutionary change (even some mainstream historians also agree with this view). Rather, in the view of the Marxist historian, Nazism was social reaction of the worst kind. This was because it reinforced traditional class structure and strengthened the position of the establishment élites, especially the powerful interests of the military and big business, at the expense of more popular institutions, such as trade unions.

Dahrendorf: Nazism as a revolution

In contrast, several historians in the West in the 1960s began to believe increasingly that in some ways the Nazi regime did produce a social revolution. The German Ralf Dahrendorf, who was a sociologist living in Britain, suggested that Nazism resulted in a social revolution which paved the way for the emergence of a liberal, democratic West Germany. In particular, he felt that the Nazi *Gleichschaltung* of German society caused the collapse of the social élites and the traditional loyalties and values that had dominated German life since the mid-nineteenth century.

Schoenbaum: Nazism as an interpreted social revolution

The American historian David Schoenbaum, in his book *Hitler's Social Revolution* (1966), argued that Nazism was a powerful modernising force in German society, but from a different perspective. His interpretation is a complex one founded on the differentiation between what he describes as 'objective' and 'interpreted' social reality. In substance, he claims that the idea of the *Volksgemeinschaft* was the *imagined* reality of the Third Reich as perceived in the minds of its citizens ('interpreted social reality'). In this sense, at least, Schoenbaum suggests the Third Reich witnessed a fundamental change in social values and attitudes, which formed the basis of a revolutionary national consensus. Thus, he concludes, Nazi society was regarded by the people as 'united like no other in recent German history, a society of opportunities for young and old, classes and masses, a society that was New Deal and good old days at the same time'.

Nazism: as a revolution of destruction

In the 1980s a new interpretation emerged from a range of historians, especially in Germany. They recognised that changes did help to modernise aspects of Germany, but they were limited and did not have enough substance to be called a social revolution. Moreover, many of the effects were contradictory and led to 'a revolution of destruction'. In that sense, the real changes came about through the destruction wrought by the effects of total war, economic collapse, genocide and political division. These had not been the aims of Nazism, but they were the effects.

'The one-pot meal'. One of the images cultivated by the Nazi leadership was the creation of the *Volksgemeinschaft* by encouraging people to eat a simple meal together.

Conclusion

So the debate over whether the Third Reich witnessed 'social revolution' or 'social reaction' is a complex one. This is because of a number of reasons:

- The definition of terms, such as 'reaction' and 'revolution', are not clear-cut and so they have become the focus of disagreement in their own right.
- Likewise, Nazism itself defies straightforward analysis. It was a unique mixture of forces that reflected a broad and varied social make-up. Therefore, when one tears away the propaganda and asks 'What were the real social aims of the Third Reich?' and 'Did the Third Reich achieve those aims?' unfortunately the answers remain very unclear.
- It is difficult to gauge the direct impact of Nazism – as opposed to the effects of other forces for change. Germany's history in the first half of the twentieth century was tumultuous and German society had been experiencing great changes in the 60 years before 1933.
- The Nazis were in power for only 12 years and six of those were spent fighting the bloodiest war in human history. Can the historian draw a line between Nazism and the war as a catalyst for social change? Should he/she try to draw that line, when it could be argued that war was a natural feature of Nazism?

Yet, bearing in mind all the above points, it seems increasingly difficult to uphold the idea of a Nazi social revolution. Schoenbaum's thesis is not easily disproved, but equally his view of a change in the German people's outlook is difficult to substantiate. However, past experience generally suggests that attempts to bring about fundamental changes in values and attitudes are notoriously difficult to effect within 12 years. Prevailing cultural traditions and social institutions, such as the family and the Churches, do not break down overnight. So it should be remembered that:

- Despite Nazi rhetorical support for the *Mittelstand* and the peasantry, both groups remained under social and economic pressure. In contrast, the traditional élites continued to dominate and property and industry stayed in private ownership. Indeed big business prospered.
- Women were supposed to stay at home and have more children, but really their role was set by the economic demands of the situation.
- The Christian Churches were expected to wither away. However, the Churches survived and enjoyed the support of the vast majority of Christians, although active opposition to the regime was actually limited.
- Nazi culture was meant to establish new roots in the *Volk*, but it exerted little more than a negative censorious role.
- It seems that the indoctrination of German youth did have some successes, especially in the pre-war years. However, even

then the effects of Nazi education have been questioned on the grounds of imposing conformity without real conviction.

• If there was a revolutionary core to Nazism, it is to be found in the obsessive nature and implementation of its racial policy and that is the focus of the subject in Chapter 4.

Some key books in the debate
I. Kershaw, *The Nazi Dictatorship: Problems and Perspectives of Interpretation*, 3rd edn (London, 1993).
J. Noakes, 'Nazism and Revolution' in Noel O'Sullivan, ed., *Revolutionary Theory and Political Reality* (London, 1983).
D. Schoenbaum, *Hitler's Social Revolution* (London, 1966).

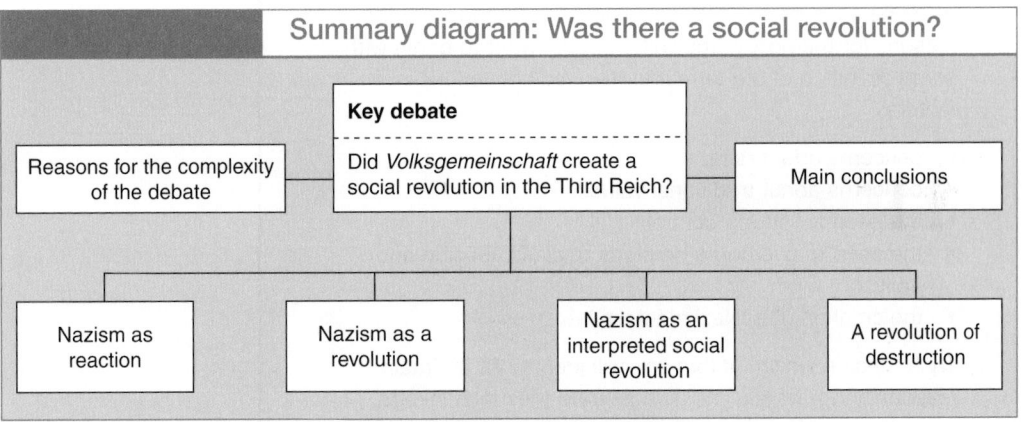

Summary diagram: Was there a social revolution?

Study Guide: AS Questions

In the style of AQA

(a) Explain why Hitler tried to introduce the policy of
Volksgemeinschaft ('a people's community') in Germany in the
period 1933–9.   (12 marks)

(b) 'The Nazis were totally unsuccessful in their attempt to
control the Churches in Germany.' Explain why you agree or
disagree with this view.   (24 marks)

Exam tips

*The cross-references are intended to take you straight to the material
that will help you to answer the questions.*

(a) Look again at pages 51–3. Remember you are not required to
describe aspects of *Volksgemeinschaft* but to identify the
reasons for the policy. You will probably want to begin with
some definition of the term and then look at various
factors:

- concerns about race
- concerns about traditional values
- the need for strong control
- the need to overcome divisions of class, religion and
  politics
- the creation of a 'Nazi mentality'.

Try to decide which factors you will identify as the main
reasons and how you will demonstrate their interlinkage.
You will need to provide a well-substantiated conclusion to
your answer.

(b) The Nazis' attempts to control the Churches are explained on
pages 66–70. You will need to consider the Nazis' aims before
you can talk about success and you should also ensure you can
cite ways in which they were successful as well as ways in which
they were not.
   Successes might include:

- the Catholic concordat
- the *Reich* Church under Müller
- the Ministry of Church Affairs
- the prevention of any co-ordinated Church opposition
  to the regime.

Failures might include:

- the German Faith Movement
- limited control and co-operation from Protestant and Catholic Churches
- opposition from Niemöller and the Pope in 1937
- Hitler's caution in his dealings with the Churches.

You will need to decide whether you are going to 'agree' or 'disagree' and provide a suitably balanced argument leading to a well-supported conclusion.

4 The Racial State

POINTS TO CONSIDER

The previous chapter considered many of the social themes covered by the concept of the *Volksgemeinschaft*, but the essential topic of Nazi racism will be the focus of this chapter. This topic can be broken down into three chronological stages, but it also raises a number of broader issues:

- The origins of anti-Semitism
- Gradualism 1933–9
- War and genocide 1939–45

Key dates

1933	April 1	First official boycott of Jewish shops and professions
1935	September 15	Nuremberg Race Laws introduced
1938	November 9–10	*Kristallnacht*: anti-Jewish pogrom
1939		Creation of the Reich Central Office for Jewish Emigration
1942	January	Wannsee Conference: 'Final Solution' to exterminate the Jewish people

1 | The Origins of Anti-Semitism

At the very centre of Nazi social policy was the issue of race and, specifically, anti-Semitism. Hitler's obsessive hatred of the Jews was perhaps the most dominant and consistent theme of his political career. The translation of such ideas into actual policy was to lead to racial laws, government-inspired violence and to the execution of the **genocide** policy that culminated in what became known as the **Holocaust**. For historians, such questions pose immense problems.

Historical background

There is a long tradition of anti-Semitism in European history. It was not the preserve of the Nazis, and it certainly has never been

Key question
How was anti-Semitism in Nazi Germany rooted in the past?

Genocide
The extermination of a whole race.

Key term

Holocaust
Generally used to describe mass slaughter – in the context of the Third Reich it refers specifically to the extermination of the Jews.

just a purely German phenomenon. It was rooted in the religious hostility of Christians towards the Jews (as the murderers of Jesus) that can be traced back to medieval Europe. And the reason went further than that. Jews being used as a scapegoat for society's problems was a long-established practice.

However, there emerged in Germany in the course of the nineteenth century a more clearly defined anti-Semitism based on racism and national resentment. By 1900 a number of specifically anti-Semitic *völkisch* political parties were winning seats in the *Reichstag* and, although they were comparatively few, their success shows that anti-Semitic ideas were becoming more prevalent and generally more respectable. One of the leaders of these right-wing anti-Semitic parties was the Imperial Court Chaplain, Adolf Stöcker, 1874–90. Some historians have seen this anti-Semitism as a by-product of the nationalist passions stirred up by the emergence of Imperial Germany as a world power under Kaiser Wilhelm II, 1888–1918. However, it should be remembered that a similar development had also taken place in German-speaking Austria, and there the political situation was very different.

Key question
How did social changes affect the development of anti-Semitism?

Social factors

In reality, the emergence of political anti-Semitism was a response to intellectual developments and changing social conditions. The Jews became an easy scapegoat for the discontent and disorientation felt by many people as rapid industrialisation and urbanisation took place. And, because many of the Jews were actually immigrants from eastern Europe, they were easily identifiable because of their different traditions. Moreover, although many members of the Jewish community were impoverished, they became the focus of envy because they were viewed as privileged. In 1933, for example, although Jews comprised less than one per cent of the German population, they composed more than 16 per cent of lawyers, 10 per cent of doctors and five per cent of editors and writers.

In the late nineteenth century, anti-Semitism also began to be presented in a more intellectual vein by the application of the racial theories of Social Darwinism (see page 51). According to such thinking, nations were like animals and only by struggling and fighting could they hope to survive. In this way, an image of intellectual and cultural respectability was given to those anti-Semites who portrayed the Jews as an 'inferior' or 'parasitic' race and the German race as superior:

- Heinrich von Treitschke, the leading historian, who publicly declared 'the Jews are our misfortune'.
- Richard Wagner, the musician and composer whose operas glorified German mythology and often portrayed Jewish characters as evil.
- Houston Stewart Chamberlain, an Englishman, who in his book, the *Foundations of the Nineteenth Century*, celebrated the superiority of the German *Volk*.

Such thinking brings one of the leading historians of Nazi Germany, J. Noakes, to suggest that by 1914:

> In the form of a basic dislike of the Jews and of what they were felt to represent, it [anti-Semitism] had succeeded in permeating broad sections of German society from the Kaiser down to the lower middle class. Ominously, it was particularly strongly entrenched within the academic community, thereby influencing the next generation.

Nazi anti-Semitism 1919–33

The emergence of right-wing racist *völkisch* nationalism was clearly apparent before 1914, but its attractions expanded in the aftermath of the First World War: the self-deception of the **'stab in the back' myth**; the humiliation of the Versailles Treaty; and the political and economic weaknesses of the Weimar Republic. So, by the early 1920s, there were probably about 70 relatively small right-wing splinter parties, e.g. the Nazi Party.

In that environment Hitler was able to exploit hostility towards the Jews and turn it into a radical ideology of hatred. He was the product, not the creator, of a society that was permeated by such prejudices. Yet, it would be inaccurate to dismiss Hitler as just another anti-Semite. Hitler's hatred of Jews was obsessive and vindictive, and it shaped much of his political philosophy. Without his personal commitment to attack the Jews and without his charismatic skills as a political leader, it seems unlikely that anti-Semitism could have become such an integral part of the Nazi movement. He was able to mobilise and stir the support of the leading anti-Semitic Nazis:

- Göring (see page 39)
- Goebbels (see pages 92 and 128)
- Himmler (see page 119)
- Streicher (see page 92)
- Heydrich (see page 98).

It is all too easy to highlight the rhetoric of Nazi anti-Semitism as the reason for the success of the Party. Certainly, 37.3 per cent of the population may have voted for Hitler the anti-Semite in July 1932, but the vast majority of Germans were motivated by unemployment, the collapse of agricultural prices and the fear of communism. Indeed, in a 1934 survey into the reasons why people joined the Nazis, over 60 per cent did not even mention anti-Semitism.

Key question
What were the causes of anti-Semitism in Nazi Germany?

Key term

'Stab in the back' myth
The distorted view that the German army had not really lost the First World War in 1918. Rather, unpatriotic elements, e.g. socialists and Jews, had undermined the war effort. It was a myth that played on certain scapegoats and severely weakened the Weimar democracy from the start.

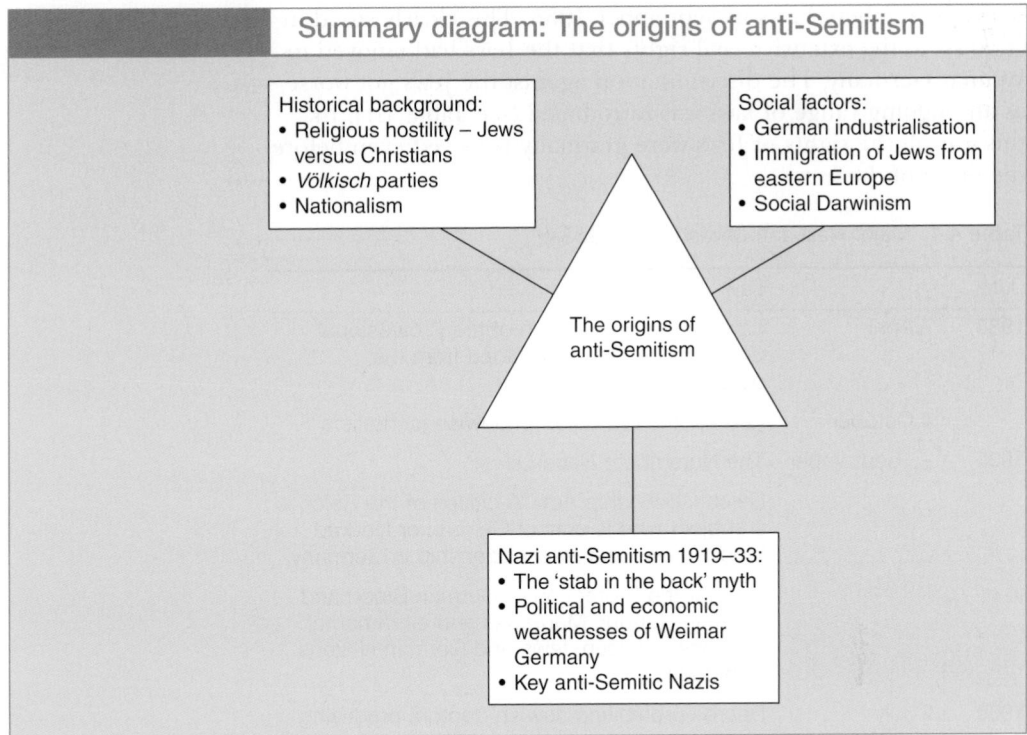

Summary diagram: The origins of anti-Semitism

Historical background:
• Religious hostility – Jews versus Christians
• *Völkisch* parties
• Nationalism

Social factors:
• German industrialisation
• Immigration of Jews from eastern Europe
• Social Darwinism

The origins of anti-Semitism

Nazi anti-Semitism 1919–33:
• The 'stab in the back' myth
• Political and economic weaknesses of Weimar Germany
• Key anti-Semitic Nazis

2 | Gradualism 1933–9

Key question
Did Nazi anti-Semitism change over time?

The Nazi approach to anti-Semitism was **gradualist**. The early moves against the Jews gave no suggestion of the end result. Indeed, for some Germans the discriminatory legislation was no more than the Jews deserved. For the more liberal minded, who found such action offensive, there was the practical problem of how to show opposition and to offer resistance. Once the apparatus of dictatorship was well established by the end of 1934, the futility of opposition was apparent to most people. Feelings of hopelessness were soon replaced by those of fear. To show sympathy for, or to protect the Jews, was to risk one's own freedom or one's own life. It was an unenviable dilemma.

Key term
Gradualism
Changing by degrees; progressing slowly.

Legal discrimination

Key date
First official boycott of Jewish shops and professions: 1 April 1933

Many radical Nazis were keen to take immediate measures against Jewish people and their businesses, but the Party's leadership was worried that it could get out of hand. And those concerns were confirmed when a one-day national boycott was organised for 1 April 1933. Jewish-owned shops, cafés and businesses were picketed by the SA, who stood outside urging people not to enter. However, the boycott was not universally accepted by the German people and it caused a lot of bad publicity abroad.

The Nazi leaders developed their anti-Semitism in a more subtle way. Once the Nazi regime had established the legal basis for its dictatorship (see pages 8–12), it was legally possible to initiate an anti-Jewish policy – most significantly by the creation of the Nuremberg Laws in September 1935. This clearly stood in contrast to the extensive civil rights that the Jews had enjoyed in Weimar Germany. The discrimination against the Jews got worse as an ongoing range of laws was introduced (see Table 4.1). In this way all the rights of Jews were gradually removed even before the onset of the war.

Table 4.1: Major Nazi anti-Jewish laws 1933–9

Date		Law
1933	7 April	Law for the Restoration of the Professional Civil Service. Jews excluded from the government's civil service
	4 October	Law for the exclusion of Jewish journalists
1935	15 September	The Nuremberg Race Laws:
		Reich Citizenship Act. 'A citizen of the Reich is a subject who is only of German or kindred blood.' Jews lost their citizenship in Germany
		Law for the Protection of German Blood and German Honour. Marriages and extramarital relations between Jews and German citizens forbidden
1938	5 July	Decree prohibiting Jewish doctors practising medicine
	28 October	Decree to expel 17,000 Polish Jews resident in Germany
	15 November	Decree to exclude Jewish pupils from schools and universities
	3 December	Decree for the compulsory closure and sale of all Jewish businesses
1939	1 September	Decree for the introduction of curfew for Jews

Propaganda and indoctrination

Nazism also set out to cultivate the message of anti-Semitism – in effect to change people's attitudes so that they hated the Jews. Goebbels himself was a particularly committed anti-Semite and he used his skills as the Minister of Propaganda and Popular Enlightenment to indoctrinate the German people (see pages 76–80 and 123–9). All aspects of culture associated with the Jews were censored. Even more worrying was the full range of propaganda methods used to advance the anti-Semitic message, such as:

• posters and signs, e.g. 'Jews are not wanted here'
• newspapers, e.g. *Der Angriff*, which was founded by Goebbels himself; *Der Stürmer*, edited by the *Gauleiter* Julius Streicher, which was overtly anti-Semitic with a seedy range of articles devoted to pornography and violence
• cinema, e.g. *The Eternal Jew*; *Jud Süss*.

A particular aspect of anti-Semitic indoctrination was the emphasis placed on influencing the German youth. The message

Poster for the anti-Semitic film *The Eternal Jew*.

was obviously put across by the Hitler Youth, but all schools also conformed to new revised textbooks and teaching materials, e.g tasks and exam questions.

Terror and violence

In the early years of the regime, the SA, as the radical left wing of the Nazis, took advantage of their power at local level to use violence against Jews, e.g. damage of property, intimidation and physical attacks. However, after the Night of the Long Knives in June 1934 (see page 19), anti-Semitic violence became more sporadic for two probable reasons. First, in 1936 there was a distinct decline in the anti-Semitic campaign because of the Berlin Olympics and the need to avoid international alienation.

Secondly, conservative forces still had a restraining influence. For example, Schacht had continued to express worries about the implications of anti-Semitic action for the economy (although he resigned in 1937 – see page 40).

However, the events of 1938 were on a different scale. First, the union with Austria in March 1938 resulted, in the following month, in thousands of attacks on the 200,000 Jews of Vienna. Secondly, on 9–10 November 1938 there was a sudden violent **pogrom** against the Jews, which became known as the 'Night of Crystal Glass' (*Kristallnacht*) because of all the smashed glass. *Kristallnacht* started in Berlin and spread throughout Germany with dramatic effects: the destruction of numerous Jewish homes and 100 deaths, attacks on 10,000 Jewish shops and businesses, the burning down of 200 synagogues and the deportation of 20,000 to concentration camps. The excuse for this had been the assassination of Ernst von Rath, a German diplomat in Paris, by Herschel Grünspan, a Jew, on 7 November. Goebbels had hoped that the anti-Semitic actions might also win Hitler's favour, and compensate for Goebbels' disreputable affair with a Czech actress. It should be noted that much of the anti-Semitic legislation (see also page 92) came in the months after the pogrom.

Forced emigration

From the start of the Nazi dictatorship a number of Jews had decided to leave Germany voluntarily. Many Jews with influence, high reputation or sufficient wealth could find the means to leave. The most popular destinations were Palestine, Britain and the USA, and among the most renowned emigrés were Albert Einstein, the scientist, and Kurt Weill, the composer.

However, from 1938 a new dimension to anti-Semitism developed – forced emigration. As a result of the events in Austria in 1938, the Central Office for Jewish Emigration was established in Vienna, overseen by Adolf Eichmann. Jewish property was confiscated to finance the emigration of poor Jews. Within six months Eichmann had forced the emigration of 45,000 and the scheme was seen as such a success that, in January 1939, Göring was prompted to create the Reich Central Office for Jewish Emigration run by Heydrich and Eichmann (see Table 4.2).

Pogrom
An organised or encouraged massacre of innocent people. The term originated from the massacres of Jews in Russia.

Key term

Kristallnacht, anti-Jewish pogrom: 9–10 November 1938

Creation of the Reich Central Office for Jewish Emigration: 1939

Key dates

Table 4.2: The Jewish community in Germany 1933–45

	Jewish population	Emigrés per annum
1933	503,000	38,000
1939 (May)	234,000	78,000*
1945	20,000	N/A

* The cumulative figure of Jewish emigrés between 1933 and 1939 was 257,000

It is therefore estimated that the Nazi persecution led to about half of the Jewish population leaving before the war. Technically, the Jews had voluntarily emigrated but they were forced to leave behind all their belongings. Given those circumstances, the remainder decided to take their chances and stay in Germany, rather than lose their homes and all their possessions.

Conclusion

Key question
Why was the year 1938 so significant?

Despite the range of anti-Semitic measures of 1933–9, it is difficult to claim that the Nazis had pursued a planned overall policy to deal with 'the Jewish question'. In many respects the measures were at first haphazard. However, on one point it is very clear – the year 1938 marked an undoubted '**radicalisation**' of Nazi anti-Semitism. The legal laws, the violence connected with *Kristallnacht* and the forced emigration came together, suggesting that the regime had reached a pivotal year – a fact confirmed by the tone of the speech in the Reichstag by Hitler on 30 January 1939:

Key term

Radicalisation
A policy of increasing severity.

> If the international Jewish financiers in and outside Europe should succeed in plunging the nations once more into a world war, then the result will not be the Bolshevising [making communist] of the earth, and thus the victory of Jewry, but the annihilation of the Jewish race in Europe.

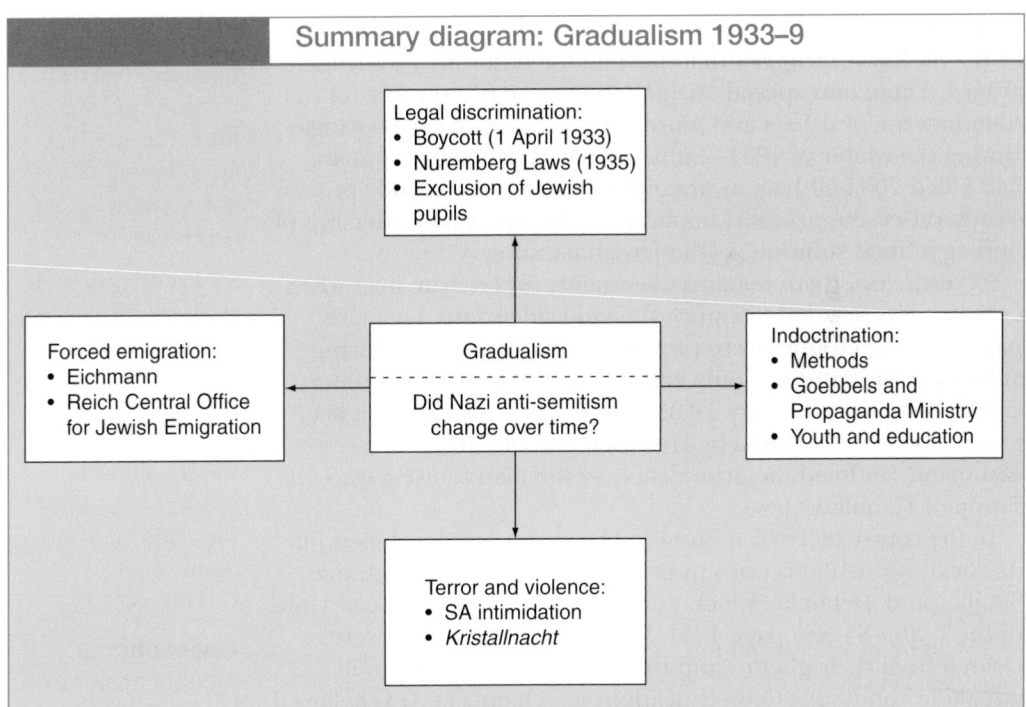

Summary diagram: Gradualism 1933–9

Legal discrimination:
- Boycott (1 April 1933)
- Nuremberg Laws (1935)
- Exclusion of Jewish pupils

Forced emigration:
- Eichmann
- Reich Central Office for Jewish Emigration

Gradualism

Did Nazi anti-semitism change over time?

Indoctrination:
- Methods
- Goebbels and Propaganda Ministry
- Youth and education

Terror and violence:
- SA intimidation
- *Kristallnacht*

3 | War and Genocide 1939–45

At the time it was inconceivable to imagine that the Holocaust was possible. Who in 1939 could have predicted the scenario of the next six years? The suggestion that millions would be systematically exterminated would have defied belief. It is an event in modern European history that even now seems almost beyond rational comprehension, although it had a terrifying logic to it. For those who lived in occupied Europe it was easier and more comfortable to dismiss the rumours as gross and macabre exaggerations – the result of war-time gossip and Allied propaganda. Yet, the unbelievable did happen and it required not only the actions of a 'criminal' minority but also the passivity of the 'innocent' majority. In Germany the moral dimension has helped to make this historical debate a particularly impassioned one.

From emigration to extermination

Germany's victory over Poland in autumn 1939 (see page 175) meant that the Nazis inherited responsibility for an estimated three millions Jews. Moreover, the beginning of a general European war made emigration of Jews to independent countries more difficult. However, plans to 'resettle' so many people placed such a great strain on food supplies and the transportation system that, in the short term, the Nazi leadership in Poland were compelled to create a number of Jewish **ghettos**, e.g. Warsaw, Krakow and Lublin.

The invasion of Russia in the summer 1941 marked a decisive development. From that time, it was seen as a racial war launched by the **SS *Einsatzgruppen*** that moved in behind the advancing armies. These four special 'Action Units' were responsible for rounding up local Jews and murdering them by mass shootings. During the winter of 1941–2 it is estimated that *Einsatzgruppen* had killed 700,000 Jews in western Russia, but the bloody process clearly raised the practical implications for the Nazi leadership of finding a '**final solution**' to the Jewish question.

Nevertheless, there remains uncertainty and debate over when exactly it was decided to launch the genocide of the Jews (see pages 100–1). Options were probably being considered during autumn 1941, but it was only agreed as a result of the Wannsee Conference on 20 January 1942. There, in no more than a few hours, a meeting, chaired by Heydrich and organised by Eichmann, outlined the grim details of the plan to use gas to kill Europe's 11 million Jews.

In the course of 1942, a number of camps were developed into mass extermination centres in Poland, most notably Auschwitz, Sobibor and Treblinka, which were run by the Death's Head Units of the *Waffen* SS (see page 120). Most of the Polish Jews were cleared from their ghettos and then 'transported' by train in appalling conditions to their death in gas chambers. It is believed that, of the original three million Polish Jews, only 4000 survived the war. In 1943–4 Jews from all over Europe were deported to face a similar fate – so that by 1945 it is estimated that six million European Jews had been murdered.

Key date

Wannsee Conference. 'Final solution' to exterminate the Jewish people: 20 January 1942

Key question
How did Nazi anti-Semitism degenerate into genocide?

Key terms

Ghetto
Ancient term describing the area lived in by the Jews in a city. Under Nazi occupation the Jews were separated from the rest of the community and forced to live in appalling and overcrowded conditions.

SS *Einsatzgruppen*
'Action Units'. Four of the units were launched in eastern Europe after the invasion of Russia. Responsible for rounding up local Jews and murdering them by mass shootings.

Final Solution
A euphemism used by the Nazi leadership to describe the extermination of the Jews from 1941.

Table 4.3: The Nazi extermination of the Jews 1940–5

Date		Event
1940		First deportations of Jews from some German provinces
1941	June	Action squads (*Einsatzgruppen*) of SS moved into the USSR behind the advancing armies to round up and kill Jews
1941	1 September	All Jews forced to wear the Yellow Star of David
1942	20 January	Wannsee Conference. Various government and Party agencies agreed on the 'Final Solution' to the Jewish problem
	Spring	Extermination facilities set up at Auschwitz, Sobibor and Treblinka
1943	February	Destruction of Warsaw Ghetto
1943–4		Transportation of Jews from all over German-occupied Europe to death camps began
1945	27 January	Liberation of Auschwitz by Soviet troops

Henri Pieck, *Behind Barbed Wire*. Painting drawn in Buchenwald concentration camp.

Profile: Reinhard Heydrich 1904–42

1904		– Born at Halle in Saxony, Germany
1922–8		– Joined the navy but discharged (probably for a sexual offence against a woman)
1931		– Joined the NSDAP and the SS
1932		– Appointed leader of the newly created SD (the Party's intelligence security service, see pages 118–20)
1934	June	– Worked closely with Himmler in the Night of the Long Knives. Appointed SS Lieutenant-General
1936		– Appointed Chief of Secret Police (but still under Himmler's authority)
1939	January	– Created Reich Central Office for Jewish Emigration
	September	– Appointed Head of RSHA (Reich Security Head Office), but still under Himmler's authority
1941		– Reich Protector of Bohemia and Moravia (Czech lands)
1942	January	– Chaired the Wannsee Conference meeting to exterminate the Jews
	May	– Assassinated by the Czech resistance in Prague

Heydrich was undoubtedly talented – he was not only physically the image of the perfect Aryan but also a very good sportsman and a talented musician and linguist. Yet, his skills gave way to the dominating traits of selfishness, ambition and brutality that earned him the title of 'the butcher of Prague'. He advanced extremely quickly within the SS, so at the age of 32 he was appointed Chief of Secret Police. With his abilities he was responsibility for:

- developing and running the policing system of surveillance and repression
- implementing the Nazi racial policy
- chairing the notorious meeting at Wannsee Conference which agreed on the Final Solution.

Gypsies

In addition to the Jews, the Gypsies (Sinti and Roma) were also subject to racial persecution and became victims of Nazi genocide. The Gypsies had been viewed as 'outsiders' throughout European history for several clear reasons:

Key question
Why were the
Gypsies persecuted?

- they were non-Christian and they had their own Romany customs and dialect
- they were non-white – because they had originated from India in the late medieval period
- their 'traveller' lifestyle with no regular employment was resented.

So, even before the Nazi dictatorship and during Weimar's liberal years, there was official hostility towards the Gypsies and, in 1929, 'The Central Office for the Fight against the Gypsies' was established.

By 1933 it is believed that the number of Gypsies in Germany was about 25,000 to 30,000 – and they, too, were beginning to suffer from the gradualist policy of Nazi discrimination:

- Gypsies were defined exactly like the Jews as 'infallibly of alien blood' according to the Nuremberg Laws of 1935.
- Himmler issued, in 1938, a directive titled 'The Struggle against the Gypsy Plague', which ordered the registration of Gypsies in racial terms.
- Straight after the outbreak of the war, Gypsies were deported from Germany to Poland – and their movements were severely controlled in working camps. Notoriously, in January 1940, the first case of mass murder through gassing was committed by the Nazis against Gypsy children at Buchenwald.

As with the Jews, the Gypsies during the war were the focus of ever increasing repression and violence but there was no real, systematic Nazi policy of extermination until the end of 1942. In the first months of 1943 Germany's Gypsies were sent to Auschwitz camp and over 1943–4 a large proportion of Europe's Gypsy population from south-eastern Europe was exterminated – a figure between 225,000 and 500,000.

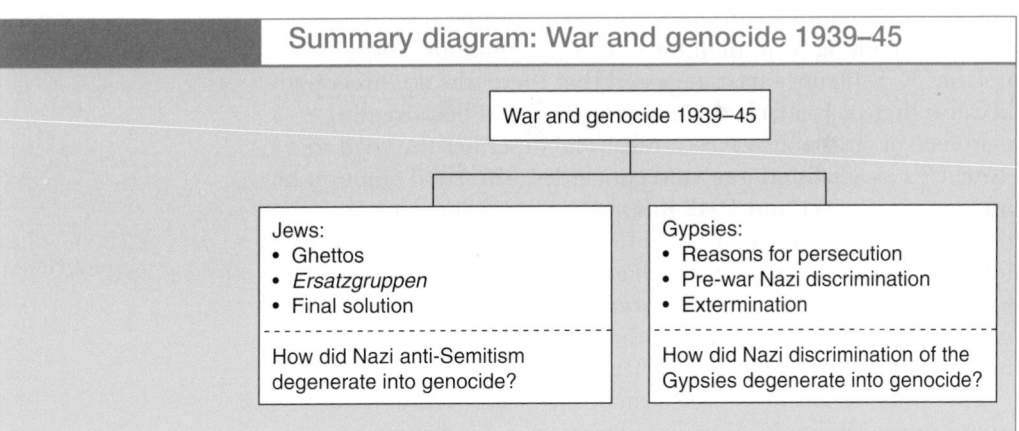

Summary diagram: War and genocide 1939–45

War and genocide 1939–45

Jews:
- Ghettos
- *Ersatzgruppen*
- Final solution

How did Nazi anti-Semitism degenerate into genocide?

Gypsies:
- Reasons for persecution
- Pre-war Nazi discrimination
- Extermination

How did Nazi discrimination of the Gypsies degenerate into genocide?

4 | The Key Debate

The issue of the Holocaust remains one of the most fundamental controversies in history. The detached rational objectivity required of historical analysis is exceedingly difficult to achieve when the subject is so emotive, and in many respects so irrational. And yet, among all the historical and moral issues, there lies one crucial question:

Why did the Holocaust happen and who was responsible?

Intentionalists

For historians of the **intentionalist** school, such as Fleming and Dawidowicz, Hitler remains the key. He is seen as having committed himself to the extermination of the Jews at an early stage in his political career. This was followed by a consistent gradualist policy that led logically from the persecution of 1933 to the gates of Auschwitz. In the simplest form they suggest that the Holocaust happened because Hitler willed it.

Even more controversially, the American historian Daniel Goldhagen has recently suggested in his book *Hitler's Willing Executioners* that the Holocaust was 'intended' because so many ordinary Germans were prepared to participate in the Third Reich's darkest deed. This is explained according to Goldhagen by the fact that within German culture there had developed a violent variant of anti-Semitism that was set on eliminating the Jews. Such a view has resurrected the old argument of 'collective national guilt and shame', although in academic circles Goldhagen's ideas have not been generally well received. He has been condemned for:

- selecting his evidence to prove his thesis
- failing to recognise other overtly anti-Semitic cultures in pre-1933 Europe
- ignoring the role of many non-Germans in the murder of the Jews.

Intentionalist
Interprets history by emphasising the role (intentions) of people who shape history.

Structuralist
Interprets history by analysing the role of social and economic forces and structures. Structuralists, therefore, tend to place less emphasis on the role of the individual.

Key terms

Structuralists

On the other hand, historians of the **structuralist** school reject the idea of a long-term plan for mass extermination. Most notably, K. Schleunes has suggested that there was no direct path because there was a lack of clear objectives and because of the existence of rival policies. As a result, he describes the road to Auschwitz as a 'twisted one' and concludes, 'the Final Solution as it emerged in 1941 and 1942 was *not* the product of grand design'. Instead, the 'Final Solution', it is suggested, came to be implemented as a result of the chaotic nature of government within the regime. As a result, various institutions and individuals improvised a policy to deal with the military and human situation in eastern Europe by the end of 1941.

Therefore, according to the structuralist interpretation, the moral responsibility for the 'Final Solution' extends beyond Hitler's intentions to the apparatus of the regime. However, nearly all structuralist historians emphasise that this in no way reduces the guilt of Hitler himself, who was in total agreement with such a policy. H. Mommsen, for example, concluded his analysis as follows: 'It cannot be proved, for instance, that Hitler himself gave the order for the Final Solution, though this does not mean that he did not approve the policy. That the solution was put into effect is by no means to be ascribed to Hitler alone, but to the complexity of the decision-making process in the Third Reich, which brought about a progressive and cumulative radicalisation'.

However, structuralists have also distanced themselves from Goldhagen's view because they cannot accept the anti-German generalisations. The reality is, that for the majority of the young men in the action squads and in the camps, their actions were not motivated by any kind of zealous anti-Semitism, but by much more mundane factors. In his chilling description *One Day in Jozefow*, Christopher Browning has detailed how one unit carried out its grim task. What emerges is that the perpetrators were influenced by peer pressure, cowardice, careerism and alcohol – all exaggerated by a brutalising context which was entirely alien to their home environment.

Conclusion

This particular historical debate has proved to be a lively one and it looks set to run for a good while yet. The controversy has generated a very close scrutiny and analysis of all the available evidence, particularly in the past 20 years. So, although the exact details are not clear, it seems fair to conclude the following points about the 'Final Solution':

- It now seems that the initial arrangements for the implementation of the 'Final Solution' were haphazard and makeshift. Hitler and the Nazi leadership did not have any clear programme to deal with the Jewish question until 1941.
- No written order for the killing of the Jews from Hitler has been found, although in January 1944 Himmler publicly stated that Hitler had given him 'a Führer order' to give priority to 'the total solution of the Jewish question'. It should be remembered that Hitler's authority was such that it encouraged initiatives from below as long as they were seen to be in line with his overall ideological vision and clearly Hitler had often spoken in violent and barbaric terms about the Jews from an early stage in his political career.
- Probably around autumn 1941 it was decided by the top Nazi leadership to launch an extermination policy and this was agreed at the Wannsee Conference in January 1942 by a broad range of representatives of Nazi organisations.

If these points are accepted, then it might be that the 'Final Solution' should be viewed as a pragmatic (practical) response to the confusion and chaos of war in 1941–2 rather than the culmination of long-term ideological intent.

Some key books in the debate

C. Browning, *Ordinary Men* (New York, 1992).

M. Burleigh and W. Wippermann, *The Racial State* (Cambridge, 1991).

L. Dawidowicz, *The War against the Jews* (Weidenfeld & Nicholson, 1975).

D. Goldhagen, *Hitler's Willing Executioners: Ordinary Germans and the Holocaust* (London, 1996).

I. Kershaw, *The Nazi Dictatorship: Problems and Perspectives of Interpretation*, 3rd edn (London, 1993).

H. Mommsen, ed., 'The realization of the unthinkable. The final solution of the Jewish question in the Third Reich', in *From Weimar to Auschwitz* (Oxford, 1991).

K. Schleunes, *The Twisted Road to Auschwitz* (London, 1970).

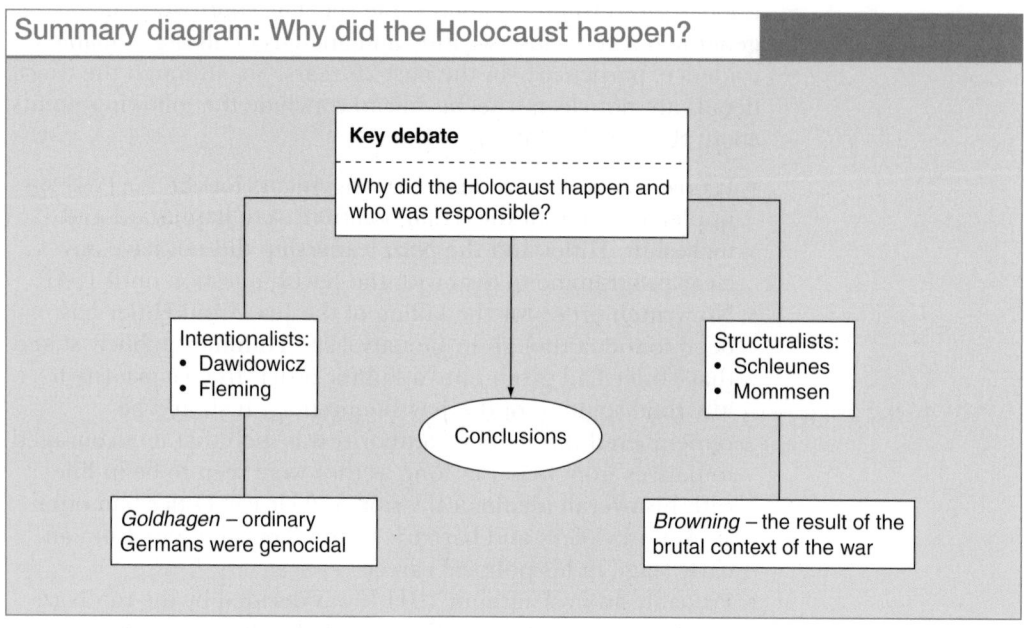

Summary diagram: Why did the Holocaust happen?

Key debate

Why did the Holocaust happen and who was responsible?

Intentionalists:
• Dawidowicz
• Fleming

Structuralists:
• Schleunes
• Mommsen

Conclusions

Goldhagen – ordinary Germans were genocidal

Browning – the result of the brutal context of the war

Study Guide: AS Questions

In the style of AQA

Read the following source material and then answer the questions that follow.

Source A

From: D. Cesarani, the introduction to The Final Solution, *1994.*

The Wannsee Conference was summoned by Heydrich, head of the Nazi Security Police, who was put in charge of Nazi policy towards the Jews. He requested the presence of some senior SS figures and key ministers at a meeting to arrange co-operation between the agencies necessary to the pursuit of the Final Solution of the Jewish question. He opened the meeting in January 1942 by announcing that emigration had failed to solve the Jewish question, so a new method would be used – 'evacuation to the east'. The significance of this conference was over-rated for many years and has since been downgraded to little more than a platform for Heydrich to display his new powers.

Source B

From: A. Farmer, Anti-Semitism and the Holocaust, *1998.*

Those attending the Wannsee Conference certainly realised that 'resettlement' meant extermination, one way or the other. At his trial in 1960, ex-SS leader Eichmann said that at the conference, the gentlemen talked about the matter without mincing their words. The talk was of killing, elimination and liquidation.

Source C

From: Heydrich talking to Göring and Goebbels on 12 November 1938.

In spite of the elimination of the Jews from economic life, the main problem, namely to kick the Jews out of Germany, remains. May I make a few proposals to that effect? ... we have set up a centre for the Emigration of Jews in Vienna and that way we have eliminated 50,000 Jews from Austria, while for the Reich only 19,000 Jews were eliminated during the same period.

(a) Use Sources A and B and your own knowledge to explain how far the views in Source B differ from those in Source A in relation to the importance of the Wannsee Conference. (12 marks)

(b) Use Sources A, B and C and your own knowledge to answer this question. How far was the Nazi policy towards the Jews 'planned' in the years 1933–42? (24 marks)

Exam tips

The cross-references are intended to take you straight to the material that will help you to answer the questions.

(a) You will need to identify points of difference between the views expressed by Farmer in Source B and those expressed by Cesarani in Source A.

- While Farmer clearly identifies the Wannsee Conference with a decision to exterminate the Jews, Cesarani talks only of a planned 'evacuation to the East' (although it is in inverted commas).
- Farmer quotes Eichmann as saying that the delegates talked 'without mincing their words' while Cesarani is much more guarded about what was discussed and suggests they talked in ambiguous language.
- Farmer implies that the conference was highly significant for the elimination of the Jews, whilst Cesarani says that is was 'over-rated' and was only a platform for Heydrich's views.

In order to 'explain how far', you will also need to look for some similarities:

- Both describe the conference as launching a new 'solution' to the Jewish problem.
- Both emphasise that it was an SS affair.
- Cesarani's use of inverted commas seems to imply that both accept there was an intention to get rid of the Jews by killing them.

You will need to make your own judgement about the extent of the difference and in writing your answer should also show your own knowledge of the context of this conference.

(b) You will need to re-read pages 91–101 and look carefully at the sources. You must include reference to the sources in your answer. The emphasis in this question is on the 'planning' and anti-Semitic policy. You may find that you want to consider changes in Nazi policy over time, but be careful not to let your answer turn into a narrative. Try to begin each paragraph with a link to the state of 'planning'. You will want to look at:

- Anti-Semitism before the war – was the discrimination part of a 'master plan'? Is there any evidence to support this?
- *Reichkristallnacht* – spontaneous or well-thought through?
- Forced emigration – why? Don't forget Source B refers to forced emigration in 1938.
- The influence of war. At what point was the decision taken to initiate the Holocaust? Refer to Sources A and B here.

This question has a number of issues to discuss. You should decide what your argument is going to be before starting to write and should ensure that you carry your view through the answer to provide a convincing conclusion.

5 The Political Structure of the Third Reich

POINTS TO CONSIDER

It is possible to assume that the consolidation of power in 1933–4 created a tightly structured dictatorship in the Third Reich, but, in fact, it became a very complex system of forces that changed over time. Therefore, the following main themes need to be considered:

- The role of Hitler
- The Party and the state
- The apparatus of the police state
- The propaganda machine
- The German army
- Big business

Key dates

1934	June	Night of the Long Knives
1936	June	Appointment of Heinrich Himmler as Chief of the German Police
	October	Introduction of the Four-Year Plan under the control of Göring; followed in the next year by the resignation of Schacht
1938	February	Forced resignation of Field Marshal Blomberg (Minister of Defence) and General Fritsch (Army Commander-in-Chief); mini-purge of army leadership
1939	September	Creation of RSHA
1942–3	Winter	Military 'turn of the tide'; German defeats at El Alamein and at Stalingrad
1944	July	Stauffenberg Bomb Plot; army purged

1 | The Role of Hitler

In theory, Hitler's power was unlimited. Nazi Germany was a one-party state and Hitler was undisputed leader of that Party. In addition, after the death of Hindenburg in August 1934, the law concerning the head of state of the German Reich combined the posts of president and chancellor. Constitutionally, Hitler was also commander-in-chief of all the armed services. (This image of Hitler was very much presented in the poster as shown on this book's front cover: *Ein Volk, Ein Reich, Ein Führer*.)

'*Führer* power'

However, if one studies contemporary documents, such as this extract from a leading Nazi theorist, E. Huber, it is clear that Hitler's personal dictatorship was portrayed in more than purely legal terms:

> If we wish to define political power in the *völkisch Reich* correctly, we must not speak of 'state power' but of '*Führer* power'. For it is not the state as an impersonal entity that is the source of political power, but rather political power is given to the *Führer* as the executor of the nation's common will. '*Führer* power' is comprehensive and total: it unites within itself all means of creative political activity: it embraces all spheres of national life.

Huber's grandiose theoretical claims for '*Führer* power' could not mask basic practical problems. First, there was no all-embracing **constitution** in the Third Reich. The government and law of Nazi Germany emerged over time in a haphazard fashion. Secondly, there was (and is) no way one individual could ever be in control of all aspects of government. Thus, Hitler was still dependent on sympathetic subordinates to put policy decisions into effect. And thirdly, Hitler's own personality and attitude towards government were mixed and not conducive to strong and effective leadership.

Hitler's character

Hitler certainly appeared as the charismatic and dynamic leader. His magnetic command of an audience enabled him to play on '**mass suggestion**'; he portrayed himself as the ordinary man with the vision, willpower and determination to transform the country.

However, this was an image perpetuated by the propaganda machine and, once in government, Hitler's true character revealed itself, as is shown in the memoirs of one of his retinue:

> Hitler normally appeared shortly before lunch … When Hitler stayed at Obersalzberg it was even worse. There he never left his room before 2.00 pm. He spent most afternoons taking a walk, in the evening straight after dinner, there were films … He disliked the study of documents. I have sometimes secured decisions from him without his ever asking to see the relevant files. He took the view that many things sorted themselves out on their own if one did not

Key question
What was the role of Hitler in Nazi Germany?

Constitution
The principles and rules that govern a state. The Weimar Constitution is a good example of a written constitution.

Mass suggestion
A psychological term suggesting that large groups of people can be unified simply by the atmosphere of the occasion. Hitler and Goebbels used their speeches and large rallies to particularly good effect.

Key terms

interfere … He let people tell him the things he wanted to hear, everything else he rejected. One still sometimes hears the view that Hitler would have done the right thing if people surrounding him had not kept him wrongly informed. Hitler refused to let himself be informed … How can one tell someone the truth who immediately gets angry when the facts do not suit him?

Hitler liked to cultivate the image of the artist and really he was quite lazy. This was accentuated further by Hitler's lifestyle: his unusual sleeping hours; his long periods of absence from Berlin when he stayed in the Bavarian Alps; his tendency to become immersed in pet projects such as architectural plans. Furthermore, as he got older he became neurotic and moody as was demonstrated in his obsession with his health and medical symptoms, both real and imagined.

Hitler was not well educated and had no experience for any role in government or administration. As cynics say, Hitler's first real job was his appointment as chancellor. He followed no real working routine, he loathed paperwork and disliked the formality of committees in which issues were discussed. He glibly believed that mere willpower was the solution to most problems.

Hitler was not even very decisive, when it came to making a choice. Thus, although he was presented to the world as the all-powerful dictator, he never showed any inclination to co-ordinate government. For example, the role of the cabinet declined quite markedly after 1934. In 1933 the cabinet met 72 times, but only four times in 1936 and the last official cabinet meeting was held in February 1938. Consequently, rivalry between the various factions of the Party and state below Hitler was rife and decision-making became, more often than not, the result of the *Führer's* whim or an informal conversation rather than rational clear-cut chains of command.

Key debate

Historians now generally agree that Hitler's government was really rather confused, but his leadership has remained the focus of great controversy and there are three schools of interpretation at the heart of this question:

Was Hitler really an effective dictator?

Intentionalist interpretation

On the one side is the so-called 'intentionalist' approach. The traditional view is that Hitler played an absolutely essential role in the development of the Third Reich. In a telling phrase N. Rich wrote: 'The point cannot be stressed too strongly. Hitler was master in the Third Reich', and many continue to uphold this view.

Intentionalists think that the division and confusion in Hitler's regime was a result of a deliberate policy of 'divide and rule' on the part of Hitler. Moreover, they claim that this strategy was successful in maintaining the *Führer's* own political authority.

Hitler took the responsibility for taking the 'big' decisions that shaped the direction of Nazi Germany, e.g. foreign policy. Moreover, although there were other power bases within the Party, Hitler preserved his own authority by tolerating only key Nazis, who were personally loyal, for example Himmler and Bormann. Finally, he hired and fired both Nazis and non-Nazis whom he could use. For example, Schacht had considerable freedom of manoeuvre for a time, but was removed when he no longer conformed. These views are outlined by Bracher and Jäckel. For such historians Nazism was in essence Hitlerism and all the vital developments of the Third Reich grew from Hitler and his 'blueprint for power'.

Structuralist interpretation

The alternative interpretation has been dubbed 'structuralist' or 'functionalist', and is expressed most forcefully in the works of Broszat and Mommsen. They believe that the Nazi regime really just evolved from the pressure of the circumstances and not from Hitler's dominant role. In fact, Hitler's personal weaknesses and limitations led to poor leadership. He was considered incapable of making effective decisions and, as a result, the government lacked clear direction. He was not able to keep the tensions in the economy and the state under control. Moreover, he was never able to control the other powerful institutions, for example, the army and the civil service. Finally, the leading Nazis exerted their own influence for their own objectives and frequently Hitler did not intervene. Indeed, Mommsen even goes as far as to describe Hitler as 'unwilling to take decisions, frequently uncertain, exclusively concerned with upholding his prestige and personal authority, influenced in the strongest fashion by his current entourage, in some respects a weak dictator'.

Kershaw's 'charismatic domination'

As a result of his research Ian Kershaw has recently outlined an interpretation that is a consensus between the structuralists and intentionalists. He has described Hitler's power as that of 'charismatic domination', which suggests that:

- Hitler was crucial because he was still responsible for the overall Nazi dream
- he had no real effective opposition to his aims
- although the government structure was chaotic, Hitler did not get lost in the detail of the day-to-day government
- he generated an environment in which his followers carried out his presumed intentions. In this way, others willingly took the responsibility 'to work towards the *Führer*'.

Therefore, in Kershaw's words, 'Hitler's personalized form of rule invited initiatives from below and offered such initiatives backing, so long as they were in line with his broadly defined goals'. In this way Hitler's personality and ideology led to a dramatic radicalisation of policy in the key spheres, such as:

- politically, by the creation of a one-party state brutally upheld by the SS-Police system
- a reorientation (re-shaping) of society by the application of racial laws, eventually followed by a policy of genocide
- and finally, in the field of foreign policy, by the drive towards a German (Aryan) world **hegemony**.

According to Kershaw's view, it is hard to envisage all these developments without Hitler at the helm.

In the light of such contradictory interpretations it is clearly necessary to consider in more detail all the other forces before drawing any conclusions about Hitler's role in the political structure of the Third Reich.

Key term

Hegemony
Political leadership and dominance.

Some key books in the debate

K.D. Bracher, *The German Dictatorship* (English translation, Penguin, 1973).
M. Broszat, *The Hitler State* (English translation, London, 1981).
E. Jäckel, *Hitler's Weltanschauung: A Blueprint for Power* (Middletown, Conn., 1973).
I. Kershaw, *The Nazi Dictatorship: Problems and Perspectives of Interpretation*, 3rd edn (London, 1993).
I. Kershaw, *Hitler Hubris* (Allen Lane, 1998).

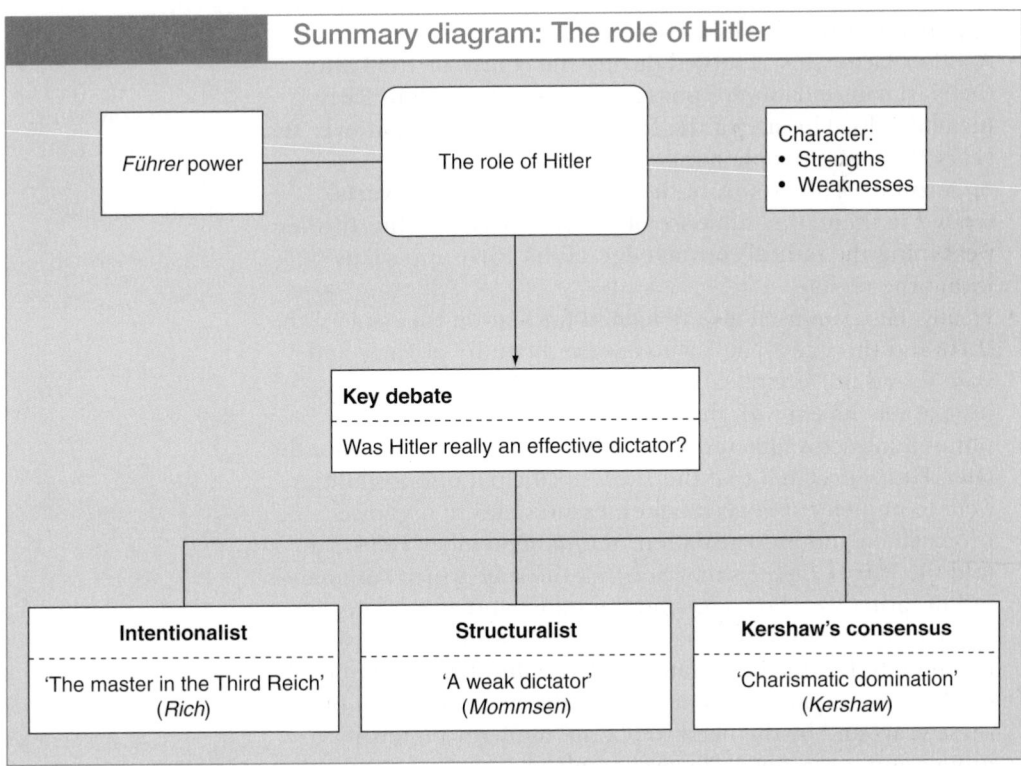

Summary diagram: The role of Hitler

Führer power — The role of Hitler — Character:
- Strengths
- Weaknesses

Key debate

Was Hitler really an effective dictator?

Intentionalist	**Structuralist**	**Kershaw's consensus**
'The master in the Third Reich' (*Rich*)	'A weak dictator' (*Mommsen*)	'Charismatic domination' (*Kershaw*)

2 | The Party and the State

By July 1933 Germany had become a one-party state, in which the Nazi Party claimed sole political authority. Nazi **totalitarian** claims, reinforced by a powerful propaganda machine, deceived many people at the time into thinking that Nazism was a clear and well-ordered system of government. The reality was very different. Fundamentally, this was because the exact relationship between the structure of the Party on the one hand and the apparatus of the German state on the other was never clarified satisfactorily. It meant that there was much confusion between the two forces in Nazi government and this clash has been given the term **dualism**.

Some of the Nazi leaders were keen to establish the Party's control over the civil service. This reflected the wishes of the revolutionary elements within the Party, which wanted to smash the traditional organs of government in order to create a new kind of Germany. However, there seem to have been three reasons why the Nazi leadership did not confront the institutions of state:

- Many recognised that the bureaucracy of the German state was well established and staffed by an educated and effective personnel. Initially, therefore, there was no drastic purge of the state apparatus. The law for the restoration of the professional civil service of April 1933 was strictly limited in its scope. It only called for the removal of Jews and well-recognised opponents of the regime (see page 92).
- Another factor that emerged during the course of 1933 after the Nazi consolidation of power was a vast increase in Party membership. The size of the Party increased three-fold over the years 1933–5 as people jumped on the bandwagon of opportunity. The growth of the so-called '**March converts**' tended to dilute the influence of the earlier Nazis, thus further weakening the radical cutting edge of the Party apparatus within the regime.
- Finally, Hitler himself also remained unclear on the issue of the Party and the state. The law to ensure the unity of Party and state issued in December 1933 proclaimed that the Party 'is inseparably linked with the state', but the explanation was phrased in such vague terms as to be meaningless. Two months later, Hitler declared that the Party's principal responsibilities were to implement government measures and to organise propaganda and indoctrination. Yet, in September 1934, he told the Party Congress that 'it is not the state which commands us but rather we who command the state', and a year later he specifically declared that the Party would assume responsibility for those tasks which the state failed to fulfil. Hitler's ambiguity on this issue is partially explained by the political unrest of these years and by the need to placate numerous interest groups and it was not really ever resolved.

Key question
Why was the relationship between the Party and the state unclear?

Key terms

Totalitarianism
A system of government in which all power is centralised and does not allow any rival authorities. The term has been applied to Nazism and also to Italian Fascism and Stalin's Russia.

Dualism
A government system in which two forces co-exist, e.g. the Nazi Party and the German state.

March converts
Those who joined the NSDAP immediately after the consolidation of power in January–March 1933.

Key question
How did the state institutions develop under the Third Reich?

Dualism: state institutions

In the German state the term for a 'civil servant' was a very broad one – it included most of the categories below on pages 111–13, including teachers. Generally, the state bureaucracy was unsympathetic to Weimar, but it was loyal to the institutions of the state. Only five per cent of the civil servants were purged and, as time passed, more and more joined the Party until it became compulsory in 1939.

Reich Chancellery

The Reich Chancellery was responsible for 'co-ordinating' government and, as the role of the cabinet declined from 1934, the Chancellery became increasingly important. Its head was Hans-Heinrich Lammers and he played a pivotal role because he:

- drew up all government legislation
- became the vital link between Hitler and all other organisations, so he in effect controlled all the flow of information.

But even as a very organised bureaucrat Lammers found it impossible to co-ordinate effectively the growing number of organisations.

Profile: Hans Heinrich Lammers 1879–1962

1879	– Born in Silesia, Germany
1921–33	– Worked as a civil servant in the Ministry of Interior
1932	– Joined the NSDAP
1933–45	– Head of the Reich Chancellery
1940	– Appointed to the honorary rank of an SS general
1943	– Formed the informal 'Council of Three' with Keitel and Bormann
1945	– Arrested and sentenced to 20 years' imprisonment at the Nuremberg Trials, but released in 1952
1962	– Died in Düsseldorf

Lammers did not actually join the NSDAP until 1932, but he had long enjoyed a senior post as a civil servant in the Ministry of Interior. He was Head of the Reich Chancellery throughout the Nazi years and in effect became the most powerful bureaucrat in the Third Reich and personally very close to Hitler. His significance was that he:

- gave legal advice
- served as a link between Hitler and the bureaucracy
- became politically more powerful, especially because of his co-operation with Bormann and Keitel from 1943, which became known as the 'Council of Three'.

Government ministries

Ministries, such as Transport, Education and Economics, were run by leading civil servants. They were generally very conservative – the most marked case was the Foreign Office.

The Ministries found themselves under pressure in the late 1930s from growing Nazi institutions: for example, the Economics Ministry was affected by the Four-Year Plan and the Foreign Office lost its position of supreme control to the so-called **Ribbentrop Bureau**. Very significantly the aristocrat Neurath was replaced in 1938 as foreign minister by the Nazi Joachim von Ribbentrop with the result that increasingly more Nazi officials were brought in.

Judiciary

In the 1920s the judiciary was hostile to the Weimar Republic. It had been ultra-conservative and in notorious cases it was biased against the left and in favour of the right. So, on one level the judiciary was reasonably content to work with the regime. Judges and lawyers were 'co-ordinated' (see pages 13–16), though not many were replaced. In fact, until 1941, the justice minister, Franz Gürtner, was not a Nazi.

However, the judiciary was not immune from Nazi interference and over the years it felt the ever-increasing power of the Nazi organisations. First of all, the structure of new courts enabled the Nazis to get round the established system of justice:

- In 1933 Special Courts were set up to try political offences without a jury.
- In 1934 the People's Court was established to try cases of high treason with a jury composed specifically of Nazi party members (7000 out of the 16,000 cases resulted in a death sentence in 1934–45).

Secondly, all legal authorities lost influence to the arbitrary power of the SS-Police system who increasingly behaved above the law (see pages 117–21). The decree **Nacht und Nebel** ('Night and Fog') of 1941 gave the SS-Police system the right to imprison without question any person thought to be dangerous. In that way, although the traditional role of the judiciary in the state continued to function, it was severely subverted.

Regional state governments

By early 1934 *Gleichschaltung* had destroyed the federal principle of government (see page 13). The Nazi Reich governors existed only 'to execute the will of the supreme leadership of the Reich', who more often than not were the local party *Gauleiters* with full powers (though their role within the Party structure was certainly not clear – see page 114).

Key terms

Ribbentrop Bureau Name given to the office created by Joachim von Ribbentrop, who ran his own personal 'bureau' to oversee foreign affairs.

Nacht und Nebel 'Night and Fog'. Name given to a decree by Hitler in December 1941 to seize any person thought to be dangerous. They should vanish into *Nacht und Nebel*.

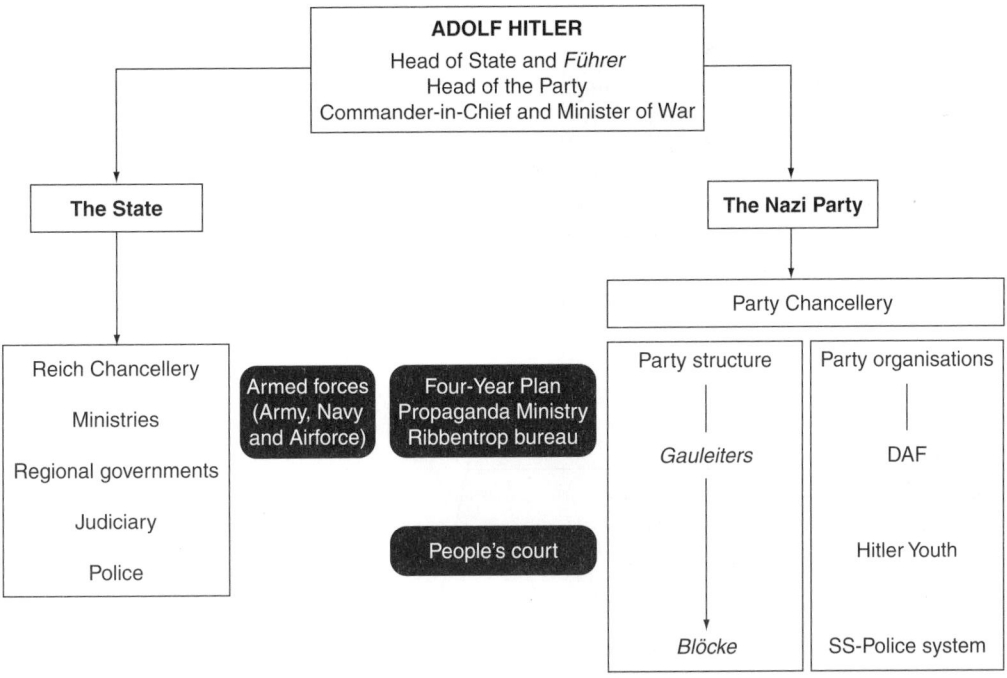

German judges swearing the oath to serve Germany and Hitler in the Berlin State Opera House.

ADOLF HITLER
Head of State and *Führer*
Head of the Party
Commander-in-Chief and Minister of War

The State

The Nazi Party

Party Chancellery

Reich Chancellery

Ministries

Regional governments

Judiciary

Police

Armed forces
(Army, Navy
and Airforce)

Four-Year Plan
Propaganda Ministry
Ribbentrop bureau

People's court

Party structure	Party organisations
Gauleiters	DAF
	Hitler Youth
Blöcke	SS-Police system

Figure 5.1: Party and state in the Third Reich. (The institutions in black were technically *not* in the state or the Party.)

Dualism: Party institutions

The role and shape of the Nazi Party were determined by its background and composition. Its organisation had been created and had evolved in order to *gain* political power and it had proved remarkably well designed for this purpose. However, the Party had to find a new role from 1933 and yet it was by no means a unified structure and not really geared to the task of government. The Party's problems arose because:

Key question
How did the Nazi Party's institutions develop under the Third Reich?

- Up to 1933 it had developed out of the need to attract support from different sections of society and it consisted of a mass of specialist organisations, such as the Hitler Youth, the SA and the NS Teachers' League. Once in power, such groups were keen to uphold and advance their own particular interests.
- Moreover, the Party became increasingly splintered. Various other organisations of dubious political position were created and some institutions were caught between the state and the Party. For example, Goebbels's propaganda machine was a newly formed ministry and the Four-Year Plan Office was an added response to the economic crisis of 1936.
- The actual membership and administrative structure of the Party were established on the basis of the *Führerprinzip* in a major hierarchy, but it did not really work in terms of effective government. The system led to the dominating role of the *Gauleiters* in the regions who believed that their only allegiance was to Hitler. As a result, they endeavoured to preserve their own interests and tended to resist the authorities of both the state and the Party (see Figure 5.2).

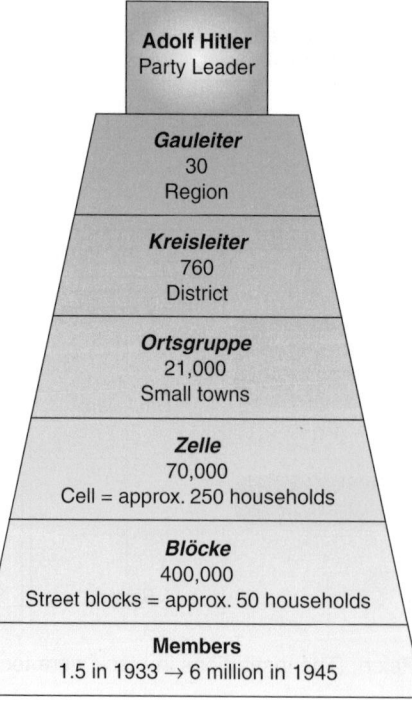

Figure 5.2: Nazi Party structure and leadership

Adolf Hitler
Party Leader

Gauleiter
30
Region

Kreisleiter
760
District

Ortsgruppe
21,000
Small towns

Zelle
70,000
Cell = approx. 250 households

Blöcke
400,000
Street blocks = approx. 50 households

Members
1.5 in 1933 → 6 million in 1945

Profile: Rudolph Hess 1894–1987

1894		– Born in Alexandria, Egypt
1914–18		– Served in the First World War in the same regiment as Hitler
1920		– Early member of the Party and secretary to Hitler
1923–4		– Took part in Munich *putsch* and helped Hitler to write *Mein Kampf* while in prison at Landsberg
1933–41		– Deputy Leader of the Party
		– Appointed to various posts, e.g. Reich Minister without Portfolio, member of the Council for the Defence of the Reich
1941	May	– Flew to Scotland on his own initiative to negotiate peace
1941–6		– Interned by British authorities
1946		– Sentenced to life imprisonment at the Nuremberg Trials
1987		– Committed suicide in prison at Spandau, Berlin

Hess may have been Deputy Leader of the Party, but he was actually of limited abilities and so he did not exert any real power. He was well known for his absolute loyalty and commitment to Hitler – which helps to explain why he was given various new appointments. Most significantly in the 1930s, he did contribute, alongside Bormann, to the development of a more influential Party bureaucracy – although the scheme was limited by the nature of the Third Reich political structure.

In one way the position of the Party certainly did improve over the years. This was mainly because Rudolf Hess, Deputy *Führer*, was granted special powers and developed a Party bureaucracy in the mid-1930s. In 1935 he was given the right to vet the appointment and promotion of all civil servants, and to oversee the drafting of all legislation. By 1939 it had become compulsory for all civil servants to be Party members. In this way, the foundations were laid for increasing Party supervision.

The other key figure in the changing fortunes of the Party was Martin Bormann, who was a skilled and hard-working administrator with great personal ambition. Working alongside Hess, he correctly analysed the problems confronting the Party and created two new departments with the deliberate aim of strengthening the Party's position (and thereby his own):

- the Department for Internal Party Affairs, which had the task of exerting discipline within the Party structure
- the Department for Affairs of State, which aimed to secure Party supremacy over the state.

The trend continued in the war years, especially from 1941 after Hess's flight to Scotland. Bormann was then put in charge of the Party Chancellery and thereafter, by constant meddling, by sheer

Profile: Martin Bormann 1900–45

1900		– Born in Halberstadt in Saxony, Germany
1918		– Dropped out of school and joined the army at the very end of the First World War
1919–20		– Involved with the actions of the Rossbach *Freikorps*
1924		– Found guilty of murder (along with the Auschwitz commandant Höss), but only served one year
1927		– Joined the Nazi Party
1928		– Made *Gauleiter* of Thuringia
1933		– Appointed chief-of-staff to Hess with the responsibility to organise the Party
1941	May	– Head of the Party Chancellery after the departure of Hess
1943	April	– Became Hitler's secretary
		– Formed the informal 'Council of Three' with Keitel and Lammers
1945		– Died trying to escape Berlin. A body found in 1973 in Berlin was confirmed in 1998 to be Bormann's after DNA testing.

Key term

Freikorps
'Free corps' who acted as paramilitaries in Germany, 1918–19. They were right-wing, nationalist soldiers who were only too willing to use force to suppress communist activity.

Despite his limited education and his brutal background, Bormann became a workaholic bureaucrat at the heart of the Party administrative machine. For the first half of the Third Reich he made no real public impact, though quietly he played an important part with Hess in improving the influence of the Party's bureaucracy over the state in the years 1933–9. His personal power increased markedly in the years 1941–5 after the departure of Hess. Bormann played a significant role because he:

- was a radical Nazi and advanced the racial policy against the Jews and the campaign against the Christian Churches
- became a manipulator who advanced the interests of the Party machine and himself. He used his position to block access to Hitler by other leading Nazis (part of the reason why relations between Bormann and Himmler and Göring were so poor).

perseverance and by maintaining good personal relations with Hitler, Bormann effectively advanced the Party's fortunes. By 1943, when he officially became Hitler's secretary, and thus secured direct access to the *Führer*, Bormann had constructed an immensely strong power-base for himself.

Conclusion

Under Bormann's influence the Party was moulded into something more than merely an organisation geared to seizing power. It had succeeded in strengthening its position in respect of the traditional apparatus of the state. Undoubtedly, it was one of the key power blocs within Nazi Germany, and its influence continued to be felt until the very end. However, it must be remembered that:

Key question
Which lost out: the Party or the state?

- the Party bureaucracy had to compete strenuously for influence over the established state institutions, and the latter were never destroyed, even if they were significantly constrained
- the internal divisions and rivalries within the Party itself were never overcome and really underlined the fact that the independence of the *Gauleiters* was one of the main obstacles to control.

Consequently, the Nazi Party never became such an all-pervasive dominating instrument as the Communist Party did in Soviet Russia and that is why the next section examines a number of other power blocs. In a telling phrase the historian J. Noakes writes: 'Perhaps the most outstanding characteristic of the political system of the Third Reich was its lack of formal structure'.

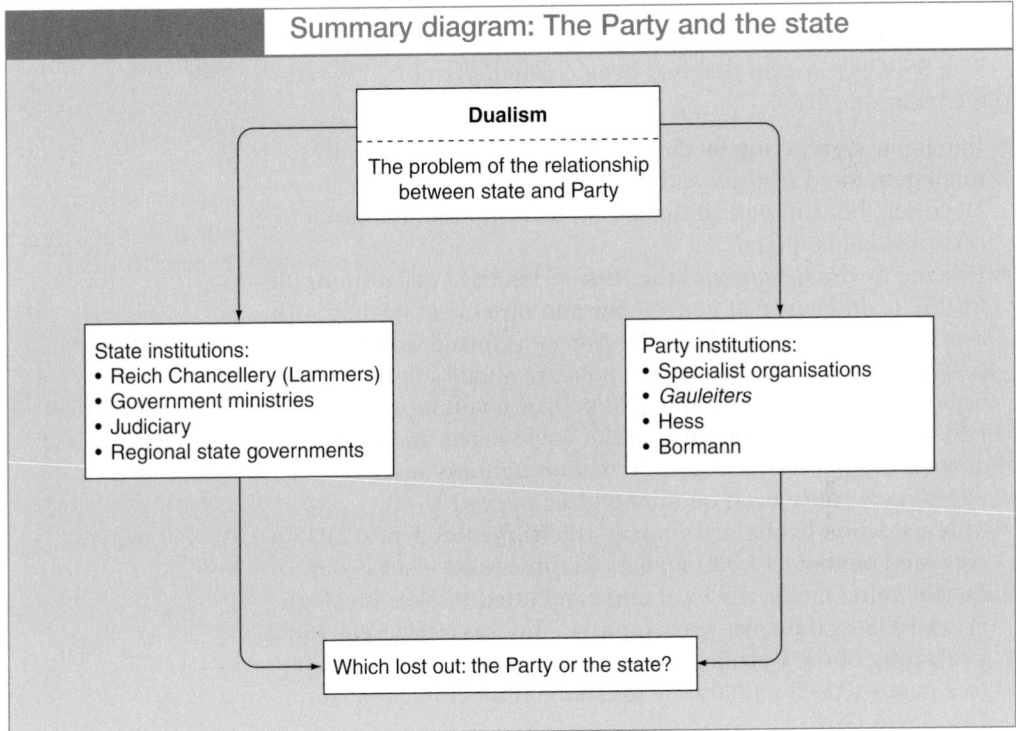

Summary diagram: The Party and the state

Dualism

The problem of the relationship between state and Party

State institutions:
- Reich Chancellery (Lammers)
- Government ministries
- Judiciary
- Regional state governments

Party institutions:
- Specialist organisations
- *Gauleiters*
- Hess
- Bormann

Which lost out: the Party or the state?

3 | The Apparatus of the Police State

Key question
How did the SS emerge?

Amidst all the confusion of the state and Party structure there emerged an organisation that was to become the mainstay of the Third Reich – the SS. The SS developed an identity and structure of its own which kept it separate from the state and yet, through its dominance of police matters, linked it with the state.

The emergence of Himmler and the SS

The SS had been formed in 1925 as an élite bodyguard for Hitler, but it remained a relatively minor section of the SA, with only

250 members, until Himmler became its leader in 1929. By 1933 the SS numbered 52,000, and it had established a reputation for blind obedience and total commitment to the Nazi cause.

Himmler had also created in 1931 a special security service, Sicherheitsdienst (SD), to act as the Party's own internal security police. In the course of 1933–4 he assumed control of all the police in the *Länder*, including the **Gestapo** in Prussia. Thus, Hitler turned to Himmler's SS to carry out the purge of June 1934 (see pages 19–20). The loyalty and brutal efficiency of the SS on the Night of the Long Knives had its rewards, for it now became an independent organisation within the Party. Two years later all police powers were unified under Himmler's control as '*Reichsführer* SS and Chief of all German Police', including the *Gestapo*. In 1939 all party and state police organisations involving police and security matters were amalgamated into the **RSHA**, overseen by Himmler but actually co-ordinated by his deputy, Heydrich (see Figure 5.3 on page 120).

The SS-Police system that had been created, therefore, served three main functions:

- Intelligence gathering by the SD. It was responsible for all intelligence and security and was controlled by its leader Heydrich, but still part of the SS. All its responsibilities grew as occupied lands spread.
- Policing by the *Gestapo* and the *Kripo*. The *Kripo* was responsible for the maintenance of general law and order, e.g. dealing with asocials and thieves. In 1936 the *Kripo* was linked with the *Gestapo*. The *Gestapo* was the key policing organisation for upholding the regime by using surveillance and repression. It had a reputation for brutality and it could arrest and detain anyone without trial – although its thoroughness and effectiveness have been questioned (see pages 121–2).
- Military action by the first units of the *Waffen* **SS**. Up to 1938 it consisted of about 14,000 soldiers in three units – but it was racially pure, fanatically loyal and committed to Nazi ideology. From 1938 its influence grew rapidly. This was affected by the weakening of the German army in the Blomberg–Fritsch crisis (see pages 131–2) and also by the more anti-Semitic policies (see pages 96–8).

It is important to keep in perspective the extent of the position of the SS in the years 1933–9. The embryonic power of the SS had definitely been created. With the take-over of territories in 1939 the creation of the '**New Order**' really began – it was from that time that the personnel and influence of the SS expanded enormously.

The SS state

As *Reichsführer* SS, Himmler controlled a massive police apparatus that was answerable only to Hitler. The SS system had grown into one of the key power blocs in the Third Reich. The SS-Police system became, in effect, in the words of E. Kogon, a '**state within a state**'. It was a huge vested interest, which numbered 250,000 in

Key terms

Gestapo
Geheime Staats Polizei: Secret State Police.

RSHA
Reich Security Office, which amalgamated all police and security organisations.

Waffen SS
Armed SS – the number of divisions grew during the war from three to 35.

New Order
Used by the Nazis to describe the economic, political and racial integration of Europe under the Third Reich.

'State within a state'
A situation where the authority and government of the state are threatened by a rival power base.

Key question
How powerful was the SS?

Profile: Heinrich Himmler 1900–45

1900		– Born in Munich in Bavaria, Germany
1917–18		– Joined the cadets, but did not face action in First World War
1919–22		– Studied agriculture at the Munich Technical University
1923		– Joined the Nazi Party
1923	November	– Took part in the Munich Beer Hall *Putsch*
1929		– Appointed leader of the SS
1930		– Elected as Nazi deputy of the *Reichstag*
1934	June	– Arranged the purge of the SA in the Night of Long Knives
1936		– Given responsibility as '*Reichsführer* SS and Chief of all German Police'
1939		– Created himself as the Commissar of the Strengthening of the German Nationhood – Formed the RSHA
1943		– Appointed Minister of Interior (replacing Frick)
1944		– Appointed as Commander-in-Chief of the Home Army
1945	May	– Arrested by British forces but committed suicide before trial

Key dates

Night of the Long Knives: 30 June 1934

Appointment of Heinrich Himmler as Chief of the German Police: June 1936

Creation of RSHA: September 1939

Himmler was in many respects a nondescript uninspiring character who before 1929 achieved little in his work or in the Party. Yet, with a reputation for an organised, obsessive, hard-working style, he became the leader of the brutally efficient SS machine which really held the Third Reich together.

When he was appointed leader of the SS he quickly converted the small group of 250 into a committed élite force of 52,000. Yet, until 1934 Himmler and the SS remained very much in the shadow of Röhm and the SA – it was his decision to take responsibility for the purge in the Night of the Long Knives that proved to be his real turning point.

From that time Himmler's political power continued to increase right until the collapse of the Third Reich. He must therefore undoubtedly take responsibility for:

- the development and control of the apparatus of terror which by surveillance and repression created the system of control
- the pursuit of his aim to create a German master-race and the development of élite institutions like *Lebensborn* and the *Ordensburgen* (see pages 75 and 62)
- the extermination of the sub-human races, such as the Jews and the Gypsies, in the concentration camps
- the exploitation of all the occupied lands for slave labour and arms production
- the development of the *Waffen* SS as an élite military force that matched the might of the German army by the end of the war.

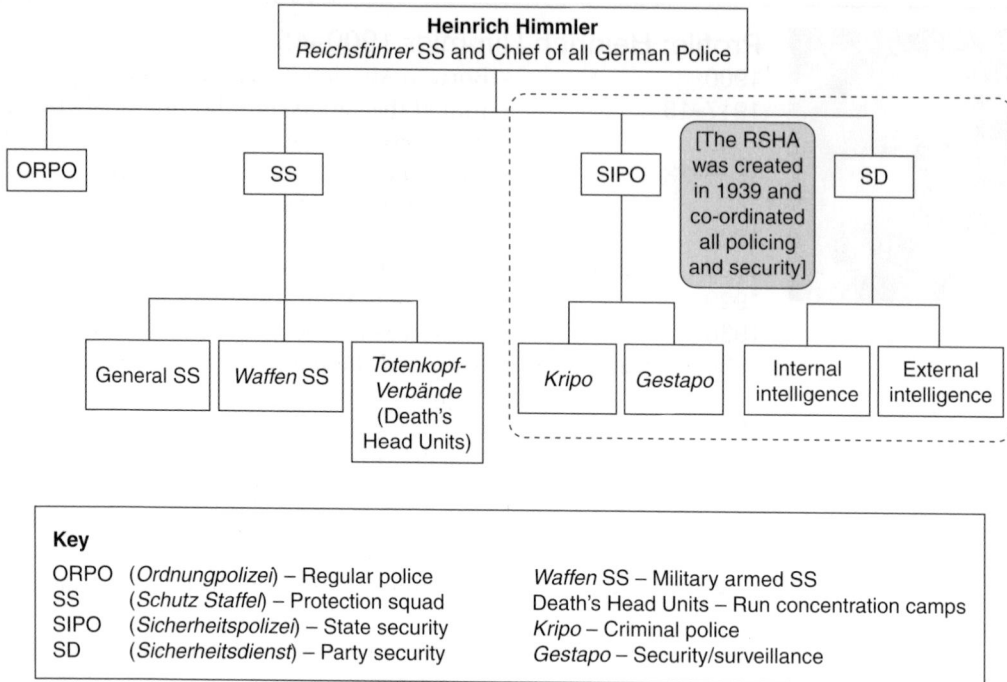

Figure 5.3: The SS-Police system in 1939

1939 and had begun to eclipse other interest groups in terms of power and influence. With the onset of war this tendency was accentuated further. As German troops gained control over more and more areas of Europe, the power of the SS was inevitably enhanced:

- Security. All responsibilities of policing and intelligence expanded as occupied lands spread. The job of internal security became much greater and SS officers were granted severe powers to crush opposition.
- Military. The *Waffen* SS increased from three divisions in 1939 to 35 in 1945, which developed into a 'second army' – committed, brutal and militarily highly rated. By 1944 the SS was so powerful it rivalled the power of the German army.
- Economy. The SS became responsible for the creation of the 'New Order' in the occupied lands of eastern Europe. Such a scheme provided opportunities for plunder and power on a massive scale, which members of the SS exploited to the full. By the end of the war the SS had created a massive commercial organisation of over 150 firms, which exploited slave labour to extract raw materials and to manufacture textiles, armaments and household goods.
- Ideology and race. The racial policy of extermination and resettlement was pursued with vigour and the system of concentration camps was widely established and run by the SS Death's Head Units (see also Chapter 4, page 96). The various 'inferior' races were even used for their economic value.

The SS was not immune to the rivalries and arguments that typified Nazi Germany. Disagreements often arose, particularly with local *Gauleiters* and the governors of the occupied territories. However, the SS state under Himmler not only preserved the Nazi regime through its brutal, repressive and often arbitrary policies of law enforcement, but gradually extended its influence. In this way it evolved over time into the key power group in the Third Reich.

Key debate

Although it has been generally accepted that the SS developed into the key power in the Third Reich, its influence over people's everyday life has been questioned. Historians have therefore asked:

Did the *Gestapo* really control the people?

In the traditional image the *Gestapo* was seen as the all-knowing totalitarian police state. This view was actually cultivated by the *Gestapo* itself, the Allied propagandists during the war and many post-war films. In many respects this interpretation was upheld in academic circles, most notably in the standard work *The History of the Gestapo* by Jacques Delarue, published in 1962. He entitled one chapter 'The *Gestapo* is everywhere' and then wrote:

> 'Never before, in no other land and at no other time, had an organisation attained such a comprehensive penetration (of society), possessed such power and reached such a degree of "completeness" in its ability to arouse terror and horror, as well as in its actual effectiveness.'

However, as a result of considerable research of local social studies of Germany, a revised interpretation of the *Gestapo* has gained great influence. The German historians Mallman and Paul, and the American historian Gellatelly have drawn attention to the limits of the *Gestapo*'s policing by revealing that:

- The manpower of the *Gestapo* was actually limited – it only had no more than 40,000 agents for the whole of Germany. This meant in practice that large cities, like Frankfurt or Hamburg, with about half a million people, were policed by just about 40–50 agents.
- The majority of the work for the *Gestapo* was actually prompted by public informers – the figures lie between 50 per cent and 80 per cent in different areas. Indeed, the information and the denunciations were actually often caused more often by gossip, which generated enormous paperwork for limited return.
- The *Gestapo* had relatively few 'top agents', so it coped by over-relying on the work of the *Kripo*.

Key term

Revisionist
In general terms revisionism is the aim to modify or change something. In this context, it refers specifically to a historian who changes a well-established interpretation.

However, in the last few years the US historian, Eric Johnson has tried to put the latest **revisionist** views into perspective through his case study of the Rhineland. He accepts the limitations of the *Gestapo*, and argues that it did not impose a climate of terror on ordinary Germans. Instead it concentrated its job of surveillance and repression on specific enemies – the political left, Jews and, to a lesser extent, religious groups and asocials. Controversially,

The oppression of Jews began early in Hitler's regime. Especially persecuted were the *Ostjuden* (Jews from eastern Europe, who had settled in Germany). Here, plainclothes *Gestapo* agents take Jews into custody.

he claims that the Nazis and the German population formed a grim 'pact' – the population turned a blind eye to the *Gestapo*'s persecution and, in return, the Nazis overlooked minor transgressions of the law by ordinary Germans.

Some key books in the debate

Eric Johnson, *Nazi Terror: The Gestapo, Jews and Ordinary Germans* (New York, 2000).
Mallman and Paul, 'Omniscient, omnipotent and omnipresent' quoted in Crew, D., ed., *Nazi and German Society, 1933–45* (1994).
R. Gellatelly, *Gestapo and German Society* (1990).

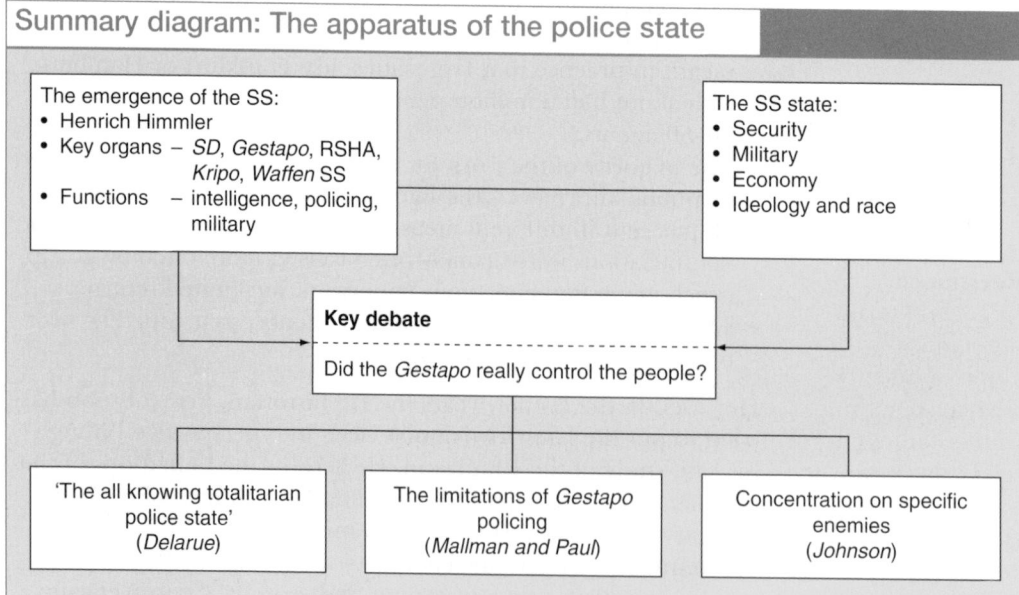

Summary diagram: The apparatus of the police state

The emergence of the SS:
- Henrich Himmler
- Key organs – *SD, Gestapo,* RSHA, *Kripo, Waffen* SS
- Functions – intelligence, policing, military

The SS state:
- Security
- Military
- Economy
- Ideology and race

Key debate

Did the *Gestapo* really control the people?

'The all knowing totalitarian police state'
(*Delarue*)

The limitations of *Gestapo* policing
(*Mallman and Paul*)

Concentration on specific enemies
(*Johnson*)

Key question
How did Nazi
propaganda use the
media?

4 | The Nazi Propaganda Machine

Despite the power of the Nazi police apparatus, it would be too simple to suggest that the regime maintained itself in power simply by the use of terror and repression. From the very start both Hitler and Goebbels recognised how important propaganda could be as a vital cog in the Nazis state. As Goebbels stated at his very first press conference on 15 March 1933:

> I view the first task of the new ministry as being to establish co-ordination between the government and the whole people ... If the means achieves the end, the means is good. Whether it always satisfies stringent aesthetic criteria or not is immaterial.

As a result considerable resources were directed towards the development of the propaganda machine in order to achieve the following aims:

- to glorify the regime
- to spread the Nazi ideology and values (and by implication to censor the unacceptable)
- to win over the people and to integrate the nation's diverse elements.

Under the Nazis all means of public communication were brought under state control.

Radio

Goebbels (and Hitler) had always recognised the effectiveness of the spoken word over the written and they had already begun to use new technology during the election campaigns of 1932–3. Up until this time, German broadcasting had been organised by regional states. Once in power, Goebbels efficiently brought all broadcasting under Nazi control by the creation of the Reich Radio Company. Furthermore, he arranged the dismissal of 13 per cent of the staff on political and racial grounds, and replaced them with his own men. He told his broadcasters in March 1933:

> I am placing a major responsibility in your hands, for you have in your hands the most modern instrument in existence for influencing the masses. By this instrument you are the creators of public opinion.

Yet, control of broadcasting was of little value in terms of propaganda unless the people had the means to receive it. In 1932 less than 25 per cent of German households owned a wireless – though that was quite a high figure compared to the rest of the world. Consequently, the Nazi government made provision for the production of a cheap set, the People's Receiver (*Volksempfänger*). Radio was a new and dynamic medium and access increased markedly. By 1939, 70 per cent of German homes had a radio – the highest national figure in the world – and it became a medium of mass communication controlled completely by the regime.

Ganz Deutschland hört den Führer

mit dem Volksempfänger

'All Germany hears the *Führer* on the People's Radio'. The cheapness and popularity of the People's Radio made it easier for the Nazis to spread their propaganda.

Broadcasting was also directed at public places. The installation of loudspeakers in restaurants and cafés, factories and offices made them all into venues for collective listening. 'Radio wardens' were even appointed, whose duty it was to co-ordinate the listening process.

Press

Control of the press was not so easily achieved by Goebbels. Germany had over 4700 daily newspapers in 1933 – a result of the strong regional identities which still existed in a state that had only been unified in 1871. Moreover, the papers were all owned privately, and traditionally owed no loyalty to central government; their loyalty was to their publishing company, religion or political party.

Various measures were taken to achieve Nazi control.

- First, the Nazi publishing house, *Eher Verlag*, bought up numerous newspapers, so that by 1939 it controlled two-thirds of the German press.
- Secondly, the various news agencies were merged into one, the DNB. This was state controlled, with the result that news material was vetted even before it got to the journalists.
- Thirdly, Goebbels introduced a daily press conference at the Propaganda Ministry to provide guidance on editorial policy.
- Finally, by the so-called Editors' Law of October 1933, newspaper content was made the sole responsibility of the editor; it became his job to satisfy the requirements of the Propaganda Ministry, or face the appropriate consequences. In this way, as one historian has explained, 'There was no need for censorship because the editor's most important function was that of censor'.

To a large extent, the Nazis succeeded in muzzling the press so that even the internationally renowned *Frankfurter Zeitung* was forced to close in 1943. However, the price of that success was the evolution of a bland and sterile journalism, which undoubtedly contributed to a 10 per cent decline in newspaper circulation before 1939.

The Berlin Olympics

The 1936 Olympic Games were awarded to Berlin in 1931, well before Hitler and the Nazis had come to power. Yet, despite Hitler's initial doubts, Goebbels was determined to exploit them as a propaganda 'gold-mine'. Initially, he saw the games as a means to present Nazi aims (see pages 51–2), but with several important caveats:

- They were not only to glorify the regime for the German people, but also for millions of people across the world, who would see Germany as the centre of attention.
- They were trying to spread Nazi ideological themes, without causing international upset. So, for example, many anti-Jewish posters and newspapers were played down.

Everything was done to present a positive image of the 'new Germany'. Over 42 million *Reichsmarks* were spent on the 130-hectare Olympics sports complex and the gigantic Olympic Stadium was built of natural stone in the classical style – the original modernist plan having been rejected. It could seat 110,000 spectators and at the time it was the world's largest stadium. The new Berlin Olympic Village was also a prototype for future games because of its excellent facilities.

Not surprisingly, the Nazi government was meticulous in overseeing all the media preparations:

- Radio: 20 transmitting vans were put at the disposal of the foreign media along with 300 microphones. Radio broadcasts at the Olympics were given in 28 languages.

- Film: the Nazis promoted and financed filming by the director Leni Riefenstahl. She brought 33 camera operators to the Olympics and shot over a million feet of film. It took her 18 months to edit the material into a four-hour film, *Olympia*, which was released in two parts beginning in April 1938.
- TV: television was in its early stages, but the games prompted a significant technical development. Broadcasts of the games were made and seen by 150,000 people in 28 public television rooms in Berlin, though the image quality was variable.

The Nazi ideal of the tall, blond, blue-eyed Aryan race was epitomised by the athlete Siegfried Eifrig lighting the torch at the start of the games in the Olympic stadium.

On the sports front, Germany successfully finished top of the medal table, gaining 89 medals with the Americans in second place with 56. However, the Nazi dream was marred by the success of the black American athlete, Jesse Owens, who won four gold medals in the 100 m, 200 m, long jump and 4 × 100 m relay.

Siegfried Eifrig lights the Olympic flame to mark the start of the 1936 games in Berlin's Lustgarten.

Hitler showed his displeasure by refusing to place the gold medal around Owens' neck.

Overall, the Berlin Olympics were a major success for the Nazis who gained praise for their excellent management and the impressive spectacle, as was recognised by the US correspondent William Shirer:

> That I'm afraid the Nazis have succeeded with their propaganda. First, the Nazis have run the Games on a lavish scale never before experienced, and this has appealed to the athletes. Second, the Nazis have put up a very good front for the general visitors, especially the big businessmen.

Nazi ritual

One final aspect of the Goebbels propaganda machine was the deliberate attempt to create a new kind of social ritual. The *Heil Hitler* greeting, the Nazi salute, the **Horst Wessel** anthem and the preponderance of militaristic uniforms were all intended to strengthen the individual's identity with the regime. This was further encouraged by the establishment of a series of public festivals to commemorate historic days in the Nazi calendar (see Table 5.1).

Table 5.1: Historic days in the Nazi calendar

30 January	The seizure of power (1933)
24 February	Party Foundation Day (1925)
16 March	Heroes' Remembrance Day (War Dead)
20 April	Hitler's birthday
1 May	National Day of Labour
2nd Sunday in May	Mothering Sunday
21 June	Summer solstice
2nd Sunday of July	German culture
September	Nuremberg Party Rally
October	Harvest festival
9 November	The Munich *putsch* (1923)
Winter solstice	Pagan festival to counter Christmas

Conclusion

Although control of the press and radio was Goebbels's major objective, he gradually extended his influence so that film, music, literature and art all came under the control of the Reich (as was shown in Chapter 3, pages 76–80). However, it is very difficult for historians to assess the effectiveness of Nazi propaganda. The extent of its influence clearly has massive implications for the whole thorny issue of public opinion (see Chapter 6).

Historians initially assumed rather too glibly that Nazi propaganda was a major achievement because it was possible to highlight the way Goebbels exploited all the means for propaganda – photographs, Party rallies, sport, festivals. This view was underlined by Herzstein's book in the 1960s, *The War That Hitler Won*. However, more recent research from oral history of local studies has raised serious doubts about its effectiveness and tended to show that the degree of success of propaganda

---

Key question
How did Nazism try to create a new social ritual?

Key term

Horst Wessel
A young Nazi stormtrooper killed in a fight with communists in 1930. The song he wrote became a Nazi marching song and later virtually became an alternative national anthem.

Key question
How effective was Nazi propaganda?

Profile: Josef Goebbels 1897–1945

1897		– Born in the Rhineland. Disabled by a clubbed foot which affected his walking
1914–18		– Excused military service on the grounds of his disability
1917–21		– Attended the university of Heidelberg and graduated with a doctor of philosophy
1924		– Joined the Nazi Party. Originally, a supporter of the radical Nazi Gregor Strasser
1926		– Broke with Strasser and sided with Hitler
		– Hitler appointed him as *Gauleiter* of Berlin
1927		– Created the Nazi newspaper *Der Angriff*
1928		– Appointed member of the *Reichstag*
1930		– Put in charge of Party propaganda
1933	March	– Joined the cabinet and appointed Minister of Public Enlightenment and Propaganda, a post which he held until 1945
	May	– Encouraged the burning of 'un-German books'
1938		– His affair with Lida Baarova undermined his position with Hitler
	November	– Issued the orders for the anti-Semitic attacks of *Kristallnacht*
1943	February	– Called for 'total war' to rouse the nation after the defeat at Stalingrad
1945	April	– Committed suicide after poisoning his children and shooting his wife

Goebbels was a man from a humble background with many talents who became one of the few intellectuals in the Nazi leadership. However, he suffered from a strong inferiority complex over his physical limitations and he became an embittered and committed anti-Semite.

He was always a radical Nazi and, originally, a supporter of the Strassers, although he became a long-term loyal supporter of Hitler from 1926. As propaganda chief of the party from 1930, he played a crucial role in exploiting every possible method to sell the Nazi image in the series of elections, 1930–3.

Once he became Minster of Propaganda, he developed the whole range of the regime's propaganda techniques that were frighteningly ahead of their time. Unscrupulous and amoral in his methods, he was mainly responsible for:

- using all possible methods to advance the idea of Nazi totalitarianism
- censoring all non-Nazi culture and media
- promoting all the main ideological ideas of Nazism.

He was a very highly skilled orator and he remained a central figure until the final collapse of the regime, though other leading Nazis, such as Göring and Ribbentrop, distrusted him.

His rivals also exploited his many love affairs to undermine his position and he became quite isolated in the years 1938–42.

But with his personal leadership and his organisational skills he played an important part in the final two years of the war in making the nation ready for total war:

- he organised help for people in the bombed cities
- he took the initiative and gave the orders to put down the July Bomb Plot (see page 133)
- he maintained civilian morale against all the odds, e.g. by visiting bombed cities (unlike Hitler)
- he took the responsibility to mobilise the last efforts to resist the Allied advance.

varied according to different purposes. Very generally it is felt that propaganda succeeded in the sense that it:

- cultivated the 'Hitler myth' of him as an all-powerful leader
- strengthened the Nazi regime after Germany's economic and political crisis, 1929–33
- appealed effectively to reinforce established family values and German nationalism.

On the other hand, propaganda failed more markedly in its attempt:

- to denounce the Christian Churches
- to seduce the working classes away from their established identity through the ideal of *Volksgemeinschaft*
- to develop a distinctive Nazi culture (see pages 76–80).

Particularly, the analysis of D. Welch claims that 'the history of Nazi propaganda during the war is one of declining effectiveness'. Such points give backing to the view that the propaganda machine was of secondary importance compared to the power and influence of the SS-Police system in upholding the Third Reich (see also pages 182–4).

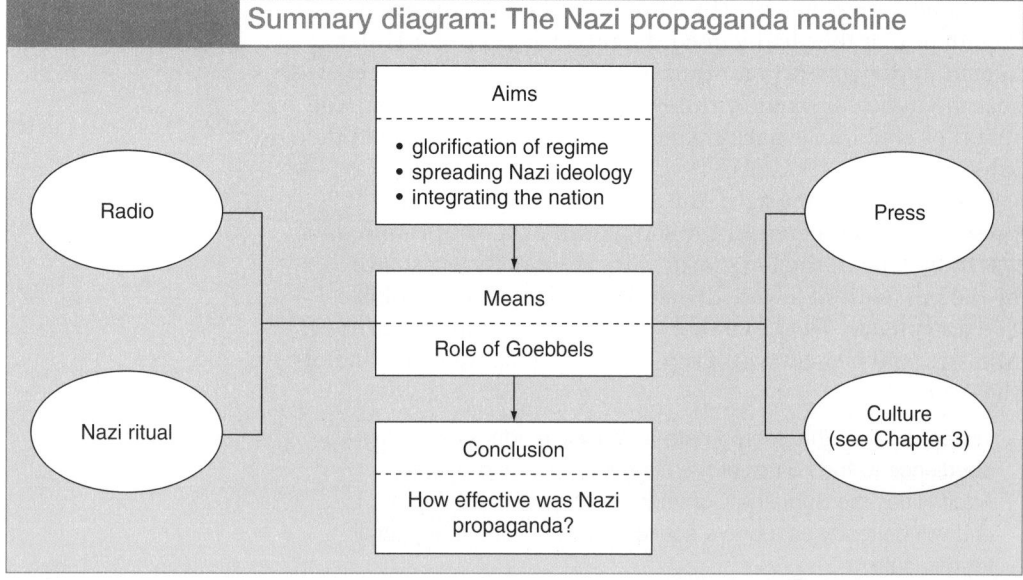

Summary diagram: The Nazi propaganda machine

5 | The German Army

In any political system, the role of the armed forces is essential for political stability. A regime that loses the support of the military will lack authority in both its domestic and foreign policies. Indeed, whenever there is a story in the media of a political *coup*, it is often the position adopted by the military that proves to be the decisive factor in the survival or overthrow of the government.

Key question
To what extent did the German army co-operate with the Nazi regime?

Background

In Germany the military tradition went back a long way into the nation's past. Above all, it was the reputation established by Prussian militarism which so often prompted comment: 'Prussia is not a country with an army: it is an army with a country', the French statesman Mirabeau had observed in the late eighteenth century.

It was the power of the Prussian military machine that had enabled Bismarck to forge German unification out of the three wars, 1864–71. Thereafter, the army was always to be found at the centre of German political life. The military élite enjoyed great social status and the leading generals exerted considerable power in Imperial Germany, 1871–1918. Yet, although the army was generally not sympathetic to the creation of the democratic Weimar Germany it cleverly maintained its influence.

So despite its suspicion of Nazism, the army accepted the Nazi accession to power and the manoeuvrings that culminated in the Night of the Long Knives (see pages 19–20).

The years of co-operation 1934–7

In the immediate aftermath of the Night of the Long Knives, it seemed as if the army was in a position of considerable strength. Unlike other institutions in Germany, it had not been 'co-ordinated' (see pages 13–19). Moreover, the generals were confident that they had gained the upper hand when Hitler agreed to the destruction of his own SA. Ironically, they believed that the radical element within Nazism had been removed and that they could now make the Nazi state work according to their interests and wishes.

However, with hindsight, the army only succeeded in preserving its influence in the short term by a compromise that was to be fatal in the long term. This is most clearly shown by the new oath of loyalty demanded by Hitler of all soldiers, and accepted by Field Marshal von Blomberg, the Defence Minister, and General von Fritsch, the Commander-in-Chief of the Army:

> I swear by God this sacred oath: that I will render unconditional
> obedience to the *Führer* of the German Reich and people,
> Adolf Hitler, the Supreme Commander of the Armed Forces,
> and will be ready as a brave soldier to risk my life at any time
> for this oath.

For a German soldier, bound by discipline and obedience, such words marked a commitment that made any future resistance an act of the most serious treachery.

In the years 1934–7 the relationship between the Nazi state and the army remained cordial. The generals were encouraged by:

- the expansion of the rearmament programme from 1935 (see page 161)
- Hitler's reintroduction of conscription in March 1935 – thereby increasing the size of the army to 550,000 (see page 161)
- the diplomatic successes over the Saar and the Rhineland (see page 162).

Blomberg even issued a number of military decrees in an attempt to adjust army training according to Nazi ideology and to elevate the *Führer*. Yet, Blomberg and the army leaders deceived themselves into believing that the army's independent position was being preserved. In fact, the power of the SS was growing fast, while Hitler himself had little respect for the conservative attitudes held by many army officers. It was merely political realism that held him back from involvement in army affairs until 1938.

The Blomberg–Fritsch crisis 1937–8

Key question
Why was the Blomberg–Fritsh crisis so significant?

The balance between the army and Hitler changed in the winter of 1937–8 after the so-called Hossbach conference meeting on 5 November 1937 (see pages 164–5). In this meeting Hitler outlined to Germany's chiefs of the armed forces his foreign policy aims for military expansion. Blomberg and Fritsch, in particular, were both seriously concerned by Hitler's talk of war and conquest – especially bearing in mind Germany's state of military unpreparedness. Their doubts further convinced Hitler that the army leadership was spineless, and in February 1938 both men were forced out of office after revelations about their private lives. Blomberg had just married for the second time, with Hitler as principal witness, but it subsequently became known that his wife had a criminal record for theft and prostitution. Fritsch was falsely accused of homosexual offences – on evidence conveniently produced by Himmler.

Key date
Forced resignation of Field Marshal Blomberg and General Fritsch. Purge of army leadership: February 1938

This sordid episode provided Hitler with the perfect opportunity to subordinate the army. He abolished the post of defence minister and he himself took the title Commander-in-Chief and Minister of War. Day-to-day leadership of all armed forces was placed in the hands of the High Command, the *Oberkommando der Wehrmacht* (OKW), headed by a loyal and subservient General Keitel. The new Commander-in-Chief of the Army was General Brauchitsch – another willing supporter of the regime. In addition to these changes, a further 16 generals were retired and 44 transferred. These changes coincided with the replacement of Foreign Minister Neurath by the Nazi Ribbentrop (see page 112). In the words of the historian Feuchtwanger:

> It was a crisis of the regime not unlike the Night of the Long Knives in 1934, although this time there was no bloodshed. Again Hitler was the undisputed winner and the national–conservative élites who had been helped into the saddle, suffered a further loss of influence.

Profile: Werner von Blomberg 1876–1946

1878	– Born in Pomerania, Germany
1914–18	– Served in the First World War and joined the General Staff
1920–33	– Served various military posts
1933 January	– Appointed by Hitler as Minister of Defence
1935–8	– War Minister and Commander-in-Chief of armed forces
1936	– Appointed as Hitler's first field marshall
1938	– Remarried to his new young wife Erna Grün – Forced to resign
1938–46	– Lived privately, but was arrested by Allies. He died awaiting the Nuremberg Trials

Blomberg's significance is as a vital member of the conservative faction that supported Hitler in 1933–8. Convinced that Hitler was the authoritarian leader who would restore German power, he backed the destruction of the SA in the Night of the Long Knives. He then played an essential role in persuading the army generals to support Hitler and take the oath of loyalty.

Blomberg's doubts about Hitler's foreign policy emerged from 1936 over the occupation of the Rhineland and the Hossbach conference. This led to his removal from office in 1938, which suited Göring and Himmler because they resented the man's influence.

In victory and in defeat 1938–45

There is little doubt that from 1938 the army's ability to shape political developments in Germany was drastically reduced. Whereas in the early years of the Nazi regime Hitler had correctly recognised the need to work with the army leadership, by early 1938 he was strong enough to mould it more closely to his requirements. That is not to say that the army was without power, but merely that it had been tamed to serve its new master. It still remained the one institution with the technical means of striking successfully at the regime. For example, it is known that in the summer of 1938 a plan was drawn up by General Beck to arrest Hitler in the event of a full-scale European war breaking out over the Czech crisis (see pages 167–70). It came to nothing.

However, from 1938–42 Nazi diplomatic and military policy was so successful that it effectively ruined the plans of any restraining officers. Moreover, once Germany found itself at war from 1939 again, resistance not only implied a lack of patriotism, it was also treasonable.

By early 1943 the military situation had changed dramatically. Defeat in North Africa had been followed by the disaster of Stalingrad. A growing number of generals came to believe that the war could not be won, and yet the army was continuing to fight on behalf of a regime that had allowed atrocities and was

Key question
Why did the war eventually result in the downfall of the German army's authority?

Military 'turn of the tide'. German defeats at El Alamein and at Stalingrad: winter 1942–3

Key date

Figure 5.4: Hitler's increasing power and the armed forces

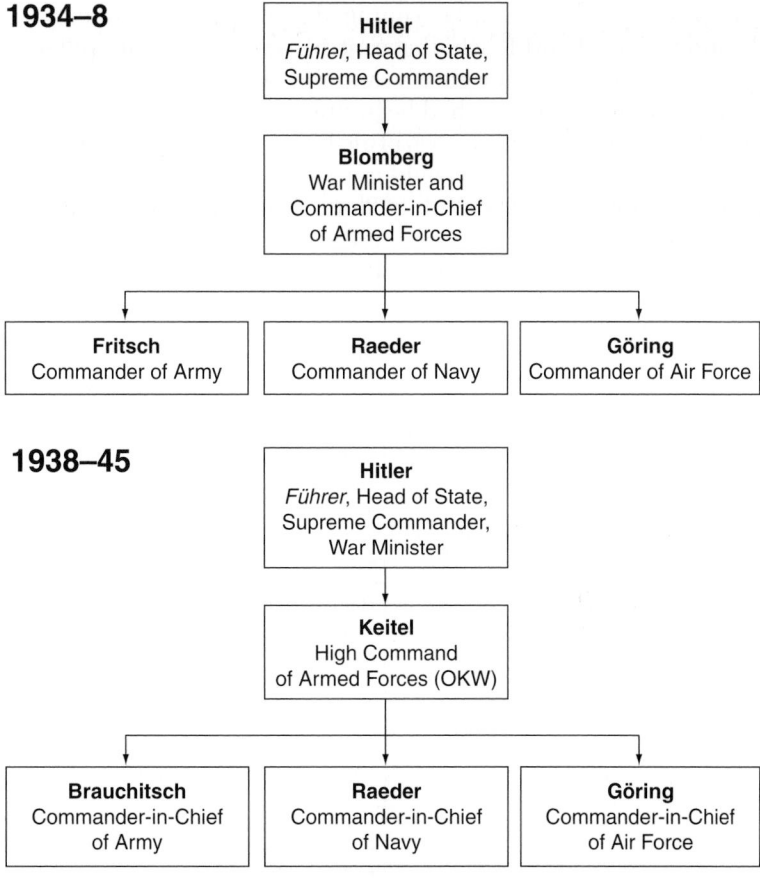

1934–8

Hitler
Führer, Head of State, Supreme Commander

↓

Blomberg
War Minister and Commander-in-Chief of Armed Forces

| **Fritsch**
Commander of Army | **Raeder**
Commander of Navy | **Göring**
Commander of Air Force |

1938–45

Hitler
Führer, Head of State, Supreme Commander, War Minister

↓

Keitel
High Command of Armed Forces (OKW)

| **Brauchitsch**
Commander-in-Chief of Army | **Raeder**
Commander-in-Chief of Navy | **Göring**
Commander-in-Chief of Air Force |

now demanding 'total war'. The involvement of some leading officers in the failed 20 July Bomb Plot (see pages 145–7) marked the end of the powerful and privileged position of the army in German society. Many officers were among those arrested or executed in the brutal *Gestapo* round-up that followed. However, perhaps even more significant than this blood purge were the orders subsequently issued:

- The Nazi salute became compulsory throughout the army.
- Political officers were appointed to oversee the indoctrination of the army.
- Himmler was appointed as Commander-in-Chief of the Home Army.

By the autumn of 1944 the army was brought under the control of the SS and the last traces of army independence had been absorbed into the Nazi regime.

Conclusion

Generally, historians have not been sympathetic to the role played by the German army during the Nazi years. Indeed, although there were different shades of opinion, it is difficult to avoid the conclusion that the army leadership played a naive and inept political game. Conditioned by their traditions of obedience,

Key date

Stauffenberg Bomb Plot – army purged: July 1944

loyalty and patriotism, and encouraged by the authoritarian position of the Third Reich, the army became a necessary pillar of the Nazi regime in the early years. Yet, even when its own power to influence events had been drastically reduced in 1938 and the full implications of Nazi rule became apparent during the war, the army's leaders could not escape from their political and moral dilemma. The 20 July Plot was a brave gesture, but the indecision of that day was a sign of the compromised position in which the army found itself by that time.

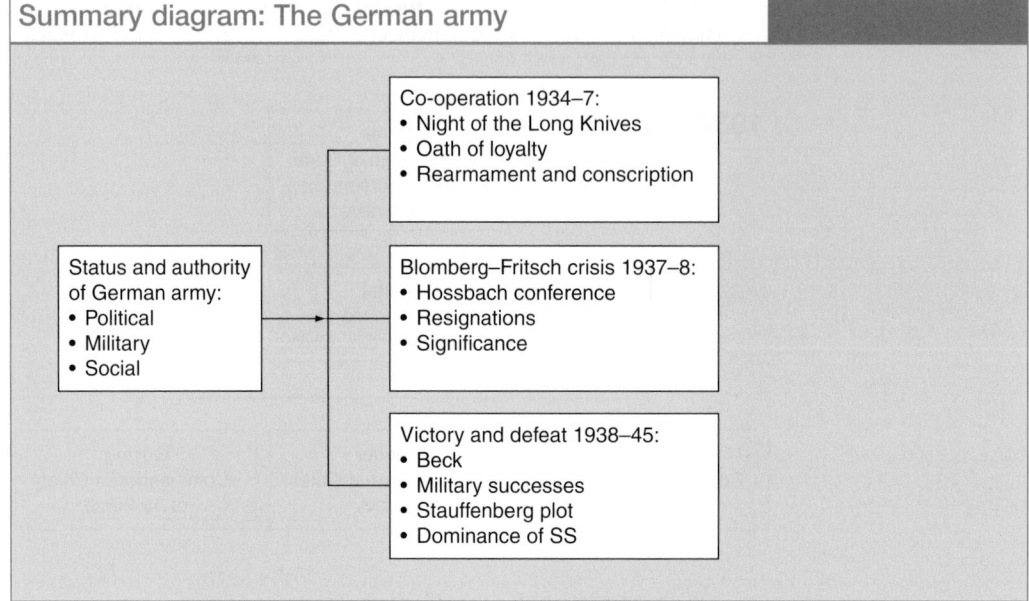

Summary diagram: The German army

Status and authority of German army:
• Political
• Military
• Social

Co-operation 1934–7:
• Night of the Long Knives
• Oath of loyalty
• Rearmament and conscription

Blomberg–Fritsch crisis 1937–8:
• Hossbach conference
• Resignations
• Significance

Victory and defeat 1938–45:
• Beck
• Military successes
• Stauffenberg plot
• Dominance of SS

6 | Big Business

The position of big business in the Third Reich has long been a focus of interest – mainly because many on the political left have believed that it dominated the Nazi regime. However, it would be wrong to see big business as a uniform interest group. There were a number of different sectors and each one was affected by the changing economic and political circumstances within that 12-year period (see Chapter 2).

Early benefits

From 1933 the position of the business community began to improve. Helped by the upturn in world trade, and encouraged by the Nazi destruction of the free trade unions, a commercial recovery occurred. However, despite all the Nazi electoral promises, small business found itself being squeezed out by the power of big business, whose support was more crucial in the creation of new jobs. Consequently, it was the building and the giant coal and steel industries that initially prospered most, while consumer goods production remained relatively depressed. So in the first few years of Nazi rule, big business was able to exert an

Key question
How influential was big business in Nazi Germany?

influence – particularly through the role of Schacht. It maintained a privileged position in its own sphere, just as the army generals did in the military field.

The significance of the Four-Year Plan

The Four-Year Plan in 1936 marked a very important development. The coalition of conservative interests between generals, business and the Nazi leadership broke up as a result of the economic crisis (see pages 36–40). According to the historian Tim Mason, this led to a 'far-reaching transformation of the economic power structure and hence a change in the relationship between economics and politics, industry and the state'. Schacht and the leaders of heavy industry urged a reduction of rearmament and an increased emphasis on consumer goods and exports. However, this was a fatal error of judgement that brought about the downfall of Schacht and the end of heavy industry's supremacy. Instead, Göring, as director of the Four-Year Plan, was now able to call the shots and the only groups able to maintain real influence were in the electro-chemicals sector because of their crucial role in rearmament:

- in the chemical industry *IG Farben* led the way with its development of synthetic substitutes
- the electrical industry was dominated by *Siemens*.

Key date

Introduction of the Four-Year Plan under the control of Göring and big business weakened: October 1936

Most telling of all was the subservient position of the so-called 'Ruhr barons' of heavy industry in coal and steel. When they refused to co-operate, Göring nationalised the iron-ore deposits and created a new state firm, the *Reichswerke Hermann Göring*, to exploit them. From 1936, the divisions in big business meant that the needs of the economy were determined by political decisions, especially those in foreign and military policy. Private property always remained in private hands, but the free market and business independence gave way to state regulation. On the whole, business accepted the controls of the political leadership, fearing that resistance to state interference would weaken their situation further.

The war years

Business had little to gain from a general European war in 1939. Access to the new markets of the conquered territories was not enough to offset the loss of overseas trade and the general economic disruption caused by war. However, the acceptance by big business of ever greater controls from the Nazi regime was telling. Labour, production, and research and development were all geared to the war economy by the second Four-Year Plan, and industry was increasingly tied by the intervention of the Nazi regime. In these ways German business was fatally compromised.

From 1942 Speer's reforms 'liberated' business to some extent, but it was still forced to operate within a political framework and the priorities were clearly set by the regime (see pages 45–9). Thus, to the very end German industry continued to work with the regime. There was no real opposition to the brutal use of forced labour and no leaders of big business were involved in the conspiracy of the July Bomb Plot of 1944 (see pages 145–7). Perhaps this was because the material benefits were on the whole just too attractive. Profits generally continued to increase until the end of the war and this was reason enough to work with the regime. However, that is not to say that they were ever directly in charge of policy. From 1936 this was clearly determined by the Nazi leadership. In a mocking simile Grunberger writes:

> German business can be likened to the conductor of a runaway bus, who has no control over the actions of the driver, but keeps collecting the passengers' fares right up to the final crash.

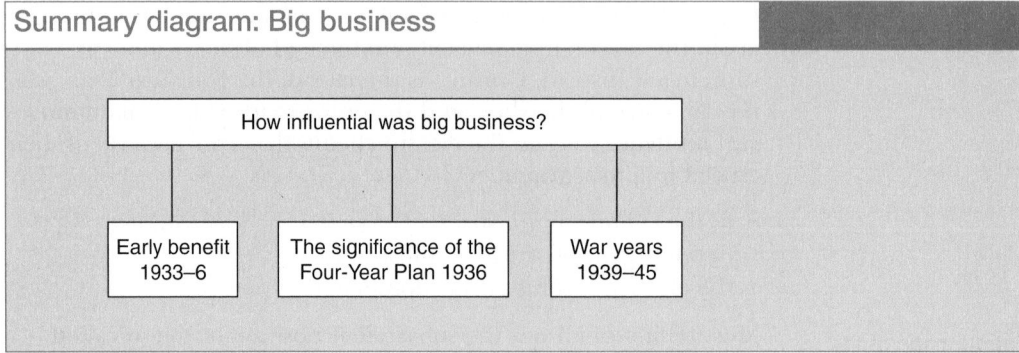

Summary diagram: Big business

7 | The Key Debate

The debate about the political structure of the Third Reich stands at the heart of nearly all aspects of Nazi Germany, but it leaves one key question:

> Where did the political power really lie in the Third Reich?

Historians have various different interpretations.

Nazism, a tool of capitalism

From the 1930s many left-wing analysts sought to explain the creation of the Nazi state (and the rise of fascism in Italy). They came to believe that there was a close connection between Nazism and the crisis of capitalism faced by Germany in 1929–33. Consequently, big business lost faith in the Weimar Republic and supported the Nazis, who were seen as mere 'agents' for the controlling capitalists who sought to:

- satisfy their desire for easy profits
- achieve their **imperialist** ambitions
- dominate a powerful political movement in order to suppress the workers.

Indeed, at the meeting of **Comintern** in 1935, fascism was defined as 'the open terroristic dictatorship of the most

Key terms

Imperialism
Rule by an emperor. It has come to mean one country taking political and economic control of another territory.

Comintern
Communist International. An international body created by Lenin and the Bolsheviks in 1919 that aimed to spread communist revolution.

Key term

Chauvinism
Aggressive
patriotism.

reactionary, most **chauvinistic** and most imperialist elements of finance capital'. And in essence this theory of a close connection between Nazism and capitalism remained the basis of Marxist studies until the collapse of communism in the Eastern bloc and the USSR.

However, non-Marxists have generally not been convinced by the evidence. Contacts did exist between Nazism and big business and there were mutual interests, but it is difficult to support the claim that the Nazis were merely the 'agents' of the capitalists. Moreover, in their attempt to explain fascism in economic terms, Marxist analysts neglected important political aspects. Greater emphasis on the 37 per cent of the population who actually voted for Hitler in 1932 would surely have convinced Marxists that Nazism was something more than just a movement of financial capitalists at a time of economic crisis.

Nazi Germany: a model of totalitarianism

In his futuristic novel *Nineteen Eighty-Four* George Orwell portrayed a political system and a society that has subsequently become a 'model' of totalitarianism. There was no place for the individual in *Nineteen Eighty-Four*; every aspect of life was controlled by the party, which in turn was dominated by the all-pervasive personality of 'Big Brother'. Orwell was writing in the late 1940s and his nightmare vision of totalitarianism had been shaped to a large extent by his observations of the dictatorial regimes of the period, especially Stalin's.

In the 1950s a number of historians and political scientists also began to interpret the Nazi regime as an example of the totalitarian model. According to such interpretations there were no fundamental differences between the regimes of Fascist Italy, Nazi Germany and Soviet Russia. Indeed, Carl Friedrich's analysis went so far as to identify six major features common to totalitarian dictatorships:

- an official ideology
- a single mass party
- terroristic control by the police
- monopolistic control over the media
- a monopoly of arms
- central control of the economy.

Although the idea of Nazism as a form of totalitarianism held great weight in the 1950s such a view is not now so readily accepted. Although the term may still be used to describe Hitler's regime, it is somewhat misleading. The term was a product of the Cold War, when liberal Western historians rather too readily assumed close similarities between Hitler's Germany and Stalin's Russia. Nazi Germany was not the single, all-powerful structure suggested by the term totalitarian, so that definition can be criticised on two major counts. First, although Germany was politically a one-party state, the Nazi Party did not have the organisation or unity to dominate affairs – unlike the Communists in the USSR. Secondly, the Nazis never established a centralised control over the economy – again in direct contrast to the situation in USSR.

The Third Reich: a polycracy

The 1960s witnessed the beginning of a remarkable growth in research into the Third Reich – partly due to the practical reason that the German archives in the hands of the Western Allies had been made readily available. By the late 1960s and early 1970s, historians, such as Martin Broszat and Hans Mommsen, had started to exert a major influence in their analysis of the structure of the Third Reich – hence their approach has been dubbed 'structuralist'.

Historians have increasingly come to accept the view that the Third Reich in its power structure was a **polycracy** and had become an alliance of different overlapping power groups. Although they did not always agree they were dependent on each other and prepared to work together as partners in power. The most important of these blocs would seem to have been the Nazi Party itself, the SS-Police system and the army, big business and the higher levels of the state bureaucracy.

However, in a way the interpretation of the Third Reich as a polycracy does not entirely satisfy the enquiring student because several key points remain:

- There were fundamental divisions and conflicts within these various groups and the key players.
- The relationship between these 'power blocs' was far from static – it changed over time in the years 1933–45.
- There was the question of the exact role and significance of Hitler himself.

Key term

Polycracy
A government system with an increasing range of competing power blocs.

Some key books in the debate
M. Broszat, *The Hitler State* (London, 1981).
C.J. Friedrich and Z. Brzezinski, *Totalitarian Dictatorship and Autocracy* (Cambridge, Mass., 1956).
I. Kershaw, *The Nazi Dictatorship: Problems and Perspectives of Interpretation*, 3rd edn (London, 1993).

Conclusion

In the early years, Hitler and the Nazis were heavily dependent on the sympathy of the army and big business and so they did not attempt to control them directly because they feared alienating them. Indeed, the destruction of the SA in 1934 was motivated very much by the need to satisfy those traditional vested interests, but it was seen as a blow by the radical Nazis in the Party. (At this stage the SS-Police system was relatively limited.) The rearmament programme and the early moves in foreign policy acted as a powerful focus of common interest – profits for industry and the restoration of prestige for the Army.

All this changed in the course of 1936–8. Hitler's personal political position was by this time much stronger and was

Key question
How did the Nazi polycracy change during the years of the Third Reich?

ruthlessly supported by the emerging power of Himmler's SS-Police system. Hitler was therefore less restricted by the need for political compromise and he could afford to pursue his aims more vigorously. Consequently, the economic crisis of 1936 led to the disappearance of Schacht and the introduction of the Four-Year Plan under Göring. This development represented a major shift in the balance of political power away from big business as a whole, although it was strongly supported by the electrochemicals sector because of its links with arms production. Despite the fact that the army had sided with the Nazi leadership in 1936, it was also severely weakened two years later by the purge of major generals after Blomberg and Fritsch had expressed their doubts about the direction of Hitler's foreign policy.

By 1938, therefore, big business, the army and other élites had been reduced to the role of junior partners in the Third Reich's power structure. This weakening of their positions was to continue in subsequent years, although at first the army gained great status from the military victories of 1939–41. It was under the pressures of war that the power and influence of the SS-Police system grew to become the dominant power bloc – so much so that some historians have gone so far as to refer to it as the emergence of the 'SS state'. This also coincided with the weakening of the traditional élites within the state bureaucracy, as the Party apparatus under Bormann's influence began to exert a greater influence. By 1945 the various organs of Nazism had become progressively more dominant, to the detriment of other agencies.

Structuralist historians have certainly succeeded in highlighting a lack of planning and organisation on Hitler's part, so that it is now generally appreciated that divisions and rivalries in the government of the Third Reich persisted throughout its 12-year life. The leading Nazis headed their own institutional empires and their aims and interests often brought them into conflict with each other. For example, the running of the German war economy was in the hands of several major wrangling leaders and their offices:

- Göring as the director of the Four-Year Plan
- Speer as the Minister of Armaments
- Sauckel as Minister for Labour
- Himmler as *Reichsführer* SS with all its economic offices and organisations.

On top of this there were personality clashes that led to personal rivalries and ambitions at the expense of efficient government. Most notably, Bormann and Himmler despised each other, and Göring and Goebbels were barely on speaking terms.

Yet, despite all this talk of individual and institutional confrontation, it is difficult to ignore the importance of Hitler or to accept the view of him as a 'weak dictator' (except perhaps in the final few months of his life). Hitler created the Party and headed a regime that was built on the principle of authoritarian leadership. It is impossible to pinpoint any major domestic development that was contrary to Hitler's wishes. Equally, it was

Hitler's own views on continental conquest and racial supremacy that determined Germany's foreign and military policy. In the final analysis, it is surely indicative that the SS-Police system emerged as *the* dominant power bloc and its guiding principle from the start had been unquestioning obedience to the will of the *Führer*.

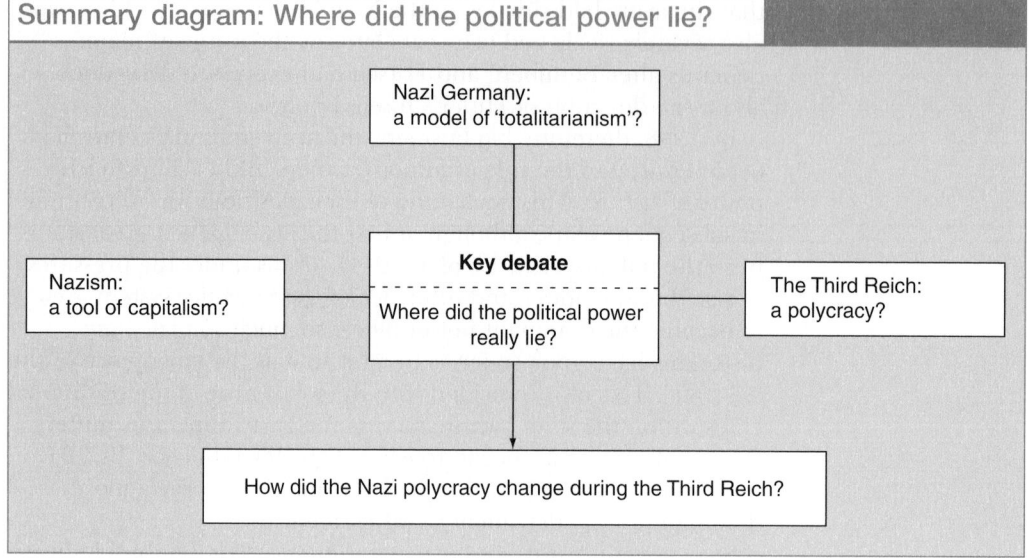

Summary diagram: Where did the political power lie?

Study Guide: AS Questions

In the style of AQA

(a) Explain why Hitler was able to extend his power over the conservative élites in the years 1936–8. (12 marks)

(b) 'The maintenance of a police state was essential for the preservation of Hitler's power in Germany between 1933 and 1939.' Explain why you agree or disagree with this view.

(24 marks)

Exam tips

The cross-references are intended to take you straight to the material that will help you to answer the questions.

(a) To answer this question you will need to define the conservative élites and you will have to consider why Hitler was able to control them. The 'conservative élites' include the army and big business, although you could also include the civil service and foreign office.

Some of the key factors to refer to are:

- The significance of the Blomberg–Fritsch crisis (pages 131–2).
- The impact of the Four-Year Plan and the resignation of Schacht (pages 38–40 and 135–6).
- Hitler's diplomatic successes 1935–8 and the resignation of Neurath (pages 160–5).

It is important to maintain an analytical approach throughout the essay and you will effectively work towards a strong conclusion with a reasoned judgement. In this way you are more likely to earn higher marks. In order to show differentiation and balance, it is also important that you prioritise between reasons, showing which were the more important and how they interlinked.

(b) The quotation is intended to be provocative and you should think of ways in which it might be challenged as well as supported. Information on the police state and its importance can be found on pages 117–22, where you are also introduced to the debate on the limitations of *Gestapo* policing. If the police state was not as efficient as was once thought, can it really have been of such significance? Try to think of other factors that helped to keep Hitler in power:

- the popularity of his policies, especially with regard to the economy
- the benefits offered to workers, women and children
- the cult of personality and the propaganda machine.

You must ask yourself the crucial question: why was there so little opposition? Was it because people were too afraid to speak out or because they had no reason to oppose? Of course, different answers may apply to different groups, but you should try to provide a thoughtful response that is well supported by factual evidence.

6 Opposition in the Third Reich

POINTS TO CONSIDER

This chapter considers the issue of opposition to the Nazi regime in its broadest sense. It should be borne in mind that the Third Reich was never static. People's attitudes changed over the years. For example, some who had started off as sympathisers with the regime eventually became outright opponents. This chapter considers the types of opposition the regime faced through three main themes:

- Active resistance
- Dissent
- The extent of the opposition

Key dates

1934	May	Establishment of Confessional Church to resist Nazi control of the Protestant Church
1935		Mass arrests by *Gestapo* of socialists and communists
1938		Planned *putsch* by General Beck if war resulted from Czech crisis
1941	August	Bishop Galen's sermon against euthanasia
1942		Red Orchestra discovered and closed down
1942–3		White Rose student group; distribution of anti-Nazi leaflets
1944	July	Stauffenberg Bomb Plot on 20 July failed to overthrow regime
	November	Execution of 12 Edelweiss Pirates in Cologne

1 | Active Resistance

Active resistance to the Nazi regime failed and the Third Reich only collapsed when Germany was defeated by the Allies. So those who organised activities aimed at subverting the regime – however gloriously and heroically portrayed – made enormous personal sacrifices without making any real impression on the Nazi stranglehold of power. The real question is why did they fail?

Communists

Key question
Why was active communist resistance to the Nazi state so limited?

Although the Communist Party (KPD) had a mass membership of 300,000 and polled 17 per cent of the popular vote in 1932, it felt the full force of Nazi repression from the very start (see pages 10–11). Over half of its members were interned during the first year of Nazi rule. By 1935 the *Gestapo* had infiltrated the remains of the party, which had tried to continue with the distribution of printed pamphlets and posters and involvement in minor acts of sabotage.

Key dates

Mass arrests by *Gestapo* of socialists and communists: 1935

Red Orchestra cell discovered and closed down: 1942

There followed a series of mass trials, although the communist underground movement was never entirely broken in spite of this onslaught. Many small communist cells continued to be formed by Wilhelm Knöckel in many of the large German cities. The most famous of the communist cells was the so-called Red Orchestra (*Rote Kapelle*), a spy network that successfully permeated the government and military through the aristocratic sympathiser Schulz-Boysen. From 1938 to 1942 it transmitted vital information back to Moscow – but all the members were eventually caught and tortured appallingly.

However, the impact of communist activities should not be overstated and German communists failed because:

- Leading activists after 1936 were also drawn away from Germany to fight for the Republicans against the Fascists in the

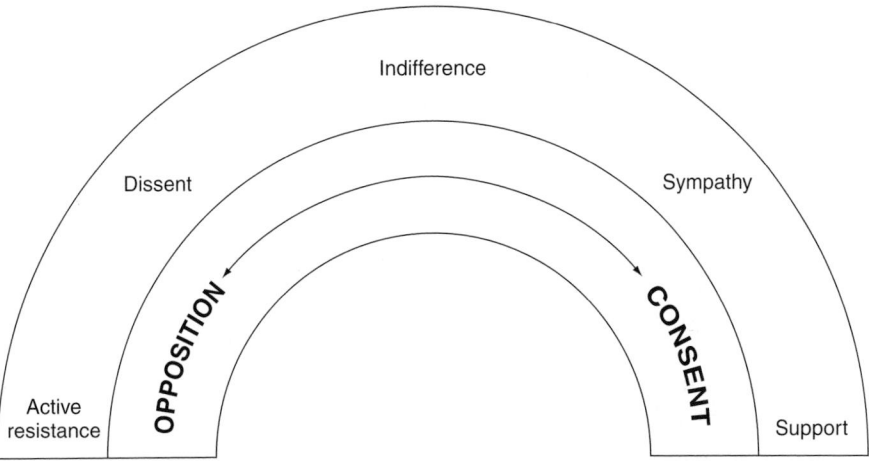

Figure 6.1: A suggested spectrum of public attitudes to the Nazi regime

Spanish Civil War in the belief that such a gesture was a more worthwhile way of resisting fascism.

- They took their orders from Moscow and yet in the 1930s Stalin purged elements of the whole communist movement.
- They were fatally compromised by the Nazi–Soviet Pact of 1939–41 (see pages 170–1).
- Even when the USSR and Germany did end up at war with each other in June 1941 the resistance groups remained isolated.

Active communist resistance to the Nazi state was limited and in the end it really became more geared towards self-preservation, so that it was ready for the day when Nazism would be defeated and the Soviet 'liberation' could take place.

Spanish Civil War The 1936–9 conflict between Republicans, who supported the democratic government, and the Nationalists/ Fascists (financially and militarily backed by Italy and Germany).

Key term

Students: the White Rose Group

The White Rose student resistance movement is probably the most famous of the youth groups because it went beyond mere dissent. It was led by brother and sister Hans and Sophie Scholl. *The White Rose* (the symbol of peace) was the name given to a series of leaflets printed in 1942–3 and distributed initially amongst the students of Munich University but in time to many towns in central Germany. The content of the leaflets was highly political and openly condemned the moral and spiritual values of the Nazi regime. One of the early leaflets was entitled 'Isn't every decent German today ashamed of his government?'

The group represented a brave gesture of defiance and self-sacrifice. However, from the start the group's security was weak and it was only a matter of time before the *Gestapo* closed in. In February 1943 the six leaders were arrested, tortured and swiftly executed. Sophie Scholl openly said to the court:

> What we wrote and said is in the minds of you all. You just don't say it aloud.

Key question
Did the White Rose Group achieve anything?

Key date
White Rose student group and the distribution of anti-Nazi leaflets: 1942–3

Conservative élites

It might seem surprising that the most influential active resistance emerged from the ranks of Germany's upper classes, who dominated the civil service and, most particularly, the officer corps. After all, these were the very same conservative nationalists who had given sympathetic backing to Nazi authoritarianism (see pages 5 and 7). Yet, the army as an institution was never fully 'co-ordinated' (until the summer 1944) and therefore it enjoyed a degree of freedom from Nazi control. Moreover, with its access to arms, the army had the real capacity to resist. For these reasons the development of the active resistance of the German élites formed around the army, although once again it was to fail in its primary objective.

The opposition of the conservative élites emerged slowly. At first, most of them could give qualified support of Nazism for:

- its attacks on the left-wing movement
- its dismantling of the democratic system and the restoration of an authoritarian rule

Key question
Why did Germany's 'active resistance' fail to undermine the Third Reich?

- its hostility towards the Treaty of Versailles
- its demands for rearmament.

Most significantly, the army gave its blessing to the Night of the Long Knives which fatally linked itself with the regime (see pages 19–21). At first, then, the conservative élites did not recognise – or did not want to recognise – the true radical nature of Nazism. They unwittingly strengthened the regime to such an extent that resistance afterwards became much more difficult.

Diplomatic and military success 1938–42

Key date

Planned *putsch* by General Beck if war resulted from Czech crisis: 1938

Key term

Appeasement
Making concessions in order to satisfy an aggressor. In this context, it refers to the Anglo-French policy of the 1930s towards Hitler's territorial demands.

The year 1938 marked the emergence of a real conservative resistance – a response to Hitler's success in gaining political supremacy over the Blomberg–Fritsch crisis (see pages 131–2). Ulrich von Hassell, the ex-ambassador in Rome, and Carl Goerdeler, Mayor of Leipzig and a one-time member of Hitler's early government, both joined the Nazi opposition at this time. More significantly, Ludwig Beck, formerly Chief of the General Staff, became convinced by the summer of 1938 that Hitler's intention to invade Czechoslovakia could only lead to a continental war against Britain and France. Plans were drawn up to stage a *coup* and overtures were also made to the British Foreign Office. As it happened, the Allied **appeasement** of Hitler at Munich cut the ground from beneath the conspirators and the planned revolt was dropped while Hitler took the glory for his diplomatic gains.

Military failings 1942–4

Effective resistance began to re-emerge in the winter months of 1942–3 with the military disasters at El Alamein and Stalingrad (see pages 176–7). The so-called Kreisau Circle was a wide-ranging group of officers, aristocrats, academics and churchmen who met at the Kreisau estate of Helmut von Moltke. The conferences discussed ideas about plans for a new Germany after Hitler and, in August 1943, a programme was drawn up. The principles of the Kreisau Circle were politically conservative and strongly influenced by Christian values. Indeed, there were pacifist elements in the group who were opposed to a *coup* against Hitler.

Nevertheless, some individual members were supporters of what became the most far-reaching act of resistance to Hitler's Germany – the Bomb Plot of 20 July 1944. A number of the civilian resistance figures made contact with dissident army officers, such as Beck and Tresckow, in order to plan the assassination of Hitler and the creation of a provisional government. In the words of Tresckow just before the attempted assassination:

> The assassination must take place, whatever the cost. Even if it should fail, the attempt to seize power in Berlin must take place. The practical consequences are immaterial. The German resistance must prove to the world and to posterity that it dares to take the decisive step.

Eventually, the lead was taken by Colonel von Stauffenberg, who came to believe that the assassination of Hitler was the only way to end the Nazi regime. He himself placed a bomb in Hitler's briefing room at his headquarters in East Prussia on 20 July 1944. Unfortunately for the conspirators, the briefcase containing the bomb was moved a few yards just a minute before it exploded. Hitler thus sustained only minor injuries. In the confused aftermath the generals in Berlin fatally hesitated, thus enabling a group of Hitler's loyal soldiers to arrest the conspirators and re-establish order. About 5000 supporters of the resistance were killed in the aftermath, including Stauffenberg, Beck, Tresckow, Rommel, Moltke and Goerdeler.

Key date

Stauffenberg Bomb Plot failed to overthrow regime: 20 July 1944

The conservative élites proved incapable of fundamentally weakening the Nazi regime and in that sense their active resistance failed. Among the reasons for this are:

- They only recognised the need to resist the regime after the crucial developments of 1934 and 1938, by which time it was too well established.
- The military oath tied the army to the Nazi regime and its leader.
- Hitler's diplomatic and military successes in 1938–42 undoubtedly blinded the élites. Even after the '**turn of the tide**' and the growing knowledge of brutal actions, the majority of army generals did not work with the resistance.
- Planning and organisation of effective action was always fraught with difficulties. Their long-term political aims lacked clarity and practical plans were inhibited by the environment of suspicion and uncertainty in a police state.

Key term

'Turn of the tide'
Used to describe the Allied military victories in the winter of 1942–3, when the British won at El Alamein in North Africa and when the Russians forced the surrender of 300,000 German troops at Stalingrad.

In the end the bad luck and confusion of the Bomb Plot of 20 July reflected these difficulties.

A photo taken of the room after Stauffenberg's bomb exploded. Despite the destruction Hitler was only slightly injured.

Profile: Claus von Stauffenberg 1907–44

1907		– Born in Bavaria, Germany, the descendant of an aristocratic military family
1926–30		– Joined the Bavarian Cavalry Regiment and commissioned as a lieutenant
1936–8		– Joined the army's War Academy in Berlin and graduated first in his class
1939–43		– Fought in Poland, France, Russia and Africa
1942		– Witnessed atrocities in Russia. Started to associate with the resistance of the Kreisau Circle along with Tresckow
1943	January	– Promoted to lieutenant-colonel
		– Badly injured when his staff car ran into a minefield in Africa. Lost his eye, two left-hand fingers and his right forearm
1944		– After his recuperation he decided to kill Hitler and draw up the plan codenamed 'Operation Valkyrie'. Several attempts were aborted in the first half of the year
	July 20	– Detonated the bomb at Hitler's headquarters at Rastenburg, in eastern Germany. Hitler was only injured. Stauffenberg was arrested and shot in the late evening

Stauffenberg was a very able and committed soldier who, like so many, initially admired Hitler. However, his strong Catholic moral outlook shaped his increasing doubts about the regime by 1941. He remained on the fringes of the Kreisau Circle in 1942–3, but he gave the resistance a real purpose from early 1944. Stauffenberg personally took the initiative to carry out the assassination, but for his failure he paid the ultimate price – along with his brother.

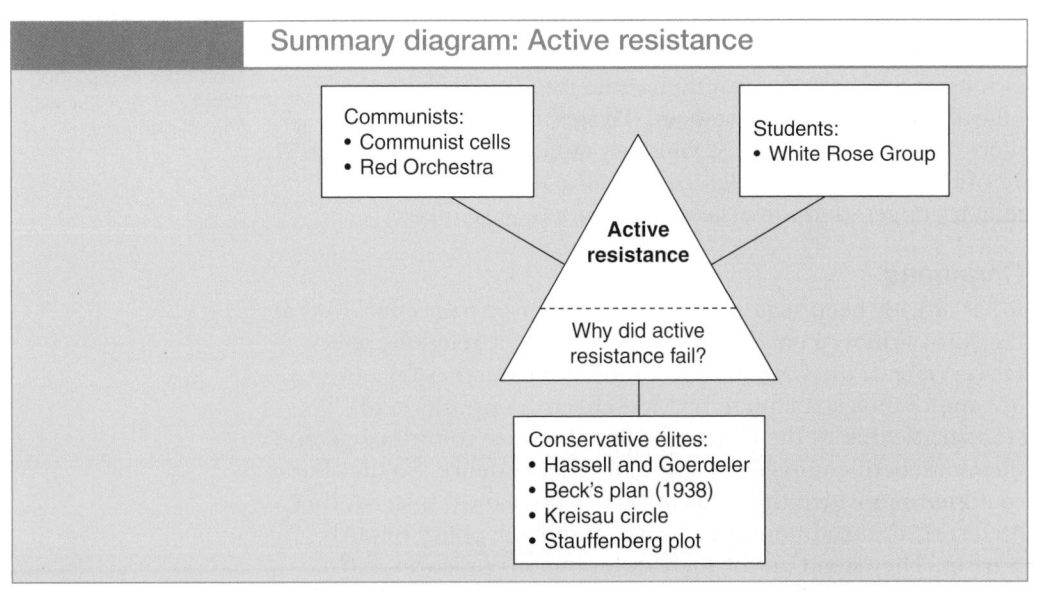

Summary diagram: Active resistance

Communists:
• Communist cells
• Red Orchestra

Students:
• White Rose Group

Active resistance

Why did active resistance fail?

Conservative élites:
• Hassell and Goerdeler
• Beck's plan (1938)
• Kreisau circle
• Stauffenberg plot

2 | Dissent

It is clear that the heroic gestures of Stauffenberg and the Scholls led the way to 'active resistance'. However, it is important to bear in mind the reality for Germans living in the Third Reich. Nazi Germany was a regime that was working towards totalitarianism, and viewed the most innocent action as unacceptable. For example, the refusal to give the 'Heil Hitler' salute could be deemed an act of opposition and held against someone. The same could be said of anyone telling anti-Nazi jokes or refusing to hang out a Nazi flag. It demanded from its people a degree of social conformity that even included the rejection of jazz and swing music as decadent and anti-German. In the end, it was even designated a criminal offence in Nazi Germany to listen to foreign radio broadcasts or to fraternise with foreign workers.

Key question
In what ways did anti-Nazi dissent reveal itself?

Youth

It is possible to be lulled into believing that German youth was a relatively secure bastion of Nazi conformity. Nazi propaganda in the newsreel pictures of the Hitler Youth cleverly portrayed images of camaraderie and youthful exuberance for the cause. However, much recent research suggests that sizeable pockets of the adolescent population had not been won over by 1939 and that, during the war, alienation and dissent increased quite markedly. The regime even established a special youth section of the secret police and a youth concentration camp was set up at Neuwied.

A number of youth groups developed which deliberately exhibited codes of behaviour at odds with the expected social values of Nazism. 'Swing Youth' was one such craze among mainly middle-class youngsters who took up the music and imagery associated with the dance-bands of Britain and the USA. The *Edelweiss Piraten* (a general name given to a host of working-class youths who formed gangs, such as the 'Roving Dudes' and 'Navajos') had been alienated by the military emphasis and discipline of the Hitler Youth. They met up and organised their own hikes and camps which then came into conflict with the official ones. In several instances, 'Pirates' became involved in more active resistance, most famously at Cologne in 1944 when 12 of them were publicly hanged because of their attacks on military targets and the assassination of a *Gestapo* officer.

Edelweiss
A white alpine flower that served as a symbol of opposition.

Key term

Execution of 12 Edelweiss Pirates in Cologne: November 1944

Key date

Christians

It has already been suggested in Chapter 3 (see pages 66–70) that the Nazis achieved only limited success in their religious policy. However, both the Catholic and Protestant Churches failed because of their inability to provide effective opposition to Nazism. Neither of the Christian Churches was 'co-ordinated' and therefore, both enjoyed a measure of independence. So they both could have provided the focus for active resistance. Instead, they preferred, as institutions, to adopt a pragmatic policy towards Nazism. They stood up for their own religious practices and

Kittelbach Pirates from 1937. 'Pirates' was the label chosen by dissenting German youth. In what ways could these boys be seen as challenging Nazi ideals?

traditions with shows of dissent, but generally they refrained from wholesale denunciations of the regime.

The reasons for the Churches' reluctance to show opposition to the regime lay in their conservatism:

- They distrusted the politics of the left that seemed to threaten the existing order of society. The most extreme form of communism rejected the existence of religion itself.
- There was a nationalist sympathy for Nazism, especially after the problems of 1918–33. For many Church leaders it was too easy to believe that Hitler's 'national renewal' was simply a return to the glorious days before 1914. This was particularly true of the Lutheran Protestant Church, which had been the state Church in Prussia under Imperial Germany.
- Both Churches rightly feared the power of the Nazi state. They believed that any gestures of heroic resistance were more than likely to have bloody consequences. In such a situation, their emphasis on pastoral and spiritual comfort was perhaps the most practical and realistic policy for them.

Effective Christian resistance, therefore, remained essentially the preserve of individual churchmen who put their own freedom and lives at risk in order to uphold their beliefs or to give pastoral assistance.

Profile: Dietrich Bonhoeffer 1906–45

1906		– Born in Breslau, Germany
1923–31		– Studied at Tübingen, Berlin, Rome, Barcelona and New York
1931–3		– Lecturer and student pastor at Berlin University
1933–5		– Worked as a pastor on the outskirts of London
1935		– Returned to Germany and joined the Confessional Church
1935–40		– Ran a college to train pastors
1935		– His college was closed
1940–3		– Banned from preaching and made contact with the active resistance movement
1943	April	– Arrested by the *Gestapo*
1943–5		– Held in various prisons and camps
1945	April	– Murdered in Flossenbürg concentration camp

From the very start Bonhoeffer was a consistent opponent of Hitler and Nazism. However, by 1940, he had moved from religious dissent to political resistance. Over the next three years he:

- helped Jews to emigrate
- was drawn into the Kreisau Circle and actively worked with the underground
- travelled secretly to Sweden to see the English bishop Bell in the hope that Britain would help the resistance (the British authorities remained very cautious).

When Bonhoeffer was sentenced to death the SS doctor later wrote: 'in nearly 50 years as a doctor I never saw another man go to his death so possessed of the spirit of God'.

It has been estimated that 40 per cent of the Catholic clergy and over 50 per cent of the Protestant pastors were harassed by the Nazis. Most famous were:

- Bishop Galen of Münster, whose outspoken sermon attacking Nazi euthanasia policy (see page 81) in 1941 proved so powerful that the authorities recoiled from arresting him and actually stopped the programme.
- Martin Niemöller, the founder of the Confessional Church, who languished in a concentration camp from 1937 (see page 69).
- Dietrich Bonhoeffer, whose opposition started as religious dissent but, from 1940, developed into political resistance which brought him into direct contact with elements of the conservative resistance (see pages 144–6).

Such heroic examples were by no means exceptional and hundreds of priests and pastors were to die in the camps for their refusal to co-operate with the regime. Their sacrifice is therefore eloquent testimony to the limits to which people would go to defy conformity. But it also bears witness to the fact that such courageous resistance was rarely able to restrain the regime.

Key dates

Establishment of Confessional Church to resist Nazi control of the Protestant Church: May 1934

Bishop Galen's sermon against euthanasia: August 1941

Workers

Although the vast majority of workers did not engage in the active resistance encouraged by the Communists, the working class had a clearly established identity and association that was at odds with Nazism. This alternative 'identity' enabled opposition to survive and occasionally to express itself. There were a number of strikes in the years 1935–6 and also, not surprisingly, in the last few months of the regime. However, industrial action proved to be ineffective and, on balance, more often than not was motivated by economic discontent rather than by political aims. Moreover, reports of low morale and poor work discipline, while not suggesting widespread support of the regime, were not sufficiently threatening to force it to change direction.

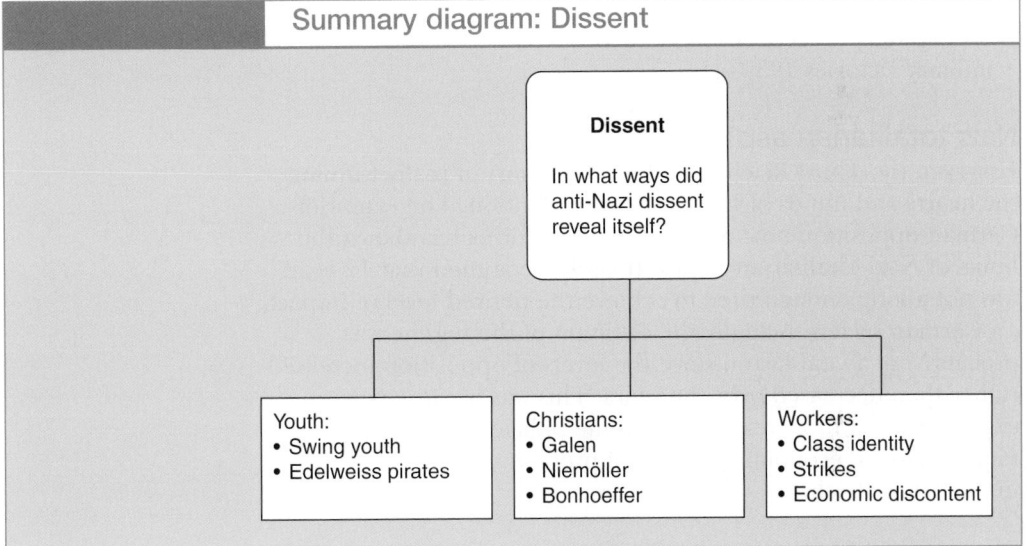

Summary diagram: Dissent

Dissent

In what ways did anti-Nazi dissent reveal itself?

Youth:
• Swing youth
• Edelweiss pirates

Christians:
• Galen
• Niemöller
• Bonhoeffer

Workers:
• Class identity
• Strikes
• Economic discontent

Key question
How much opposition was there among the German population to the Nazi regime?

3 | The Extent of the Opposition

The limitations of the opposition

The real threat posed by those who opposed the regime was fairly limited. Active resistance to undermine the Nazi state could only ever have come from the élites and the disillusioned elements did not act together until the late 1930s. It is also clear that the conservative opposition did not enjoy a sufficiently strong and broad base of support at any time. There remains considerable doubt about whether, even if Stauffenberg's bomb had killed Hitler, the plotters would have received the level of support required to bring an immediate end to the Nazi regime. Obviously, conspiracy required isolation, but in the final analysis the extent of opposition was unlikely ever to provide a sufficiently powerful surge of support for the likes of Stauffenberg. It was even less likely to weaken Nazi policies or threaten the security of the Nazi state. One of Germany's leading historians in this area, Hüttenberger, has written:

Whatever the perceptible reserve and discontent of the workers, sections of the middle class, and the peasantry, the fact cannot be ignored that the leadership of the Third Reich largely succeeded in producing such a degree of conformity, indeed readiness to collaborate, that its plans, especially preparation for war, were not endangered from within.

Sympathy for the regime

It is also evident (see Chapters 3 and 7, pages 51–60 and 160–78) that groups of people did sympathise with and support the Nazi regime at times. It is therefore important to remember the following key factors:

- the economic recovery and, particularly, the creation of jobs
- the 'Hitler myth' which glorified him as an effective leader, almost like a 'saviour'
- the diplomatic successes of 1936–8
- military victories 1939–41.

Nazi totalitarian aspirations

However, the Third Reich fell a long way short of really winning the hearts and minds of the German population. The extent of German opposition now revealed in all its forms has shown the limits of Nazi totalitarian hopes. It could be argued that 12 years was not a long enough time to achieve the desired level of impact on German society. Actually the duration of the regime was probably not a vital factor, since the levels of opposition increased rather than decreased over the years. This was because Nazism expressed itself in increasingly extreme policies that caused even more personal, economic and moral problems for all those living in the Third Reich.

The nature of the problem

Even so, it required, in the words of Kershaw, 'a quantum leap in attitude and behaviour' to cross the boundary from dissent to active resistance. After all, the Third Reich was a regime built on terror and backed by systems of surveillance and censorship. It was also supported by a propaganda machine that effectively upheld the myth of Hitler's invincibility to the very end. For many, it was perhaps easier to believe the propaganda than to question it.

With the advantages of hindsight, one can dismiss the impact of the propaganda or sneer at the gullibility of those who were taken in. To have lived in a society where only one point of view was disseminated must have blunted one's powers of judgement. Those individuals who were able to cross the boundary, like the Scholls, must have known that their actions were only a gesture that would end in personal sacrifice and without real effect. Finally, many people could push to one side their doubts about the regime because of its perceived successes. Very few Germans had the moral courage to make the 'quantum leap' required. Those who did deserve our respect, but one should be wary of morally condemning the many who could not.

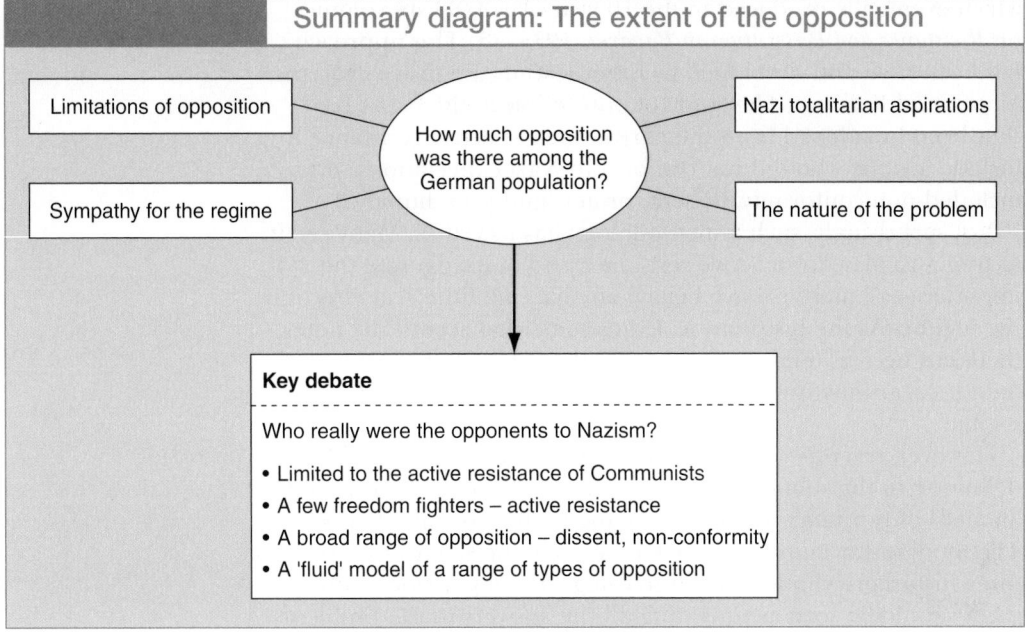

Summary diagram: The extent of the opposition

Limitations of opposition

Sympathy for the regime

How much opposition was there among the German population?

Nazi totalitarian aspirations

The nature of the problem

Key debate

Who really were the opponents to Nazism?

- Limited to the active resistance of Communists
- A few freedom fighters – active resistance
- A broad range of opposition – dissent, non-conformity
- A 'fluid' model of a range of types of opposition

The Key Debate

Historical interpretations about the nature of the opposition to the Third Reich have changed quite dramatically, though there remains one fundamental question:

Who really were the opponents to Nazism?

In the 25 years after the Second World War numerous studies were published of what was termed 'active resistance'. So, Marxist historians from East Germany concentrated almost exclusively on the role of the internal communist opposition and portrayed it as the means to Germany's liberation from fascism by the Soviet Union.

On the other hand, in West Germany, the historical writings of Hans Rothfels, *The German Opposition* (1948), and Gerhard Ritter, *The German Resistance* (1958), tended to highlight those famous individuals who valiantly fought for freedom and liberalism. Consequently, the focus of research, though not ignoring the Churches and students, was on the role of the traditional élites and conservatives. The leading English historians Namier and Wheeler-Bennett also focused on the importance of the same individuals, though they argued that the motivation of the army officers in the bomb plot was not idealistic, but self-serving.

However, a new generation of historians in the 1970s started to question the nature of the opposition to Nazism by a completely new historical methodology. The historian H. Mommsen adopted new research techniques to examine people's attitudes and beliefs at the grass-roots of society through oral history. This was initiated by the so-called Bavaria Project led by him and Hüttenberger, which eventually produced in the 10 years 1973–83 six volumes on *Resistance and Persecution in Bavaria, 1933–45*. This approach has been used and developed by other leading English historians, Mason and Kershaw. The study of opposition to the Nazis has thus been broadened from the narrow area of active resistance to include anyone who did not conform to Nazi expectations. It has included non-conformity, dissent, protest and even humour.

Not surprisingly, such a methodology has its critics. Many see it as trying to play down active resistance and to exaggerate the importance of mere passive behaviour that had little real effect on the regime. As the historian R. Evans somewhat sceptically notes, there has been a 'tendency to expand the concept of resistance until it covers anything short of positive enthusiasm for the regime'.

However, recently some historians, in an attempt to give clearer definition to the subtle differences of opposition, have proposed 'models' of resistance similar to the methods of social scientists. The models shown in Figure 6.2 are merely the suggestions of three historians who have tried to categorise opposition. None of them should be seen as providing all the answers to the problems raised. Indeed, they are probably best viewed as starting-points for discussion and analysis.

Once again, a lot clearly depends on the particular meanings applied to specific words. More significantly, there are dangers in the drawing of clear-cut boundary-lines because what emerges from all the research is that any individual's behaviour was rarely clear-cut. More often than not, any one person exhibited a broad mixture of attitudes – variously shaped by religious, financial, moral or personal influences.

For example, according to Housden's levels of action, it was quite feasible for a Catholic priest to show opposition in the following ways:

- to protest publicly over the Nazi euthanasia policy
- to carry on traditional Catholic customs within the community deliberately.

However, the priest could at the same time:

- be generally supportive of Nazi foreign/military policy
- sympathise with the more authoritarian nature of Nazi government.

It should also be borne in mind that attitudes were rarely static – circumstances changed dramatically in the 12 years of the Third Reich. Therefore it should be no surprise that any attempt to make general statements about public opinion must take into account change over time. Indeed, some of the most important figures in the active resistance among the conservative élites had initially supported the Nazi regime.

In this way, the models show how all the different aspects of opposition in the Third Reich overlap. They reveal that the situation was a lot more 'fluid' than assumed previously. It means that there are no easy answers to the question of who really were the opponents, but at least the models present a more accurate interpretation.

Figure 6.2: Models of resistance

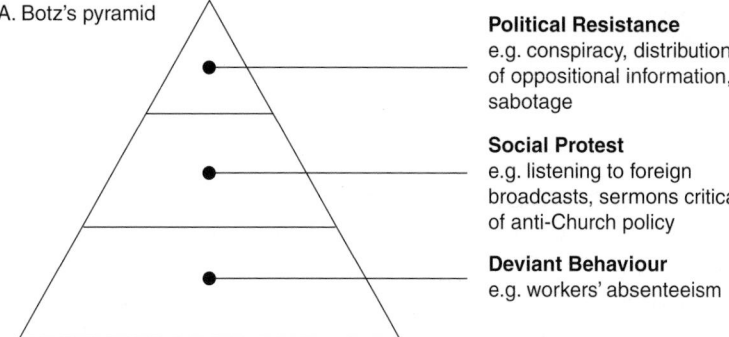

A. Botz's pyramid

Political Resistance
e.g. conspiracy, distribution of oppositional information, sabotage

Social Protest
e.g. listening to foreign broadcasts, sermons critical of anti-Church policy

Deviant Behaviour
e.g. workers' absenteeism

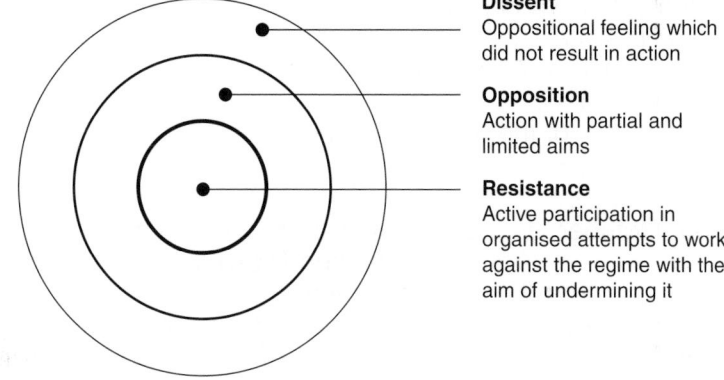

B. Kershaw's concentric circles

Dissent
Oppositional feeling which did not result in action

Opposition
Action with partial and limited aims

Resistance
Active participation in organised attempts to work against the regime with the aim of undermining it

C. Housden's levels of action

1. Personal mental protection.
2. The deliberate carrying on of traditional community life in the face of Nazi preferences to the contrary.
3. Anti-Nazi discussions with a close circle of friends.
4. Open dissent.
5. Public protest.
6. Concerted conspiracy using low-key means (e.g. the secret distribution of leaflets) to subvert Nazi policies.
7. Open rebellion against elements of the Hitler state.
8. Revolution against the whole Hitler state.

Some key books in the debate

M. Housden, *Resistance and Conformity in the Third Reich* (1997).

I. Kershaw, *The Nazi Dictatorship: Problems and Perspectives of Interpretation*, 3rd edn (London, 1993).

D. Peukert, *Inside Nazi Germany: Conformity, Opposition and Racism in Everyday Life* (1989).

H. Rothfels, *The German Opposition* (1948).

---

7 German Foreign Policy 1933–45

POINTS TO CONSIDER

There is a lot of detail in this chapter and you must be careful not to get too lost in it. Moreover, this chapter cannot be taken in isolation. Many aspects of Nazi domestic policy are closely connected with the foreign policy of the Third Reich. This chapter focuses on foreign policy between 1933 and 1945 through the following themes:

- The framework of Nazi foreign policy
- The Nazi challenge to the Versailles Treaty 1933–7
- The road to war 1937–9
- Germany at war 1939–45
- The impact of the war on Germany

Key dates

1933	October	Germany withdrew from League of Nations and Disarmament Conference
1934	January	German–Polish non-aggression pact
1935	March	Reintroduction of military conscription
1936	March	Remilitarisation of Rhineland by German troops
1937	November	Hossbach Conference: Hitler's address to the chiefs of armed services and Neurath
1938	March	*Anschluss* with Austria
	September	Munich Agreement ceded Sudetenland to Germany
1939	March	Invasion of Czechoslovakia: Munich Agreement undone
	August	Nazi–Soviet Pact
	September 1	German invasion of Poland
	September 3	Britain and France declared war
1941	June	'Operation Barbarossa' – German invasion of USSR
	December	German declaration of war on USA following Pearl Harbor: continental war 'globalised'
1943	January	German surrender at Stalingrad
1944	June	Allied landings in Normandy
1945	May	German surrender: division of Germany

1 | The Framework of Nazi Foreign Policy

Key question
Was Germany's international position weakened after the First World War?

Despite the restrictions of the Treaty of Versailles and the country's difficult economic conditions created by the Depression, Germany was able to pursue a major continental war within seven years of Hitler's assumption of power in 1933. This remarkable transformation in her fortunes was the result of two key factors. First, Hitler was prepared to pursue his foreign affairs policy with ambitious aims. Secondly, the continental **balance of power** that emerged from 1918 actually tilted towards Germany's advantage.

Key term

Balance of power
The political idea that the best way of ensuring international order is to have power so evenly distributed among states that no single state is able to have a dominant position.

The international context
The First World War and the peace settlements of 1919–20 dramatically changed the European map. The great empires of Russia, Austria–Hungary and Turkey had collapsed, creating a power vacuum in central and eastern Europe.

- The USSR was relatively weak and initially mainly concerned with its own modern industrialisation. It was isolated from the Western world although it had signed the Rapallo Treaty (1922) with Germany. This was not an alliance, only a treaty of friendship establishing full diplomatic relations between the two countries. Moreover, after the establishment of the Nazi dictatorship, relations between Russia and Germany deteriorated quickly.

Figure 7.1: Germany's borders

- The successor states of the Austria–Hungary empire were unstable and relatively minor powers: Austria, Czechoslovakia and Hungary.
- The new Turkish republic was a modernising and inward-looking state.

Moreover, the major European powers of Britain and France had been decisively weakened by the effects of total war:

- Britain had to pay for the enormous economic costs of the war and found it increasingly difficult to maintain her overstretched empire.
- France was determined to maintain its continental status and to uphold the terms of the Treaty of Versailles. However, it faced ongoing political and economic problems.

Very significantly, the USA showed little inclination to uphold the European order that it had done so much to create between 1917 and 1919. Instead it retreated into **isolationism** in the inter-war years and did not even join the **League of Nations**.

Nazi aims

In the international world, the recovery of Germany with its vast economic potential and manpower was always probable. Indeed, the revision of the Versailles settlement and the re-emergence of Germany as a great power had already begun under the Weimar Republic. However, under the Nazi regime the pace and direction of foreign policy were changed.

In the decade after the **Nuremberg Trials** of 1946 it was widely assumed that the expansionist aims of Nazi foreign policy dated from the so-called Hossbach Conference in 1937 (see pages 164–5). Hitler's address to the chiefs of the armed service and to Foreign Minister Neurath seemed to mark the turning point from a **revisionist policy** to one of aggressive expansion. Such a view is not now generally accepted.

As far back as 1960, the English historian Hugh Trevor-Roper, in his article 'Hitler's War Aims', drew attention to the systematic nature of Hitler's ideas on foreign policy from the start of his political career. Such an interpretation has been more fully developed by the so-called **programme school** of historians in Germany. In their view, Hitler had a clearly defined set of objectives, which amounted to a 'stage by stage plan' (*Stufenplan*):

- The destruction of the Treaty of Versailles and the restoration of Germany's pre-1914 boundaries.
- The union of all German-speaking peoples such as Austria, western Poland, the borders of Czechoslovakia (the Sudetenland) and provinces in Hungary and Romania.
- The creation of *Lebensraum*: the establishment of a Nazi racial empire by expanding into eastern Europe at the expense of the Slavic peoples, particularly in Poland and Russia.

Key terms

Isolationism
The foreign policy of the USA after the First World War when it withdrew from international politics. The USA decided not to join the League of Nations.

League of Nations
An international body based on the idea of US President Wilson to create to encourage disarmament and to prevent war.

Key question
What were the aims of Nazi foreign policy?

Key terms

Nuremberg Trials
The international military tribunal set up by the Allies to try major war criminals.

Revisionist policy
The aim to modify or change an agreement. Here it refers specifically to the policy of changing the terms of the Treaty of Versailles.

Programme school
A title given to some intentionalist historians who concentrate on Hitler's foreign policy.

However, there remain conflicting opinions over the precise extent of Hitler's ambitions.

- The 'continentalists' believe that planned expansion was to be limited to the establishment of a hegemony within Europe.
- The 'globalists' go further and support the thesis that Hitler aspired to German supremacy in the Middle East and Africa (in particular, at the expense of British colonial territories) and finally to a struggle with the USA for world domination.

The 'programme' school has achieved an unusually high degree of acceptance within academic circles. Even the dispute between the 'globalists' and the 'continentalists' is rather artificial – since it does not revolve around what actually happened but is based on the significance of some rather vague statements from Hitler himself on Germany's future world role. Yet, on essentials both interpretations are in agreement:

- They uphold the central place of Hitler himself in the creation of Nazi foreign policy.
- They emphasise the racialist framework of that foreign policy.
- They view the creation of *Lebensraum* as the basis for Hitler to build Germany's status as a great power and to destroy Soviet Russia.

Although historians now accept the view that Hitler had a 'programme' in mind in his foreign policy, they differ over the analysis of the actual events between 1933 and 1945. This is the subject of the next few sections.

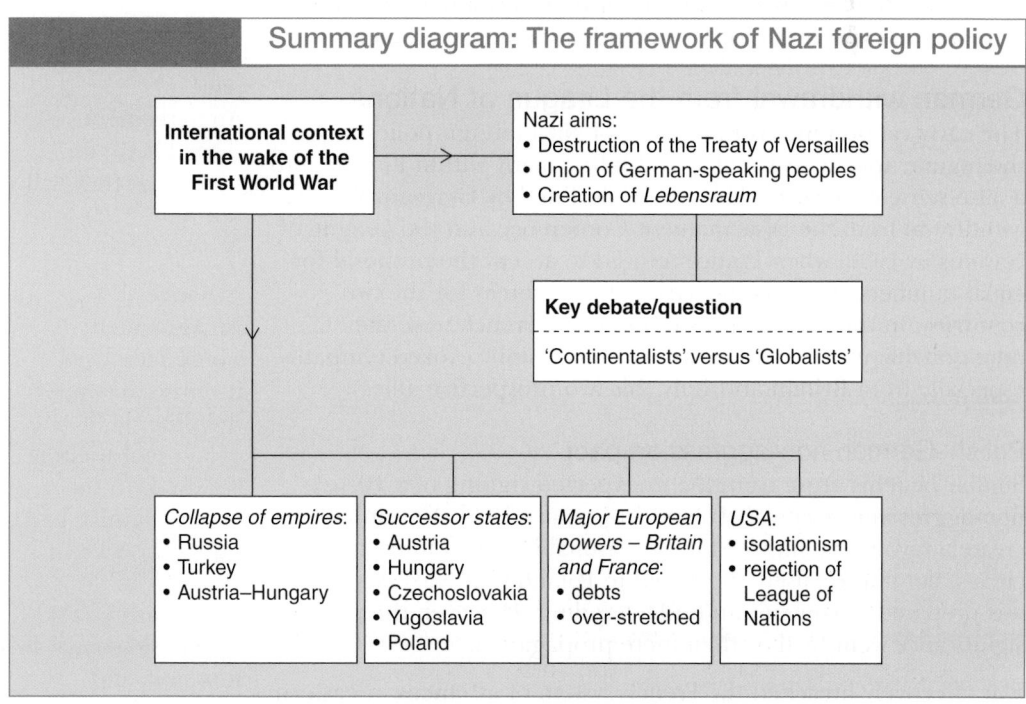

Summary diagram: The framework of Nazi foreign policy

International context in the wake of the First World War

Nazi aims:
- Destruction of the Treaty of Versailles
- Union of German-speaking peoples
- Creation of *Lebensraum*

Key debate/question

'Continentalists' versus 'Globalists'

Collapse of empires:
- Russia
- Turkey
- Austria–Hungary

Successor states:
- Austria
- Hungary
- Czechoslovakia
- Yugoslavia
- Poland

Major European powers – Britain and France:
- debts
- over-stretched

USA:
- isolationism
- rejection of League of Nations

2 | The Nazi Challenge to the Versailles Treaty 1933–7

Hitler's appointment as chancellor did not immediately usher in a new era in German foreign policy. Indeed, the post of foreign minister remained in the hands of Constantin von Neurath, a conservative nationalist, which suggested continuity rather than change. Such a public perception suited Hitler. Economic and military circumstances also demanded a cautious approach: Germany's unemployment still stood at about six million and its army was still limited to 100,000 men. Moreover, the priority was the establishment of the dictatorship at home rather than extravagant diplomatic actions abroad.

The beginnings of Nazi foreign policy

Bearing in mind Germany's isolation, Hitler's objectives in the early years of Nazi foreign policy were limited to cultivating friendship with Britain and Italy and weakening French power and influence wherever possible. However, Hitler was helped in this by the changing international situation, which was moving in Germany's favour.

- The Japanese invasion of Manchuria in 1931 had not only highlighted the ineffectiveness of the League of Nations, but had also underlined the strategic dilemma facing Britain. Namely, how could it uphold its global commitments to the Empire, act as 'world policeman' for the League, and also play a major role in maintaining political stability in Europe?
- The severity of the Great Depression exacerbated the problems faced by the USA, Britain and France. As a result, each country tended to concentrate on its individual domestic problems.

German withdrawal from the League of Nations

The early caution in this first phase of Nazi foreign policy made the regime appear reasonable and lulled many within Europe into a false sense of security. This was underlined by Germany's withdrawal from the Disarmament Conference and the League of Nations in 1933, when France refused to accept the proposal for equal numbers and military parity of land forces for the two countries. In this way, it appeared as if the French were the unreasonable party, while Hitler had successfully evoked sympathy, especially from Britain and Italy (his two prospective allies).

Polish–German non-aggression pact

Similar benefits arose from the unexpected signing of a 10-year **non-aggression pact** with Poland in January 1934. Not only did it create a favourable impression of reasonableness in international circles, but it also falsely suggested to Poland that Nazi Germany was prepared to come to an understanding. However, the pact's significance went further than mere propaganda.

- It effectively breached the French system of **alliances** in eastern Europe.

Key question
Did Hitler strengthen Germany's diplomatic position in the first two years of power?

Key dates

Germany withdrew from League of Nations and Disarmament Conference: October 1933

German–Polish non-aggression pact: January 1934

Key terms

Non-aggression pact
An agreement signed between states that they will not fight each other. Not an alliance.

Alliance
An agreement where members promise to support the other(s), if one or more of them is attacked. In this context France had signed a series of alliances in the 1920s with Poland, Czechoslovakia, Romania and Yugoslavia.

Key terms

Buffer state
The general idea of two rival countries being separated by a territory between them, e.g. the Rhineland demilitarised zone, 1919–36.

Plebiscite
A vote by the people on one specific issue – like a referendum. In the Peace Settlement 1919–20, it was decided to hold a series of plebiscites to decide the future of some territories. In this context, the Treaty of Versailles stated that a plebiscite should be held on the Saarland in January 1935.

- It secured Germany's eastern flank while diplomatic problems were being dealt with in the south and west, e.g. the Rhineland and Austria.

However, in the long term, Hitler did not envisage any place for an independent Poland, as he believed it simply served as the gateway to the creation of *Lebensraum* in the east.

Such successes did not result in any kind of formal agreement with Britain and Italy in the course of 1934. Although Britain showed considerable sympathy with Germany's revisionist demands, sympathy was not like a military or strategic understanding. So several high-level diplomatic Anglo-German missions failed to achieve any kind of breakthrough. An alliance with Italy also seemed a long way off. The attempted *coup* by the Austrian Nazis in July 1934 probably enjoyed only moral support from Berlin, but it frightened Mussolini into moving 40,000 troops to the Austro-Italian frontier at the Brenner Pass, since he regarded Austria as an important **buffer state** between Germany and Italy. This incident was a clear indication of the limits of Nazi power at this time.

By the end of 1934 Hitler had secured his domestic position and the economy was recovering rapidly. His prestige was further enhanced in January 1935 when the Saarland, which for the previous 15 years had been under the control of the League of Nations, voted in a free and fair **plebiscite** to return to German rule. It represented a great propaganda success for the Nazis. However, if Hitler was to loosen the constraints of Versailles, it seemed that he would require greater military power than was permitted by the treaty. Therefore, it is a reflection of Hitler's great diplomatic skills that within the next two years, 1935–7, the Versailles Treaty was effectively dead and the continental balance of power had shifted in favour of Germany without a single shot being fired.

Breaking free from Versailles

Key question
How was Hitler able to dismantle the treaties of Versailles and Locarno?

Key date
Reintroduction of military conscription: March 1935

Germany's declaration in March 1935 of the existence of a *Luftwaffe* was followed shortly afterwards by the introduction of conscription and a peacetime army of 550,000. These decisions went directly against the terms of the Treaty of Versailles and led to a combined verbal condemnation by Britain, France and Italy in a statement, the so-called Stresa Declaration. Yet, in an uncertain international atmosphere in June 1935 Britain and Germany signed a naval agreement, which ignored the terms of the Versailles Treaty and allowed Germany to have a navy 35 per cent of the strength of the British fleet. In this way Hitler had successfully:

- detached Britain from the other two friends of the Stresa Front
- managed to increase German naval military power
- laid the basis for an improved Anglo-German understanding.

The remilitarisation of the Rhineland, March 1936

Yet, the real turning point in Nazi foreign policy in the years 1933–9 was Hitler's decision in March 1936 to order his troops to re-occupy the demilitarised Rhineland. He seized this initiative because of the changing international atmosphere:

Remilitarisation of the Rhineland by German troops: March 1936

Key date

- Mussolini ordered in October 1935 the invasion of Abyssinia (now known as Ethiopia), one of the two remaining independent African states. Italy's act of war and its violation of the League of Nations destroyed the last remains of unity with Britain and France.
- When it became clear that the aggressor had triumphed, it also underlined the impotence of the League of Nations in major international incidents.
- The crisis focused Anglo-French diplomacy on Italy and on threats to the world order outside Europe.
- The British government (and public opinion) did not see the Rhineland as a major issue – after all, it was legally German territory.
- France had a general election pending and showed no inclination to intervene.

As a result international condemnation was limited to verbal protests, more directed at Hitler's methods than at his aims.

The remilitarisation of the Rhineland was a bold gamble by Hitler, which initially did not enjoy the full support of the army generals. They believed that the risk of military retaliation was too great. Such pessimists were proved wrong and Hitler was proved right. With hindsight, it is clear that the remilitarisation of the Rhineland was a decisive turning point in European international relations in the years 1933–9.

- In diplomatic terms, not only the Versailles Treaty, but also the **Locarno Pact**, had been overturned (the Locarno Pact was a voluntarily agreed treaty, unlike Versailles).
- Most significantly, the strategic advantage of the demilitarised buffer between France and Germany had been lost completely.
- French military thinking had reflected the loss of purpose in its political leadership. It had been shown to be purely defensive and clearly incapable of taking any kind of aggressive military initiative east of the **Maginot Line**.
- In addition, Hitler's personal standing within Germany had been enormously enhanced. As one journalist commented, '… this observer, who covered the "election" from one corner of the Reich to the other, has no doubt that the vote of approval for Hitler's *coup* was overwhelming. And why not? The junking of Versailles and the appearance of German soldiers marching again into what was, after all, German territory were things that almost all Germans naturally approved.'

Key terms

Locarno Pact
A series of treaties that became known as the Locarno Pact in 1925. The main points were to accept the Franco-German and Belgian–German borders and to recognise as permanent the demilitarisation of the Rhineland.

Maginot Line
The name given to the extensive defence fortifications built on the Franco-German frontier by the French governments in the 1930s. It was intended to resist any German offensive military action.

The Rome–Berlin Axis

The diplomatic pendulum continued to swing in Germany's favour during 1936. A civil war broke out in Spain. This caused further political uncertainty, which was worsened by the military

THE GOOSE-STEP

"GOOSEY GOOSEY GANDER,
WHITHER DOST THOU WANDER?"
"ONLY THROUGH THE RHINELAND—
PRAY EXCUSE MY BLUNDER!"

A British cartoon condemning Germany's **remilitarisation of the Rhineland** and the overturning of the treaties of Versailles and Locarno.

Remilitarisation of the Rhineland
In the Treaty of Versailles (1919) the Rhineland was to be demilitarised from the French frontier to a line 32 miles east of the Rhine, although legally it was still part of Germany. In March 1936 German troops 're-occupied' the territory and re-established German military control.

Rome–Berlin Axis
An understanding signed in 1936 based on political, economic and ideological co-operation. It did not involve any military commitments.

involvement of Italy, Germany and the USSR. Britain and France, fearing that the war could provide the spark for a major international conflict, struggled to maintain a policy of non-intervention. All this suited Hitler's purpose, for attention was again directed away from central Europe. It also provided a common focus for Italian and German interests which culminated in the emergence of the **Rome–Berlin Axis** in November 1936 – an understanding although not yet a military alliance.

By the end of 1936 Germany's international status had undergone a remarkable transformation. France's previously dominant position on the continent had withered away and the diplomatic and military initiative had passed to Germany. The constraints of Versailles and Locarno had been struck off at no cost. Moreover, Germany was no longer isolated – Mussolini had been detached from France and Britain and was moving ever closer to an understanding with Hitler.

The Hossbach Conference

However, Hitler's position was not without problems. Political and economic developments in the Nazi regime had important implications for the evolution of his foreign policy because:

Key question
Was Hitler set for war?

- In the autumn of 1936 the economic crisis revealed the weaknesses of Germany's economic expansion (see pages 36–41). Hitler was not yet in a position to risk fighting a war – hence the creation of the Four-Year Plan under Göring to create a war economy.
- There was also the problem of conservative forces in the army and the foreign ministry. Certain elements in both these institutions had already advised a more cautious policy. If Hitler wished to raise the diplomatic stakes higher, he needed guaranteed support from such quarters.
- There remained the problem that Germany had not secured an alliance with Britain and voices within the Party were promoting alternative diplomatic strategies. In particular, the leading Nazi Joachim von Ribbentrop, who ran his own personal 'bureau', was keen to develop a **tripartite** understanding between Germany, Japan and Italy. Hitler was not convinced, despite the developing co-operation between these three powers, and he remained committed to the idea of the British alliance as a way of securing his long-term aim of crushing the USSR. He sent Ribbentrop to London as Germany's new ambassador in the autumn of 1936 with the specified objective of securing an agreement with Britain.

Tripartite
An agreement of three parties.

Key term

These problems partly explain the relative inactivity of 1937 that stands out as a dividing line between the diplomatic *coups* of 1935–6 and the pre-war crises of 1938–9. However, in November 1937 at the so-called Hossbach Conference (named after Hitler's adjutant who took the surviving notes), Hitler addressed Foreign Minister Neurath, War Minister Blomberg and the three commanders-in-chief of the armed forces and he outlined three war scenarios:

- to take action after the period 1943–5 when military preparations would be nearly complete
- to exploit French internal problems and to take action against Czechoslovakia
- to take action if France became involved in a war with another country which would prevent her defending herself against Germany.

The significance of the meeting has been the focus of considerable controversy. It was used by the prosecution at the Nuremberg Trials and by some post-war historians to suggest, in the words of Shirer, that from this point 'the die was cast. Hitler had communicated his irrevocable decision to go to war'. At the other extreme, the meeting has been dismissed as simply a

Profile: Joachim von Ribbentrop 1893–1946

1893	– Born in Wesel, Germany
1914–17	– Served in the First World War, seriously wounded and awarded the Iron Cross First Class
1920–45	– Ran a successful wine and champagne trade company and travelled widely
1932	– Joined the Nazi Party
1933	– Created the Ribbentrop Bureau to advise Hitler on foreign policy
1935	– Negotiated the Anglo-German Naval Agreement
1936–8	– Served as German ambassador to Britain
1938–45	– Appointed as Foreign Minister, replacing the aristocratic Neurath
1939 August	– Negotiated the Nazi–Soviet Pact
1946	– Hanged at the Nuremberg Trials

Ribbentrop was well educated and travelled widely in his commercial career in North America and Europe. He was a great socialiser who learned the skill to advance his position by making important contacts. Although he only joined the Party in 1932 he rose quickly and soon won favour with Hitler mainly because he said the right things. His main significance was that:

- he created the Ribbentrop Bureau that undermined the traditional supremacy of the foreign ministry
- he played an important role in the negotiations that led to the diplomatic gains of 1936–9
- he maintained his status to 1945, but he lost real influence from 1939 after his diplomatic role declined with the beginning of the war.

Key date

Hossbach Conference – Hitler's address to Blomberg and the chiefs of armed forces and Neurath: November 1937

manoeuvre in domestic affairs to overcome the conservatives' doubts about the pace of rearmament. According to the historian A.J.P. Taylor, Hitler's ideas were 'in large part day-dreaming unrelated to what followed in real life … There was here no concrete plan, no directive for German policy in 1937 and 1938'.

It is likely that the pressures of the traditional interest groups at home did prompt Hitler's statement and, certainly, it is true that actual events did not unfold as outlined in Hitler's scenarios. So the Hossbach memorandum does not provide a blueprint for Nazi foreign policy. However, it would be wrong simply to dismiss its contents out of hand. It does show how Hitler's policy was changing from one centred on diplomacy to one where military force could play a much greater part. This view is supported by two subsequent developments:

- Blomberg's and Neurath's criticisms of Hitler resulted in their resignation (see pages 131–2) and so the army high command was restructured and Ribbentrop was appointed as foreign minister.
- It was decided to develop an offensive war plan against Czechoslovakia.

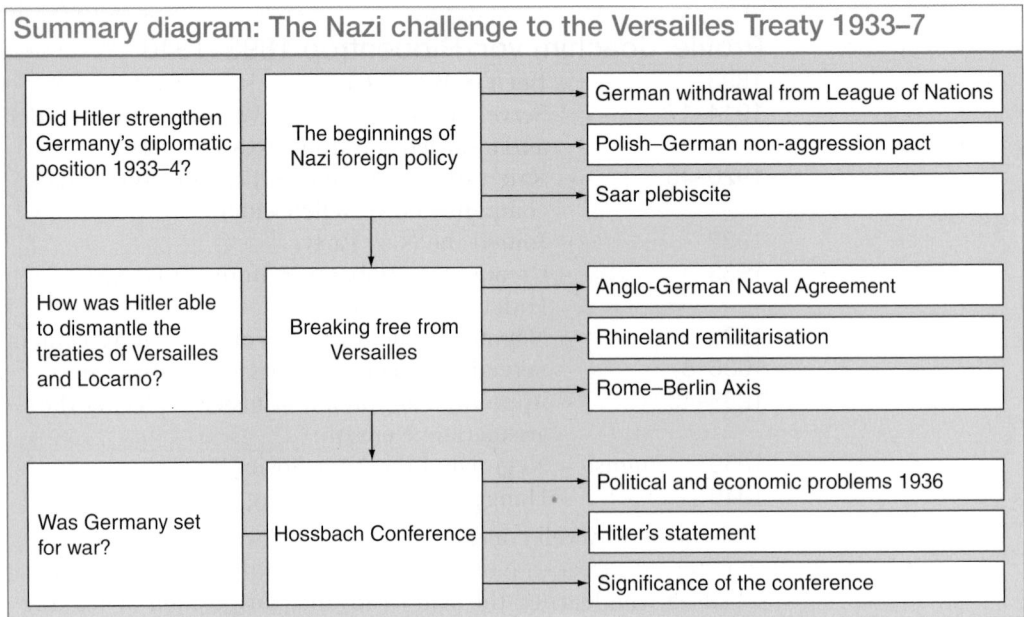

3 | The Road to War 1938–9

Austria's independence was guaranteed by the Versailles Treaty. Its position had been protected by Mussolini's desire to maintain a pro-Italian buffer on his northern frontier. However, by early 1938 the Austrian Nazi movement had re-established itself as a powerful and disruptive force following the failed *putsch* of 1934. Mussolini's growing friendship with Hitler suggested that an agreement over Austria would be possible. Even more significantly, Britain and France implied in diplomatic circles that Nazi Germany's unification with German-speaking Austria was not an issue to go to war over.

The *Anschluss* March 1938

Hitler was therefore hopeful that diplomatic pressure and internal disruption could bring about a peaceful *Anschluss* without major conflict. For example, Schuschnigg, the Austrian chancellor, conceded to Hitler in February 1938 that the Austrian Nazi leader, Seyss-Inquart, would be appointed minister of interior. However, Schuschnigg soon became concerned that the Austrian Nazis were exploiting the concessions and he suddenly tried to strengthen his position by organising a national referendum to appeal to the Austrian people.

Hitler was furious because he was frightened that a vote against the union would undermine his claims and so he was forced into a rushed and poorly executed invasion of Austria on 12 March 1938. This was technically legal because the Austrian government was forced to issue an invitation to the Nazis to invade.

The *Anschluss* with Austria represented a spectacular foreign policy triumph for Hitler, after a period of relative inactivity, and it had important consequences:

Key question
Why did Germany's unification with Austria not lead to war?

Key question
How significant was the *Anschluss*?

Anschluss
'Union'. In the years 1919–38, it referred to the paragraph in the Treaty of Versailles which outlawed any political union between Germany and Austria, although the population was wholly German speaking.

Key term

Key date

Anschluss with
Austria: 12 March
1938

- Diplomatically, the *Anschluss* had again shown Britain and France to be unwilling to stand up to Germany, while Mussolini had been willing to accept the loss of his Austrian buffer for the sake of German friendship.
- There were also economic advantages for the Third Reich. Austria's gold reserves and mineral deposits of iron-ore, copper and lead were of great value in the light of Germany's recurring balance of payment problems.
- Most importantly, Hitler had successfully overturned the strategic balance of power in central Europe. The take-over of Austria meant the western half of Czechoslovakia was now encircled, and control of the Danube valley from Vienna provided a gateway into south-eastern Europe (see the map on page 168).

Key question
Why did
Czechoslovakia
become the focus of
an international
crisis?

The Czech crisis

Having gained such a dramatic triumph over Austria, Hitler's attention turned almost immediately towards Czechoslovakia. The Czech crisis was to last almost a year and was to bring Europe very close to war. Hitler made clear his intention to use military force in his statement, written at the beginning of the military plan on 30 May 1938 for the attack on Czechoslovakia: 'It is my unalterable decision to smash Czechoslovakia by military action in the near future'.

In the face of Hitler's increasingly aggressive demands, Czechoslovakia's chances of survival depended on:

- the maintenance of its democracy (in contrast to all the other eastern European states)
- the natural geography provided by the mountains in the border territory of the Sudetenland backed up by fortifications
- her reasonably modern army
- her military alliances with France (1924) and Russia (1935), which meant support could be requested in the event of war.

However, the existence of 3.5 million Sudeten Germans in the border region of Czechoslovakia, actively stirred up by the propaganda of the Nazi Sudeten German Party and its leader Henlein, provided the means to undermine the Czech state from within. At the same time, the behaviour of Britain and France suggested that they would not interfere militarily in any territorial readjustments in the region. Hitler may not have been able to secure the desired alliance with Britain, but the diplomatic messages coming out of London convinced him that the government there was prepared to appease Germany by concessions to Czechoslovakia for the sake of peace.

The crisis came to a head in September 1938 – with constant clashes between Sudeten Germans and Czechs, with German and Czech troops poised on their respective frontiers (see the box 'The Czech crisis 1938' on page 169). With the possibility of Britain and France being dragged into the war, Hitler settled for a diplomatic solution by accepting the Munich Agreement, which ceded the Sudetenland to Germany. The whole incident was

Figure 7.2: German annexations 1938–9

portrayed as another success for the *Führer*. Yet, Hitler himself was not entirely pleased that his 'entry into Prague had been spoilt'. He had been aiming to destroy the Czech state in its entirety, but he backed down from a military invasion and accepted a negotiated settlement because he estimated that the risk of a more widespread continental war had become too great.

Consequences of the Munich Agreement

The outcomes of the Munich Agreement were many and complex and spread across Europe. For Germany there were considerable political, economic and strategic advantages:

- The Sudetenland was rich in natural deposits of coal, copper and lignite (brown coal); and it was also a strong manufacturing centre for textiles, chemicals and machine tools. All these assets now passed to Germany.
- It was a major success for Hitler and the regime. It seems that German public opinion was apprehensive of the possibility of

Key date

Munich agreement ceded Sudetenland to Germany: 30 September 1938

Key question
Why was the Munich Agreement so significant?

The Czech crisis 1938

28 March	Hitler encouraged Henlein to make excessive demands on the Czech government that could never be satisfied
20–22 May	War scare. Czech troops mobilised and Hitler refrained from invasion
30 May	Germany's military plan 'Operation Green' was revised with the aim 'to smash Czechoslovakia by military action' by 1 October
12 September	In Hitler's address he demanded 'justice' for the 'oppressed' Sudetens with the result of many disturbances in the Sudetenland
15 September	Chamberlain met Hitler at Berchtesgaden in the hope of preventing war by recommending the Czechs to make some concessions
22 September	The basis for an agreement was made by Britain, France and the Czechs, but when Chamberlain came to Bad Godesberg Hitler increased his demands and the negotiations collapsed
29–30 September	With a European war looking very likely a Four Power Conference was held at Munich between, Britain, France, Germany and Italy, though Czechoslovakia and USSR were not invited. Hitler claimed that the Sudetenland was his 'last territorial demand in Europe' and on that promise: • the Sudetenland was handed over to Germany • the province of Teschen was handed over to Poland • the province of Southern Slovakia was handed over to Hungary

Major characters

Germany	Hitler (*Führer*)	Ribbentrop (Foreign Minister)
Britain	Chamberlain (Prime Minister)	Henderson (British Ambassador)
France	Daladier (Prime Minister)	
Italy	Mussolini (*Duce*)	Ciano (Foreign Minister)
Czechoslovakia	Beneš (Prime Minister)	Hacha (President)
	Henlein (the leader of the Sudeten German Party)	

war, but the political gains achieved without conflict further reinforced Hitler's position. Certainly, it completely undermined those generals led by Beck who had been planning to arrest Hitler if war broke out (see page 145).

- Czechoslovakia had constructed its frontier defences within the mountains of the Sudetenland. They too were simply taken over by Germany, thus removing any real defensive capacity from the remains of the Czech state.

In addition, the crisis had profound implications for European diplomacy and the continental balance of power:

- Hitler's ultimate objective was still the creation of *Lebensraum* at the expense of the USSR. However, he hoped this could be eased by Britain developing its appeasement policy into a more general acceptance of Germany's dominant position in central and eastern Europe.
- The USSR saw its exclusion from the decision-making process at Munich as a clear sign that the western democracies were not prepared to work with Russia together on an anti-fascist coalition. Consequently, in the wake of the Sudeten crisis, Soviet foreign policy began to realign itself. From that time it began to consider the possibility of an understanding with Nazi Germany that would be aimed at preserving its own national security.

Key terms

Protectorate
A weak state that is dependent on a stronger one.

Pact of Steel
The military alliance signed between Italy and Germany in May 1939.

Poland: the outbreak of war

Expectations of a fundamental peace in the winter months 1938–9 disappeared very suddenly in March 1939. Germany had used diplomatic and military threats to secure the destruction of the weakened Czech state so the provinces of Bohemia and Moravia were annexed to Germany and Slovakia was reduced to a German **protectorate**. This was a vital development because it showed clearly that Hitler had acted far beyond his early territorial claims to unite the German-speaking population.

The western democracies did not respond militarily to this overturning of the Munich Agreement; it resulted in a few months of peace but frenzied diplomatic activity. Chamberlain understandably felt he had been duped and so an Anglo-French military guarantee was drawn up on 31 March 1939 to uphold Poland's independence. This clearly lessened Hitler's chances of a free hand in eastern Europe and yet, he most definitely did not want a war with Britain and France.

Key question
Why and with what result did Hitler break the Munich Agreement?

Key dates

Invasion of Czechoslovakia: March 1939

Nazi–Soviet Pact: August 1939

Nazi–Soviet Pact

In May 1939 Hitler did manage to secure an alliance with the **Pact of Steel** with Italy, but this was of limited military significance. It was the hope of neutralising Britain and France that drove Hitler into the arms of Stalin. Anglo-French negotiations with the USSR had made limited progress and Stalin was becoming increasingly convinced that the Western democracies had no real sympathy for the security concerns of the USSR. This created a suitable atmosphere in which trade talks between Germany and the USSR could be re-established in July. Only a month later, a 10-year

Key question
How did Hitler hope to avoid a conflict while pursuing his claims on Poland?

RENDEZVOUS

A British cartoon drawn soon after the signing of the Nazi–Soviet Pact. It mocks the two dictators for making the cynical political agreement. The body lying between them represents Poland.

Nazi–Soviet non-aggression pact was signed with additional secret clauses that allowed for eastern Europe to be divided between the spheres of influence of the two powers.

German invasion
Hitler was now confident that Western military intervention would not follow a German invasion of Poland. Even while the negotiations were still taking place, Hitler told an assembly of senior army commanders that he had no diplomatic or military doubts:

> … The enemy had another hope, that Russia would become our enemy after the conquest of Poland. The enemy did not reckon with my great strength of purpose. Our enemies are little worms. I saw them in Munich …

Confident of success he therefore ordered Germany to attack her eastern neighbour on 1 September 1939 as planned. However, Britain and France stood by their guarantee to Poland, and two days later they declared war on Germany. Germany had become involved in a major continental conflict that would involve military action on both its Eastern and Western fronts.

Key dates

German invasion of Poland: 1 September 1939

Britain and France declared war on Germany: 3 September 1939

The significance of Germany's invasion of Poland

By the end of 3 September 1939 Germany was at war not only with Poland, but also with Britain and France. Ironically, neither of these two countries had any real desire to take the military initiative against Germany, but they reluctantly felt obliged to declare war and the first eight months were marked by military inactivity on the Western front. So, how and why did Germany find itself in this unwanted situation?

Key question
Why did the German invasion of Poland result in a continental war?

It is hard to escape the conclusion that the fundamental cause lies with Hitler's grand foreign and racial policies. His desire for continental hegemony and the creation of *Lebensraum* at the expense of eastern Europe could only realistically be achieved (as he knew very well) by military force. The outbreak of some kind of war was inevitable as long as Hitler continued to direct German foreign policy, simply because he wished to overturn the existing *balance* within Europe (and perhaps, beyond). This was clearly not acceptable to many other European countries. However, in 1939 Germany was neither economically nor militarily prepared for a major continental war. Hitler only expected to fight a small-scale localised war against Poland, which would help to bolster Germany for the greater conflict to come with Russia.

Hitler was convinced (mainly as a result of advice from Ribbentrop) that the Western democracies would not intervene. In this analysis he was shown to be wrong. Above all, Hitler failed to appreciate Britain's position. From the outset he had desired an alliance with Britain and, although this was clearly not a possibility by 1937, he continued to believe that some sort of understanding was at least feasible. Undoubtedly, Chamberlain's own hostility to the USSR and his policy of appeasement over Czechoslovakia contributed to Hitler's misapprehension. It was entirely logical of Hitler to believe that, having sacrificed Czechoslovakia, Britain and France would be even less willing to fight over Poland.

However, one of the traditional principles of British foreign policy had long been to prevent one power dominating the continent of Europe. The annexation of Bohemia and Moravia in March 1939 convinced many in Britain that Germany under Hitler could no longer be trusted. Thus, despite Chamberlain's personal reservations, attitudes in Britain towards Germany changed fundamentally and this made a repeat of the appeasement at Munich an impossibility.

Therefore, in 1939 Britain and France guaranteed the independence of Poland in the hope of restraining Hitler. Moreover, although they were in an even weaker diplomatic position after the Nazi–Soviet Pact, they continued to stand by that guarantee. Consequently, when German forces did attack Poland, Britain and France – against the expectations of Hitler – actually did declare war on Germany.

Key debate

Pages 158–9 draw attention to the way historians have looked at Hitler's foreign policy aims, some even believing that he had a prepared programme. However, considerable debate continues among historians over the analysis of the actual events. This leads to the question:

Did Hitler really have a war plan or was he an opportunist?

A.J.P. Taylor

Of course, the programmists, such as Jäckel and Hillgrüber, claim that Hitler's aims actually provide the explanation behind the foreign policy. However, as early as 1961 the English historian A.J.P. Taylor generated a vigorous debate through his book *The Origins of the Second World War*. He dismissed the belief that Hitler was a planner, and claimed that his ideas were really no more than day-dreaming. Moreover, he suggests that Hitler's foreign policy was more that of a pragmatist who essentially reacted to situations. In that way, he even implied controversially that it was the Anglo-French policy of appeasement that gave Hitler the real opportunity to exploit Nazi expansionism.

M. Broszat

To some extent this reflected the interpretation of those historians who support the polycratic view of the Third Reich and see their foreign policy as generally lacking any consistency (see pages 138–40). They see merely a confused variety of aims – 'expansion without object'. Broszat even goes as far as to suggest that Hitler's goals were 'utopian' and that it was the dynamism of the Nazi movement, with its incessant demands for change, which transformed *Lebensraum* from an idea into political reality.

T. Mason

Another point of view, posed by the historian Tim Mason, links the evolution of Nazi foreign policy to the domestic economic pressures which were building up in the second half of the 1930s (see page 41). He suggested that it was the internal discontent created by the constraints of Nazi economic policy that really shaped Nazi foreign policy. In order to preserve his own political supremacy at home, Hitler was forced to accelerate his war ambitions in 1938–9.

A. Bullock

Some historians have warned against seeing too much order and design in the shaping of Nazi foreign policy. They also highlight the dangers of Hitler-centred interpretations. As a result, it is now possible to consider compromise positions. For example, Bullock writes that Hitler had overall aims, but was prepared to adapt and show flexibility. In Bullock's words, Nazi foreign policy combined 'consistency of aim with complete opportunism in methods and tactics'. In addition, Kershaw has continued to claim that German foreign policy was not solely directed by Hitler's aims and personality, but by a range of other domestic factors and influences as well.

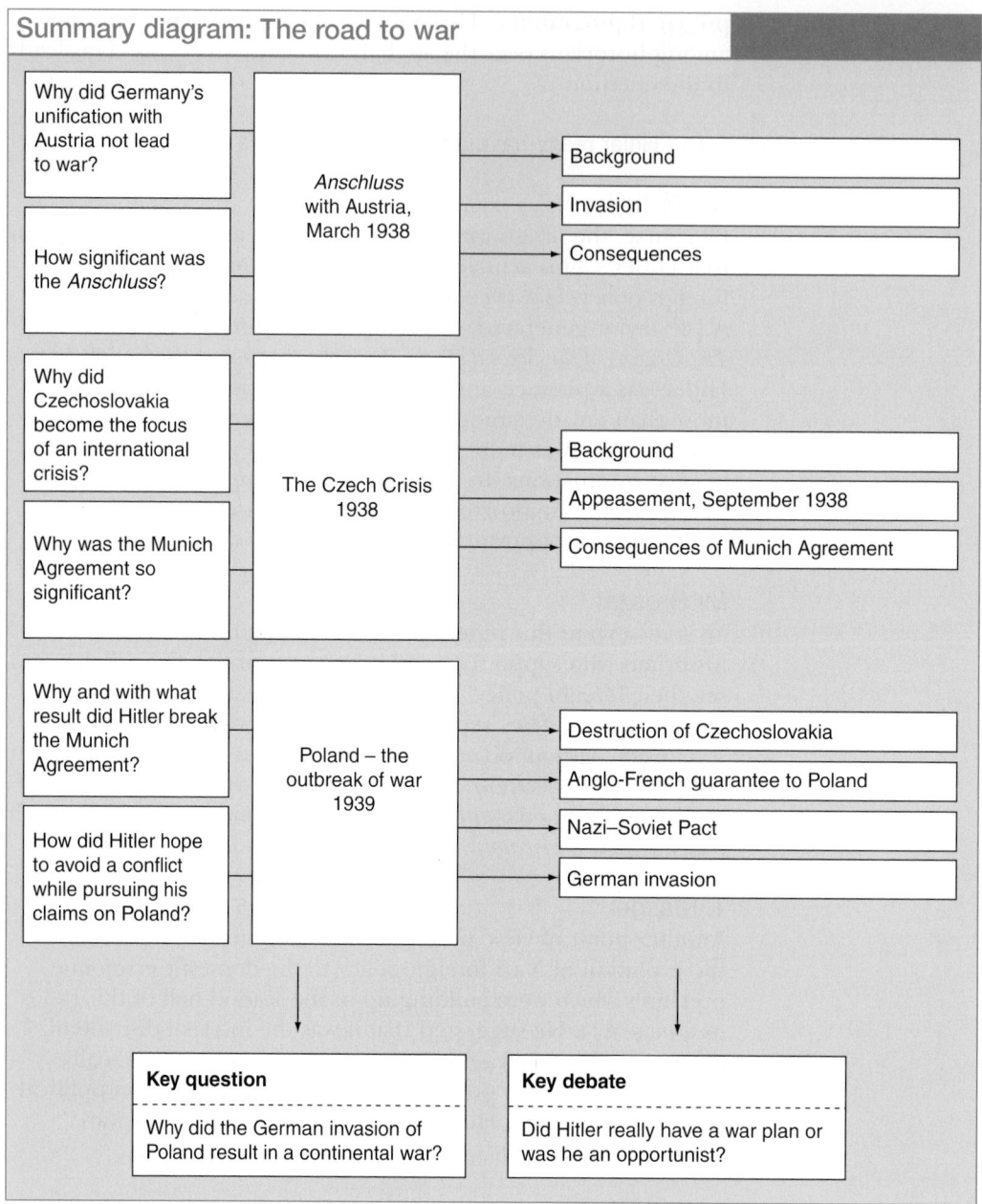

Summary diagram: The road to war

Anschluss with Austria, March 1938
- Why did Germany's unification with Austria not lead to war?
- How significant was the *Anschluss*?
  - Background
  - Invasion
  - Consequences

The Czech Crisis 1938
- Why did Czechoslovakia become the focus of an international crisis?
- Why was the Munich Agreement so significant?
  - Background
  - Appeasement, September 1938
  - Consequences of Munich Agreement

Poland – the outbreak of war 1939
- Why and with what result did Hitler break the Munich Agreement?
- How did Hitler hope to avoid a conflict while pursuing his claims on Poland?
  - Destruction of Czechoslovakia
  - Anglo-French guarantee to Poland
  - Nazi–Soviet Pact
  - German invasion

Key question

Why did the German invasion of Poland result in a continental war?

Key debate

Did Hitler really have a war plan or was he an opportunist?

4 | Germany at War 1939–45

Although Germany found itself committed to a major war in the autumn of 1939, which Hitler had not expected to wage until the mid-1940s, Germany was not militarily destined to fail from the start. The string of victories from September 1939 to November 1941 bear witness to the military power exerted by the Nazi war-machine and suggests that Germany did not have to go down the road to total collapse. However, by early 1943 Germany faced serious military reverses, but Germany's eventual defeat was in no sense inevitable. It has to be explained, not merely assumed.

Key question
Why was Germany so
successful in
1939–41?

Initial victories

Without direct help from Britain or France, Poland was crushingly defeated by Germany's *Blitzkrieg* tactics within a few weeks. This gave the Germans access to valuable raw materials and labour as well as the aid received from the USSR under the terms of the Nazi–Soviet Pact. Hitler was, therefore, keen to maintain the military momentum and planned for an invasion of France to take place as early as November 1939. But the German attack was postponed several times, mainly because of the lukewarm attitude of senior army generals towards such an operation.

The 'phoney war'

The German attack on the Western front did not finally take place until May 1940, thus prolonging the Anglo-French '**phoney war**' for eight months. Hitler's thinking seems to have revolved around the idea of removing the threat posed by the Western democracies before turning east again. To that end Germany needed 'to destroy France' and to make Britain accept German aspirations on the continent. In this way it was hoped to force Britain, under the pressure of military circumstances, into a 'deal' with Germany.

The Low Countries and France

The German defeat of the Low Countries and France within six weeks was a dramatic triumph for both the armed forces and Hitler. Diffident generals could hardly fail to be impressed by the *Führer*'s military and political handling of events. German popular opinion was relieved and triumphant. Hitler ruled not only in Berlin but also in Paris, Oslo, Vienna, Prague and Warsaw, while the Third Reich was bordered by the three 'friendly' powers of Spain, Italy and the USSR. It was assumed by many that the war was as good as over.

The Battle of Britain

If self-interest had prevailed, Britain would have settled with Germany. However, the new British prime minister, Churchill, refused even to consider negotiations. The implications of this stubbornness for Germany were clear-cut: Germany needed to secure air superiority in order to invade Britain and to disable her military and strategic potential. Thus, Germany's failure to win the **Battle of Britain** in the autumn of 1940 was significant. Yet, even more so was Hitler's personal decision to switch the military focus, and to start preparing for the invasion of the USSR even before Britain had been neutralised.

Operation Barbarossa

On 18 December 1940 Hitler issued Directive No. 21 for 'Operation Barbarossa', stating that 'The German armed forces must be prepared to crush Soviet Russia in a quick campaign even before the end of the war against England'. This decision can only be explained by Hitler's belief that *Blitzkrieg* tactics could

Key terms

Phoney war
Used to describe the war period from September 1939 to April 1940 because there was no real aggressive activity on the Western front.

Battle of Britain
Name given to the air battle fought over the skies of southern England between the Royal Air Force and the *Luftwaffe*, July–October 1940.

also succeed in bringing a quick victory against the USSR, as they had against Poland, France and the Low Countries.

The German invasion of the Soviet Union eventually took place on 22 June 1941. It was delayed by the need to invade Yugoslavia and Greece in order to secure Germany's southern flank. At first all went well. Vast tracts of Russian territory were occupied and thousands of prisoners were taken, so that by November 1941 German troops were only a short distance from Moscow and Leningrad.

Reasons for success

The German military advance was the highpoint of the war and in the years 1939–41 it was phenomenally successful for the following reasons:

- France and Britain failed to take the initiative and Poland was left to fight alone.
- Germany's *Blitzkrieg* strategy of rapid advances outmanoeuvred all of its enemies in the first two years.
- The French defensive strategy was based on the Maginot Line and it proved to be powerless in the face of German *Blitzkrieg* tactics. As a result the French political and military leadership lost the will to resist.
- Germany's expansion (from 1938) allowed her to exploit all the labour and resources of those countries for her own purposes.
- The USSR was taken by surprise by the German attack and was not really prepared.

Key dates

'Operation Barbarossa' – German invasion of USSR: 22 June 1941

German declaration of war on USA following Japanese attack at Pearl Harbor.

Continental war 'globalised': December 1941

However, despite Germany's successes, the military advance halted in December 1941. The Russians had never lost the will to carry on fighting, while Anglo-American aid and the snows of Russia combined to consolidate the Eastern front. Hitler's gamble to break the USSR by launching a *Blitzkrieg* invasion had failed and Germany was now faced with the prospect of a long war on two fronts.

The 'turn of the tide'

December 1941 was significant in another sense too, for, in that month, the Japanese attack on the USA's naval base at Pearl Harbor 'globalised' the conflict. Although Hitler was not obliged to do so, he aligned Germany with Japan and declared war on the USA. This move was perhaps prompted by the US involvement in the **Battle of the Atlantic** even before Pearl Harbor. However, it did not fit easily with Germany's existing strategy and above all it turned the industrial capacity of the world's greatest power against it. It is tempting therefore to suggest that by the end of 1941 Hitler had lost the military and diplomatic grasp which had previously allowed him to shape international developments. Events were now very much running out of the *Führer*'s control.

Yet, although it appears that the events of December 1941 were the vital turning point for German fortunes in the war, this was certainly not apparent at the time. Throughout 1942 German forces pushed deep into the Caucasian oilfields with the objective

Key question
When and why did the military balance turn against Germany?

Battle of the Atlantic
The naval struggle between the Allied convoys and the German U-boats (submarines) in the northern Atlantic.

Key term

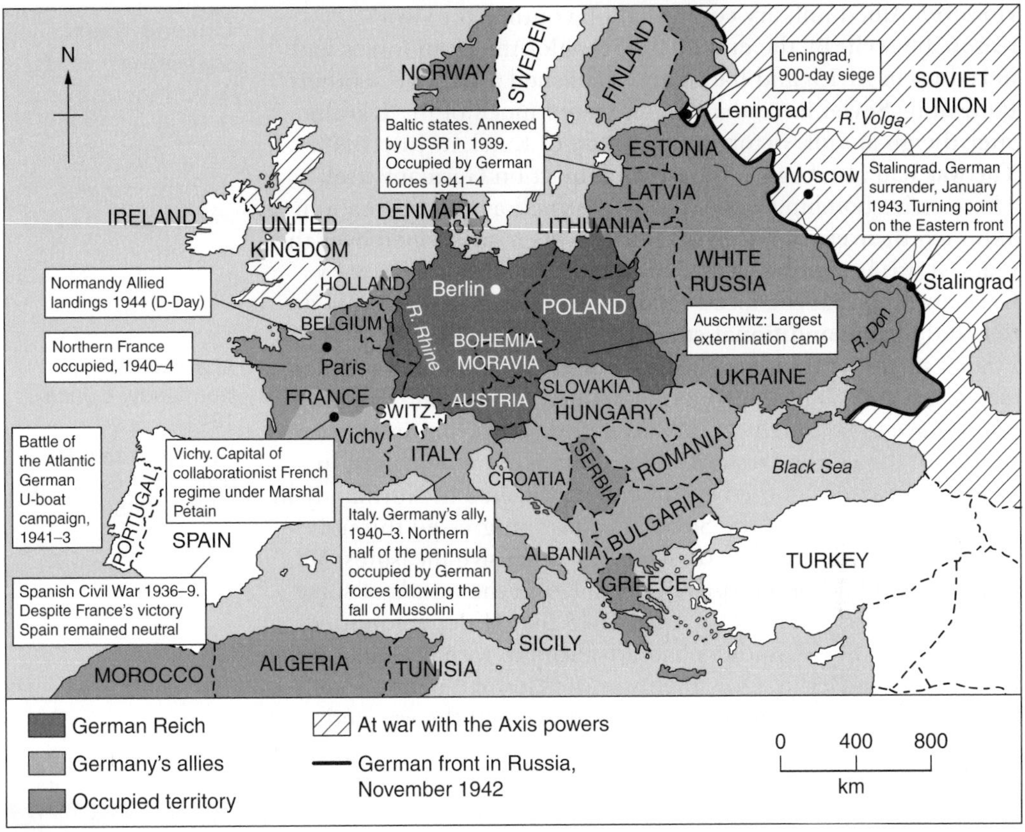

Figure 7.3: Europe, showing Nazi Germany at its height in 1942

German defeat at El Alamein: November 1942

German surrender at Stalingrad: January 1943

of capturing Stalingrad, while the Afrika Korps drove the British back across North Africa into Egypt. It was the eventual failure of these two offensives which enabled contemporaries to see the winter of 1942–3 as 'the turning of the tide': the British victory at El Alamein eventually led to the ejection of German forces from North Africa; and the encirclement and surrender of 300,000 troops at Stalingrad marked the beginning of the Soviet counter-offensive.

Defeat

Key question
Why could not Germany resist the Allied advance?

From 1943 Germany's strategy was essentially defensive. Hitler was determined to protect 'Fortress Europe' from Allied invasion, but possibly his strategic and political thinking was losing touch with reality. Increasingly it became shaped by his belief in German invincibility and his own ideological prejudices about race and communism. For example, in spite of all the military difficulties, the creation of the new racial order continued – there was no postponement of the Final Solution. Hitler deluded himself into thinking that the alliance of the USSR and the Western Allies could not last and that this would then allow Germany to play off one against the other.

However, Allied military co-ordination continued to work reasonably well. By the end of 1943 Anglo-American forces had linked up in Africa and had then established a hold on southern Italy, while Soviet forces had reconquered much of the Ukraine after the great tank victory at the battle of Kursk in July 1943. The war had also begun to have an impact on Germany itself. The massive bombing raids caused destruction and dislocation, although their exact strategic value has been questioned over the years. It was becoming clear that the war could not be won by Germany and that she faced total devastation unless the Allied demand for **unconditional surrender** was accepted.

Such realities prompted the attempted assassination of Hitler (see pages 145–7) in July 1944. Its failure meant that the war would have to be fought to the bitter end. Thus, strong German resistance forced the Western Allies to fight extremely hard in order to break out of the beach-head established in Normandy in 1944, while in the east the Soviet advance progressed through eastern Europe in the face of desperate defensive measures. Yet, even then a blind optimism still prevailed in the minds of some Germans. It was not until 30 April 1945 that Hitler committed suicide, when Soviet soldiers had advanced to within a mile of the Chancellery in Berlin. Only then was the German nation freed from the *Führer*'s command and only then could the war end.

Key term

Unconditional surrender
A statement made by Roosevelt and Churchill in 1943 that the Allies would not accept a negotiated peace.

Key dates

Allied landings in Normandy: 6 June 1944

German surrender: division of Germany: 7 May 1945

Summary diagram: Germany at war 1939–45

Phoney war	Battle of Britain	German declaration of war on USA	Defeat at El Alamein	Battle of Kursk	Normandy landings
Poland	Low Countries and France	Invasion of USSR	Battle of Atlantic	Surrender at Stalingrad	Aerial bombing	Battle of Berlin

Key question: Initial victories	Key question: 'Turn of the tide'	Key question: Defeat
Why was Germany so successful in 1939–41?	When and why did the military balance this against Germany?	Why could Germany not resist the Allied advance?
Reasons for success: • *Blitzkrieg* tactics • Maginot Line failure • British and French inaction – phoney war • German resources • Poor preparations of USSR	German problems: • Soviet resistance • Germany over-stretched • Economic mobilisation of Allies – labour – resources	Reasons for defeat: • Economic dislocation and destruction in Third Reich • Superior military and economic capacity of Allies

Profile: Adolf Hitler 1889–1945

1889	April	– Born in Braunau-am-Inn in Austria
1905		– Left school with no real qualifications
1907–13		– Lived as a dropout in Vienna
1914		– Joined the German army
1918	August	– Awarded the Iron Cross First Class
	October	– Gassed and stayed in hospital at the time of Germany's surrender
1919	September	– Joined the DAP led by Drexler
1920	February	– Drew up the Party's 25-Points Programme with Drexler. The Party was renamed as the NSDAP
1921	July	– Appointed leader of the Party
1923	8–9 November	– Beer Hall *putsch* at Munich
1924		– Found guilty of treason and sentenced to five years, reduced to nine months. Wrote *Mein Kampf*
1925–33		– Committed the Party to a legality policy
		– Re-structured the Party
1930	September	– Nazi electoral breakthrough
1932	July	– Nazis elected the largest party
1933	30 January	– Appointed chancellor of coalition government by Hindenburg
	23 March	– Enabling Act
1934	30 June	– The Night of the Long Knives
	2 August	– Combined the posts of chancellor and president. Thereafter, called *Der Führer*
1935		– Creation of *Luftwaffe*
		– Declaration of military conscription
1936	March	– Remilitarisation of the Rhineland
1937	November	– Hossbach Conference
1938	February	– Blomberg–Fritsch crisis
1938	March	– *Anschluss* with Austria
	September	– Czech crisis over
1939	March	– Occupation of Bohemia and Moravia
1939	1 September	– Ordered the invasion of Poland
1941	22 June	– Ordered the invasion of the USSR
	11 December	– Declared war on the USA
1944	20 July	– Stauffenberg Bomb Plot
1945	30 April	– Committed suicide in the ruins of Berlin

Background

Hitler's upbringing has provoked much psychological analysis and his character has been seen as repressed, lonely and moody. It also seems that his outlook on life was shaped by his unhappy years in Vienna, when he failed to become an art student. It was here, too, that the real core of his political ideas was firmly established – anti-Semitism, German nationalism, anti-democracy and anti-Marxism. Hitler only found a real purpose in the First World War. His belief in German nationalism and the camaraderie of the troops combined to give him direction. However, the shock of hearing of Germany's surrender confirmed all his prejudices.

The early years of the Nazi Party 1919–29

Hitler in 1919 was drawn to the DAP, which was one of many ultra-right-wing racist parties in post-war Germany. His dynamic speeches and his commitment quickly resulted in his becoming the NSDAP's leader by 1921 and it was he who prompted many of the Party's early features, which gave it a dynamic identity. Nevertheless, Hitler was still only the leader of a fringe political party in Bavaria. So when Germany hit major problems, Hitler over-estimated the potential of the *putsch* in November 1923 and it ended in disaster.

Hitler exploited his trial by turning himself into a hero of the right-wing nationalists and in prison he wrote *Mein Kampf*. He also re-assessed his long-term strategy to one based on legality. The following years were relatively stable and economically prosperous for Weimar and the election results and the Nazi Party in 1928 were very disappointing. Nevertheless, he managed to restore his leadership and restructure the Party and its organisation.

The road to power 1929–33

The Great Depression created the environment in which Hitler could exploit his political skills. His charisma, his speeches and his advanced use of propaganda, directed by Goebbels, were the key features of his political success. Nevertheless, although he emerged by 1932 as the leader of the largest party, he was only invited to be chancellor in January 1933 when he joined a coalition with other nationalists and conservatives.

Dictator 1933–45

Hitler established his dictatorship with immense speed. He was given unlimited powers by the Enabling Act, and he destroyed the dissident faction in his own Party at the Night of the Long Knives. After the death of Hindenburg, he styled himself *Führer*.

Hitler was portrayed as the all-powerful dictator, but there has been considerable debate about the image and reality of his direction of daily affairs (see pages 106–8). Nevertheless, it is fair to conclude that Hitler leadership directed German events:

- by creating a one-party state maintained by the brutal SS-Police system, which was totally loyal to him (see pages 117–22)
- by supporting the gradualist racial policy (see pages 91–5)
- by pursuing an expansionist foreign policy to establish a 'greater Germany' by means of *Lebensraum* (see pages 158–9).

Below the surface Hitler's regime was chaotic – but the cult of the *Führer* was upheld by Goebbels's propaganda machine as well as by the diplomatic and military successes from 1935 to 1941. However, the winter of 1942–3 marked the 'turn of the tide' and Hitler increasingly deluded himself and refused to consider surrender. It was only when the Red Army closed in on the ruins of Berlin that the spell of the *Führer*'s power was finally broken – by his own suicide in the bunker on 30 April 1945.

5 | The Impact of the War on Germany

By May 1945 Germany lay in ruins. Nazi foreign policy had reached its destructive conclusion. Its ambitions had been extensive:

- to establish a 'greater Germany', which went well beyond Germany's 1914 frontiers
- to destroy Bolshevik Russia
- to create a new order based on the concept of Aryan racial supremacy.

The means to these ends had involved the acceptance of violence and bloodshed on a massive scale.

Key question
Did Germany have to lose the war?

Germany's military defeat

On a superficial level Hitler's final failure in his ambitions could be explained by his strategic bungling. Hitler had always believed (along with most generals going back to Imperial Germany) that a war on two fronts had to be avoided. To this end he needed an alliance with Britain and/or France – or at least their neutrality – so that he could be free to launch an unrestrained attack in the east. Consequently, when Germany failed to secure either British neutrality or a British surrender in 1940–1, before attacking the USSR, the foundations for defeat were laid.

Germany had become engaged in a conflict for which it was not fully prepared. As has been seen earlier, at the start of the war Germany did not exploit fully the available resources and manpower. The alliance with Mussolini's Italy was also of little gain. Indeed, Italian military weakness in the Balkans and North Africa proved costly, since it diverted German forces away from the main European fronts. Yet, Hitler was driven on ideologically to launch an attack on the USSR with another *Blitzkrieg*.

The failure to defeat the Soviets before the onset of winter in 1941, combined with the entry of the USA into the war, now tipped the balance. Britain was still free to act as a launch-pad for a western front and also, in the meantime, could strike into the heart of Germany by means of aerial bombing. The USSR could maintain the eastern front by relying on its geography and sacrificing its huge manpower. As Stalin himself recognised, the Allied victory could be summarised in these few words: 'Britain gave the time; America the money; and Russia the blood'.

Hitler had militarily misjudged the antagonists, and now all the resources and the industrial capacity of the world's two political giants were directed towards the military defeat of Germany. The following economic factors counted against Germany:

- The Four-Year Plan. In 1936 it was meant to make Germany 'fit for war within four years' but the German economy was not really ready for a long war in 1939. Its capacity was only strong enough to sustain a couple of short campaigns (see pages 43–5).
- Anglo-American bombing. German industry peaked in the production of weapons in summer 1944, yet the German

armed forces could not fully benefit from this because of the detrimental effect of Allied air raids.

- From the start Germany was short of labour. Millions of workers were required to keep up the industrial and agricultural production, and the gaps were only partially filled by forced labourers and an increase in female employment.
- Germany was deeply in debt. The reserves in gold and foreign currencies were almost completely used up by 1939 and the Nazi state had run up a debt of roughly 42 billion *Reichsmarks*.
- The US economy was just too powerful. In 1944 the ratio of Germany's fuel supply compared to the supply of the Western allies was 1:3. The USA sent massive support to the Allies, especially to the USSR which received 13,000 tanks and 15,000 planes.
- Soviet resources. The Soviet economy had undergone a ruthless industrialisation programme in the 1930s under Stalin and despite its limitations, Russia had vast resources of human manpower and raw materials, such as oil, coal and iron.

Such explanations might make historical analysis of Germany's defeat in the Second World War seem like a relatively straightforward exercise. However, before accepting such a simple view, it should be borne in mind that, even in 1942, Germany came very close indeed to capturing Stalingrad and to defeating Britain in Egypt. Such successes would have changed the course of the war and the final outcome might have been very different.

The 'Home front'

Many of the features of the Nazi dictatorship affecting the German people have been covered in earlier chapters. Table 7.1 summarises some of the key points and important references.

Key question
How did the war change the German people's attitudes?

Generally, the onset of the war underlined the totalitarian nature of the Nazi regime. The leadership no longer needed to show any regard for international opinion. However, *within* Germany the Nazis remained very aware of public opinion and the importance of keeping up the nation's morale.

The declaration of war in September 1939 was not met with the patriotic frenzy of August 1914. Rather the mass of people seemed to be resigned and apprehensive. However, the German strategy of *Blitzkrieg* was incredibly successful and the victories of 1939–40 gave the impression of military and economic strength. Most of the people's doubts about Hitler were, therefore, put to one side. On his return journey from France back to Berlin he was met by ecstatic crowds, which were cleverly recorded in the newsreels.

The Nazi economy was not really ready for a major war from 1939 (see page 44) and as a result, from the earliest days, the Nazis had to introduce the rationing of food, clothes and basics like soap and toilet paper. Although the German population was adequately fed – even up until early 1944 its rations were about 10 per cent above the minimum calorific standard – the diet was very boring and restricted. By 1942 consumer goods began to

Table 7.1: The 'Home front'

Features	References	Major developments in the war
Role of Hitler	pages 106–9	'Hitler myth' was glorified even more during initial victories Personal authority retained almost to the end
War economy	pages 43–8	Despite *Blitzkrieg* victories, economic mobilisation was limited at start of war Speer's reforms from 1942 expanded arms production Effects of 'blanket bombing'
Propaganda	pages 123–9	Increased government censorship Failure of propaganda to compensate for declining military situation Glorification of war through films, e.g. *Kolberg*
Security/policing	pages 117–22	SS extended its power and influence and resorted to ever more brutal and arbitrary policies Limitations of *Gestapo* personnel
Youth	pages 60–5	HJ compulsory by 1939 and increased emphasis on military drill and discipline HJ appeal increasingly polarised between fanatics and the disaffected During the war the standard of teachers and HJ leaders declined
Women	pages 71–6	Contradiction between theory and practice of female employment Increased personal pressures – work, home, bombing and absentee husbands
Opposition	pages 142–51	Dissent increased, e.g. Christians, youth Active resistance failed, e.g. Stauffenberg plot
Churches	pages 66–70	Initially cautious policy on the Churches Persecution intensified from 1941 Religion remained a sensitive political issue, as shown by the increase in church attendance
Jews and outsiders	pages 91–9	Radicalisation of racial policies against Jews leading to genocide Gypsies and other outsiders Euthanasia stopped in response to Catholic opposition

decline and in the final 12 months of the war the situation worsened very dramatically with clear human consequences, for example:

- food rationing led to real shortages (and real hunger by 1945)
- clothes rationing was ended, but only because of the decline in clothes production
- boots and shoes were in short supply
- small luxuries, like magazines and sweets, were stopped.

By 1942 Germany found itself at war with Britain, the USSR and the USA and it faced a long, drawn-out conflict. Under the leadership of Speer, the Minister of Armaments, the German economy was geared even more to fighting a 'total war' (see pages 45–8). This meant that every part of German society was focused on the war effort and would have to make real sacrifices:

- industry was organised more efficiently
- working hours were increased
- more women were drafted into work
- millions of foreign workers were encouraged to work (but under controls)
- non-essential businesses were closed.

During the winter 1942–3 it became impossible for Nazi propaganda and censorship to disguise the reality of the military defeats of Stalingrad and El-Alamein. Moreover, on the home front, the Anglo-American bombing began to hit the great urban centres day and night. Most famously on the night of 24 July 1943 a massive raid on Hamburg created a fire-storm which killed 30,000 civilians and left approximately one million homeless. By 1945 it is estimated that as a result of the air-raids:

- 300,000 Germans were killed
- 800,000 were wounded
- 3.6 million homes were destroyed (20 per cent of the total housing).

The effects of the Allied bombing on the German civilian (as opposed to the effects on industry, see pages 45–8) have been the subject of considerable discussion. Some have claimed that despite the difficult circumstances faced by most Germans in the final two years of the war, there was no real sign of a decline of morale leading up to the collapse of the regime itself. Indeed, in the face of Allied mass bombing many people came together against the enemy. Rumpf therefore claims, 'Under the terrible blows of that terror from the skies the bonds grew closer and the spirit of solidarity stronger'.

However, research of the SD on civilian morale and public opinion from 1939 tends to confirm that, from 1943, people became increasingly resigned to the coming disaster and by 1944 there had developed a major loss of confidence in the regime. There was a growing mood of grumbling and complaint. Very interestingly, the source below highlights the deepening cynicism in the nation about the political and military situation after Stalingrad and there was broad criticism of the state and Hitler.

> A large section of the nation cannot imagine how the war will end and the telling of vulgar jokes against the state, even about the *Führer* himself, has increased considerably since Stalingrad. (An SD report, 1943)

So although it is true that active resistance to the war remained very limited (see pages 142–7), popular dissent in various forms developed, as Welch writes in his conclusion to *The Third Reich: Politics and Propaganda*:

> The debacle of Stalingrad undoubtedly affected the morale of the German people. It forced them to question Nazi war aims and led to a crisis of confidence in the regime amongst broad sections of the population.

Table 7.2: Three phases of the war in Germany

Phases	Key military events	Developments in Germany

1939–41
The years of
Nazi victories
	Nazi control over Poland
	  and northern and western
	  Europe
	German invasion of USSR
	  leading to control of most
	  of western USSR
		Introduction of food and clothing rationing
		Casualties limited

1941–3
The 'turn of
the tide'
	German declaration of war
	  on USA following Japanese
	  attack at Pearl Harbor
	German defeat at El-Alamein
	German surrender at Stalingrad
		'Final solution' started to exterminate Jews
		Speer's reforms to mobilise the war
		  economy
		More resistance developed, but isolated
		Creation of Kreisau Circle
		White Rose group of students at Munich

1943–5
'Total war' and
defeat
	Western allies invasion of
	  France: D-Day
	USSR gained control of eastern
	  Europe, including Berlin
	German surrender. Western
	  allies occupation of western
	  Germany
		Goebbels's speech rallied the people for a
		  'total war'
		Allied mass bombing of Germany, e.g.
		  Hamburg fire-storm
		Manufacture of clothes ended and clothes
		  rations suspended
		Stauffenberg's 'July plot' failed
		Auschwitz liberated by USSR
		Food only available on black market
		Dresden bombing – thousands killed in two
		  nights by Allies
		Hitler's suicide in Berlin

Key question
How serious was
Germany's condition
by 1945?

Germany in 1945

In the weeks before the capital fell to the Soviets a typical Berliner's joke began to circulate: 'Enjoy the war while you can! The peace is going to be terrible.'

It is no exaggeration to say that the German state had ceased to exist by May 1945. Hitler, Goebbels and a number of other Nazi leaders had committed suicide, while others had either fled or been captured and arrested (see the profiles of the main characters). Therefore, central government had broken down. Instead, Germany and Berlin had been divided by the Allies into four zones, each one with their own military commander giving orders and guidelines for the local economy and administration.

But, in the short term, the most telling problem facing Germany in that spring was the extent of the social and economic crisis.

Population displacement

At the end of the war it is estimated that one in two Germans were on the move:

- Roughly 12 million German refugees fleeing from the east.
- Ten million of the so-called 'displaced persons', who had done forced labour or had been prisoners in the various Nazi camps.
- Over 11 million German soldiers, who had been taken as prisoners of war – 7.7 million in camps in the west were soon

released whereas the 3.3 million in the USSR were kept in captivity until the 1950s, of which one-third did not survive.

All these people posed a serious problem to the British and the Americans because of a lack of food.

Urban destruction

Major German cities, especially Cologne, Hamburg and Berlin, had been reduced to rubble because of Anglo-American bombing and Soviet artillery (see the photo below). Twenty per cent of housing had been completely destroyed, and a further 30 per cent badly damaged which led many to accept sheltered accommodation or to escape to the countryside.

Food and fuel shortages

Food was the immediate problem, but it was soon to be exacerbated by the onset of winter at the end of 1945. The average recommended consumption of 2000 calories sank to 950–1150 and, if it had not been for emergency relief from the Western allies and care parcels from charities, starvation would have been far worse. This level of malnourishment led to illnesses like typhus, diphtheria and whooping cough.

The ruins of Berlin in May 1945

A US Army soldier plays the part of Hitler on the famous balcony in the ruins of the chancellery in Berlin. It was from here that the former Nazi leader had proclaimed his 1000-year empire.
A British and Soviet soldier stand on each side, while their comrades cheer them on.

Economic dislocation

Surprisingly, the economy had not completely broken down, but it was very badly dislocated. Industrial capacity had obviously declined dramatically, but its destruction was exaggerated at the time. Moreover, the infrastructure of bridges and railways and the utilities, like gas and water had broken down during the end of the war. Also, the state had massive debts, so Germany was once again facing the problem of a rising inflation causing a major black market in the supply of food and other goods.

The Third Reich had been destroyed in May 1945, but that left Germany in ruins. Violence, destruction and dislocation had brought it to **zero hour**.

Zero hour
Used in German society to describe Germany's overall collapse at the end of the Second World War.

Key term

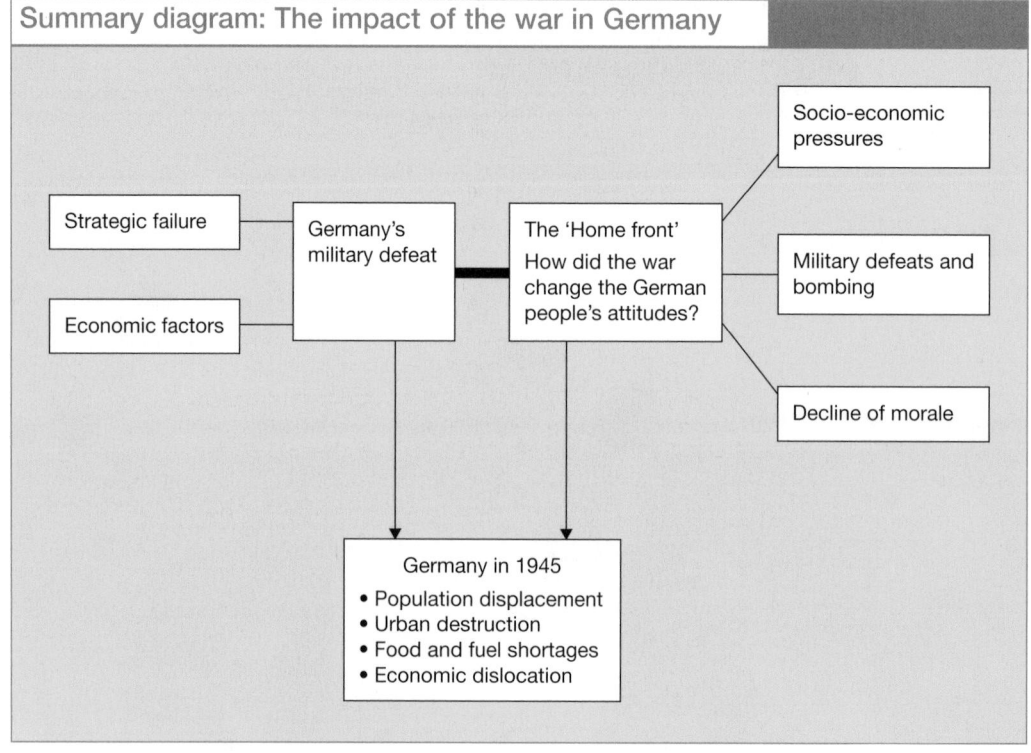

Summary diagram: The impact of the war in Germany

Socio-economic pressures

Strategic failure

Economic factors

Germany's military defeat

The 'Home front'
How did the war change the German people's attitudes?

Military defeats and bombing

Decline of morale

Germany in 1945
• Population displacement
• Urban destruction
• Food and fuel shortages
• Economic dislocation

Study Guide: AS Questions

In the style of AQA

(a) Explain why the Nazis had to ration food from 1939.

(12 marks)

(b) 'During the years of war between 1939 and 1944, the morale of the German civilian population remained high.' Explain why you agree or disagree with this view. (24 marks)

Exam tips

The cross-references are intended to take you straight to the material that will help you to answer the questions.

(a) Clearly the introduction of food rationing was linked to the outbreak of war and this will be one of the first points you should explain. However, a good answer will go further and refer to the state of the German economy in 1939, the unpreparedness for war and the limitations of the Four-Year Plan and schemes of autarky (pages 36–40). The difficulty of obtaining imports and the limitations to economic mobilisation will need to be discussed. You should try to show some overall judgement in your answer, perhaps stressing Hitler's lack of concern for the ordinary person in relation to his grand schemes of conquest.

(b) A good answer will look at points of both agreement and disagreement and balance these against one another to provide a convincing and well-supported conclusion. You have read in this chapter (and Chapter 6) how there appeared quite strong morale in these years. This may be accounted for by:

- early victories and the strength of the Hitler 'myth'
- a feeling of solidarity in adversity – through rationing, longer hours of work and particularly when bombing campaigns began
- the power of government censorship and propaganda
- the use of the SS and the compulsory Hitler youth.

In disagreement, it may be pointed out that dissent increased, e.g. among Christians and the youth (White Rose), there was some active resistance especially in the army (Stauffenberg) as well as Catholic opposition to euthanasia. Perhaps the best conclusion would be to stress the Germans' feelings of resignation by 1943 and sense of disillusionment by 1944 as Germany came to suffer more from wartime damage and failure. Whichever way you to choose to argue, do ensure all points are well-supported by factual detail.

The Third Reich and German History

POINTS TO CONSIDER
More than any other chapter in the book this one is intended to form the basis for further thought and discussion. It tries to describe and explain a variety of interpretations of the Third Reich by historians. So you must keep in mind the key issue of how the Third Reich has been thought to fit into the broader context of German history in the nineteenth and twentieth centuries.

From the outset, the development of the Nazi regime presented observers not only with important political and economic questions but also with serious moral issues to resolve. For example, most left-wing and liberal intellectuals saw Nazism as an essentially evil (and therefore morally condemned) movement. This moral dimension has not disappeared with the passage of time, even though Nazism is now a historical issue. Indeed, with the revelations of the full extent of the Nazi horror in 1944–5, the continued reference to war anniversaries in the media and still the occasional story of 'war criminals', it is almost impossible to explain the Third Reich without giving consideration to its moral implications.

1 | The Key Debate

At the very heart of these issues, historians have continued to raise the thorny question:

Was the Third Reich inevitable?

Anti-German determinists: Hitler, the inevitable result of German history

Clearly, anti-German feelings can be put down to the requirements of wartime propaganda in Britain. Nevertheless, some academic historians after the war portrayed Nazism as the natural product of German history. The renowned English historian A.J.P. Taylor wrote in *The Course of German History* in 1945:

It was no more a mistake for the German people to end up with Hitler than it is an accident when a river flows into the sea.

Anti-German determinists
Believed that the collapse of Weimar democracy and the rise of Nazi dictatorship were bound to happen because of Germany's long-term history and the national character of its people.

The culmination of this kind of **anti-German determinist** view was probably reached with the publication in 1959 of William Shirer's *Rise and Fall of the Third Reich*. This monumental work, written by an American journalist who had worked as a correspondent in Germany between 1926 and 1941, had a profound impact on the general public. In it Shirer explained how Nazism was 'but a logical continuation of German history'. He argued that Germany's political evolution, its cultural and intellectual heritage and the people's national character all contributed to the inevitable success of Hitler.

Gerhard Ritter: Nazism, the result in Germany of a 'moral crisis' in Europe

Not surprisingly, anti-German sentiments were not kindly received in Germany, especially amongst those intellectuals who had opposed Hitler. As a consequence, there emerged in the post-war decade in West Germany a school of thought that emphasised the 'moral crisis of European society'.

It was epitomised above all by the writings of Gerhard Ritter, who focused on the European circumstances in which Nazism had emerged. In his view, it was hard to believe that Germany's great traditions, such as the power of the Prussian state, or its rich cultural history could have contributed to the emergence of Hitler. Instead, Ritter emphasised the events and developments since 1914 in Europe as a whole. It was the shock given to the traditional European order by the First World War that created the appropriate environment for the emergence of Nazism. The decline in religion and standards of morality, a tendency towards corruption and materialism and the emergence of mass democracy were all exploited by Hitler to satisfy his desire for power.

Fischer: Nazi foreign policy aims reflected Imperial Germany

However, the easy calm within West German historical circles was shattered by the publication of a book not even on the subject of Nazi Germany. Fritz Fischer's *Griff nach der Weltmacht* (*Germany's Aims in the First World War*), first published in Germany in 1961, suggested in his major thesis that Germany's objectives in 1914 had undoubtedly been offensive and had been intended to establish Germany's hegemony over continental Europe. The implications of this thesis were profound, for it clearly suggested a similarity between the foreign policy aims of Imperial Germany and the Third Reich and upheld the idea of a continuity in development between the two regimes.

However, it was not only Fischer's message but also his historical method. His interpretation was based on an analysis of the strong connection between the Kaiser's domestic and foreign policies, and in particular on the role of the traditional élites in German society. Fischer, in effect, ushered in the emergence of the 'structuralist' historians.

Structuralists: Nazism, a result of Germany's *Sonderweg*

The 1960s witnessed the beginning of a phenomenal growth in research on the Third Reich – partly for the practical reason that the German archives in the hands of the Western Allies had been made available to scholars. By the late 1960s and early 1970s, historians such as Martin Broszat and Hans Mommsen had started to exert a major influence on our understanding of the rise of Hitler and the Third Reich and their approach has been dubbed 'structuralist' (see page 108).

In essence, the structuralist interpretation suggests that Germany's failure to develop liberal systems in the nineteenth century meant that Germany had developed a ***Sonderweg*** in contrast with the rest of Western Europe. It argues therefore that from the 1850s to 1945 Germany had remained dominated by authoritarian forces in Germany's society and economy, such as the armed services and the bureaucracy, and had not really developed democratic institutions. As a result, the power and influence of such conservative vested interests continued to dominate Germany – even after the creation of the Weimar Republic – and therefore, these conservatives sympathised with the Nazi movement, which provided the means to uphold a right-wing authoritarian regime.

Key term

Sonderweg
Special (or peculiar) path of development. An interpretation of German history by structuralists which argues that Germany's continuity reflected the dominance of its social and economic 'structures' in the years 1848–1945.

Intentionalists: Nazism, a result of Hitler's ideology and his evil genius

However, some historians have continued to argue that there is no escape from the central importance of Hitler the individual in the Nazi seizure of power. Indeed, 'intentionalists', like Klaus Hildebrand and Eberhard Jäckel, believe that the personality and ideology of Hitler remain so essential that Nazism can really be directly equated with the term Hitlerism. This is because although the intentionalists accept the special circumstances created by Germany's history, they emphasise the indispensable role of the individual – Hitler – as is shown in the many writings of K.D. Bracher.

Alltagsgeschichte: patterns of social behaviour in the Third Reich

From the early 1980s there has been a growing interest in *Alltagsgeschichte* (the history of everyday life), which focuses not on the political centre but on the grassroots of society. A range of studies has now been published about the experiences of different social groups in different regions in Nazi Germany in an attempt to comprehend the behaviour and experiences of ordinary people. They have studied a range of issues: sexual behaviour; the role of women; family structure; and attitudes towards death and crime.

Undoubtedly, in an attempt to create a more 'total' and more 'human' history, *Alltagsgeschichte* has provided new and very different insights into the complexities of the Third Reich. Moreover, sympathisers of *Alltagsgeschichte*, like Broszat, have said that it was indeed time to 'normalise' the Third Reich and to

A German postcard produced during the Third Reich emphasising Hitler's role in the continuity of history. ('What the king conquered, the prince formed, the field-marshal defended, was saved and united by the soldier').

Hans vom Norden
Nachdruck verboten

Was der König eroberte, der Fürst formte, der Feldmarschall verteidigte, rettete und einigte der Soldat.

'historicise' the topic in a proper fashion. However, critics of this *Alltagsgeschichte* see it as tending to view the Third Reich as if it was simply just another period of German history.

Some key books in the debate

K.D. Bracher, 'The role of Hitler: perspectives and interpretations', in W. Lacquer, ed., *Fascism* (Penguin, 1979).

M. Broszat, in P. Baldwin, ed., *Reworking the Past* (Boston, 1990).

F. Fischer, *Germany's Aims in the First World War* (English translation, London, 1966).

I. Kershaw, *Hitler* Vols 1 and 2 (1998 and 2000).

G. Ritter, *Europa und die Deutsche Frage* (Munich, 1948).

A.J.P. Taylor, *The Course of German History* (London, 1945).

Key question
Was the Third Reich a natural outgrowth of German history?

2 | Continuity and Change

Few historians would now support the view that German history made Nazism inevitable. However, it would be equally naive to portray it as an 'abnormality' divorced from Germany's history. Such an interpretation would make the Nazi retention of power for 12 years almost inexplicable.

Continuity

Key term

Treaty of Brest–Litovsk
Signed by Germany and Soviet Russia in March 1918, i.e. eight months before the end of the First World War. Germany annexed large areas of Russia, Poland and the Baltic states.

It now seems safe to assume that the Third Reich can be linked very clearly with several important features of Germany's past. Significantly, in the crucial area of foreign affairs it can be seen that the initial thrust of Nazi foreign policy was to restore German continental power and to create *Lebensraum* in the east. This corresponded very closely with the aims of Imperial Germany at the start of the First World War and was briefly achieved by the terms of the **Treaty of Brest–Litovsk** in 1918 that annexed large areas of Russia, Poland and the Baltic states.

Moreover, this aspect of continuity helps to explain why the Nazi regime enjoyed the backing of the country's traditional élites who had played such a central part in the nation's development since 1871. Rapid industrialisation and urbanisation had created social pressures that the conservative and authoritarian élites were unwilling to relieve by granting political reform until forced to do so by Germany's military defeat in 1918. Although these élites were partly eclipsed during the Weimar Republic, they were to be revived in 1933 by their sympathy with National Socialism. Moreover, despite the increasing radicalisation of the Nazi system their support was never entirely withdrawn. Thus, in the years 1933–45 there was no fundamental social transformation and the essential traditional structure of society remained intact.

Change

The above points of important strands of continuity need to be set alongside some fundamental differences between the Third Reich and earlier German history. Imperial Germany did not seek to destroy the federal tradition within Germany. Nazism did (see page 13). Imperial Germany operated according to a constitution and its values were squarely in the tradition of what Germans call the *Rechtsstaat* (the constitutional state). Citizens enjoyed certain legal rights, which meant, for example, that only civilian courts could take away an individual's liberty. The Third Reich, despite the so-called 'legal revolution', behaved in a totally unrestricted fashion, which permitted (even encouraged) imprisonment without trial and state violence on a barbaric scale.

As for Nazi ideology, it is true that most of its political and racial ideas, especially anti-Semitism, pre-dated the Third Reich, but then there is absolutely nothing in Germany's earlier history to suggest the horrors of Auschwitz and all that it represents. The Holocaust is surely on an entirely different scale to any anti-Semitic precedents – it therefore marks a fundamental change rather than merely a difference in degree.

Finally, although Nazi foreign policy had common links with imperial ambitions, it was founded on an entirely different premise: namely that the Third Reich would create a racist utopia (a 'new order') which would eventually lead to world domination by Germany.

The significance of Hitler

If one accepts that the Third Reich can be understood only by appreciating its 'roots' in German history, while also recognising that that it stands out in sharp relief to both Weimar and Imperial Germany, it is tempting to assume, as 'intentionalists' would have us believe, that the crucial difference lies in the role of Hitler himself.

Only the most committed 'structuralist' could now portray Hitler as a mere agent or puppet. Hitler's power was very real, although it was not exerted in the ordered authoritarian fashion projected by the propaganda machine.

Kershaw's biography of Hitler has had great influence because he has successfully integrated the structuralist and intentionalist approaches. He has described Hitler's power as that of 'charismatic domination' by which all forms of legal and rational government were undermined by a readiness 'to work towards the *Führer*'(see page 108). In other words, Hitler generated an environment in which his followers carried out his presumed intentions.

In this way it remains true that Hitler's personality and ideology led to a dramatic radicalisation of policy in the following key spheres: the creation of a political one-party state; the establishment of a racial state leading to a policy of genocide; and the drive towards a German (Aryan) world hegemony. It is hard to envisage these developments without Hitler at the helm.

Yet, the house inherited and built by Hitler collapsed under his leadership. By 1945 Germany as a modern nation-state had in effect ceased to exist. This was the empty inheritance left by Hitler's Third Reich and in that sense 1945 was an even greater turning-point than 1933 or 1918.

So, the Third Reich should be seen as a watershed in German history. Under the influence of Hitler, it was able to emerge and then to distort certain tendencies within Germany. However, the Nazi machine could not be sustained and the intended new racial world order was never established (albeit as a result of its defeat because of the Allies' military power). Instead, the Third Reich collapsed in an orgy of destruction and as a result Germany developed along very different lines. If any point in history deserves the title of zero hour then surely Germany in 1945 has a particularly good claim. Indeed, it is difficult to pinpoint anything positive or creative in the legacy of the Third Reich. Perhaps, this is why, even at the start of the twenty-first century, the history of the Third Reich continues to exert such a powerful fascination among historians, students and the general public.

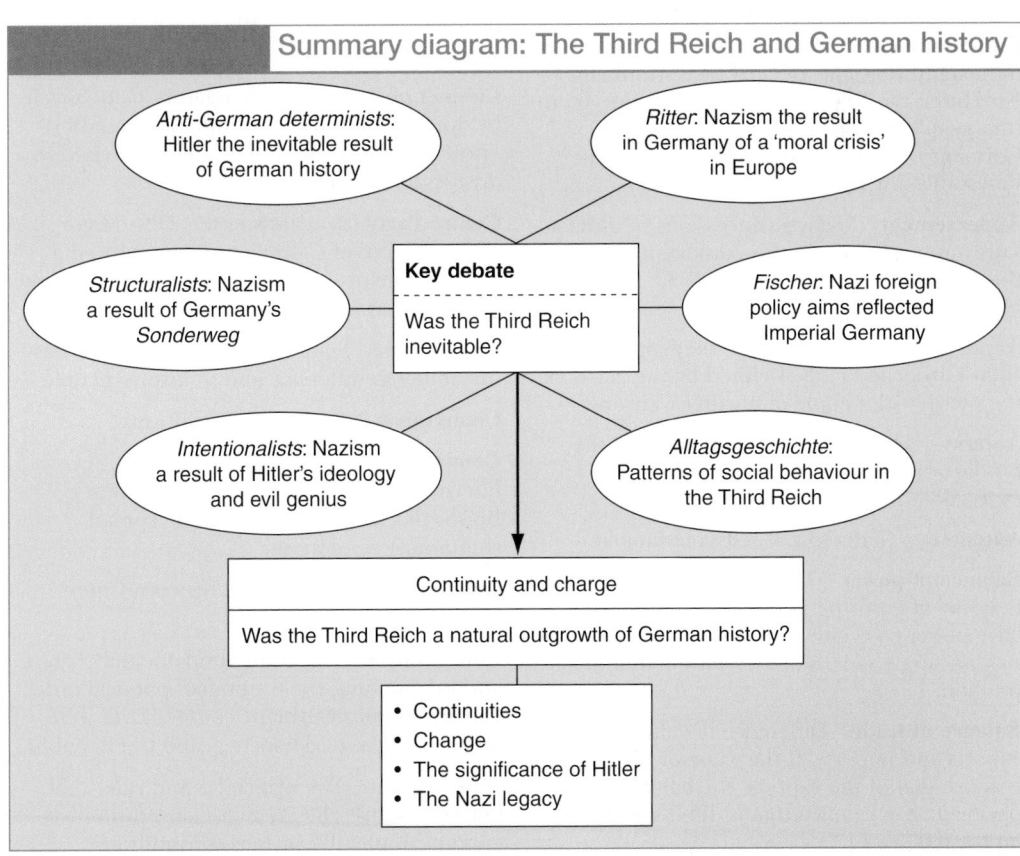

Summary diagram: The Third Reich and German history

Anti-German determinists: Hitler the inevitable result of German history

Ritter. Nazism the result in Germany of a 'moral crisis' in Europe

Structuralists: Nazism a result of Germany's *Sonderweg*

Key debate

Was the Third Reich inevitable?

Fischer. Nazi foreign policy aims reflected Imperial Germany

Intentionalists: Nazism a result of Hitler's ideology and evil genius

Alltagsgeschichte: Patterns of social behaviour in the Third Reich

Continuity and charge

Was the Third Reich a natural outgrowth of German history?

- Continuities
- Change
- The significance of Hitler
- The Nazi legacy

Glossary

Alliance   An agreement where members promise to support the other(s), if one or more of them is attacked. In this context France had signed a series of alliances in the 1920s with Poland, Czechoslovakia, Romania and Yugoslavia.

Anschluss   'Union'. In the years 1919–38, it referred to the paragraph in the Treaty of Versailles which outlawed any political union between Germany and Austria, although the population was wholly German speaking.

Anti-feminist   Opposing female advancement.

Anti-German determinists   Believed that the collapse of Weimar democracy and the rise of Nazi dictatorship were bound to happen because of Germany's long-term history and the national character of its people.

Anti-modernism   Strand of opinion that rejects, objects to or is highly critical of changes to society and culture brought about by technological advancement.

Anti-Semitism   Hatred of Jews. It became the most significant part of Nazi racist thinking. For Hitler, the 'master race' was the pure Aryan (the people of northern Europe) and the Germans represented the highest caste. The lowest race for Hitler was the Jews.

Appeasement   Making concessions in order to satisfy an aggressor. In this context, it refers to the Anglo-French policy of the 1930s towards Hitler's territorial demands.

Aryan   Refers broadly to all the peoples of the Indo-European family. Defined by the Nazis as the non-Jewish people of northern Europe.

Autarky   The aim for self-sufficiency in the production of food and raw materials, especially when at war.

Autonomy   The right of self-government.

Balance of power   The political idea that the best way of ensuring international order is to have power so evenly distributed among states that no single state is able to have a dominant position.

Balance of trade   Difference in value between exports and imports. If the value of the imports is above that of the exports, the balance of the payments has a deficit that is often said to be 'in the red'.

Battle of Britain   Name given to the air battle fought over the skies of southern England between the Royal Air Force and the *Luftwaffe*, July–October 1940.

Battle of the Atlantic   The naval struggle between the Allied convoys and the German U-boats (submarines) in the northern Atlantic.

Blitzkrieg   Literally 'lightning war'. It was the name given to the military strategy developed to avoid static war. It was based on the use of dive-bombers, paratroopers and motorised infantry.

Brownshirts   So called because of the colour of their uniform. They were the SA (*Sturm Abteilung*) and also became known in English as the Stormtroopers. They were organised and set up in 1921 as a paramilitary unit led by Ernst Röhm.

Buffer state   The general idea of two rival countries being separated by a territory between them, e.g. the Rhineland demilitarised zone, 1919–36.

Cabinet of Barons   A derogatory name given by opponents to the government created by Franz von Papen because it was dominated by aristocrats and businessmen.

Centre Party (Zentrumspartei, ZP)   Major political voice of Catholicism, but enjoyed a broad range of support. In the 1920s it became more sympathetic to the right wing.

Charismatic   Suggests a personality that has the ability to influence and to inspire people.

Chauvinism   Aggressive patriotism.

Comintern   *Com*munist *Intern*ational. An international body created by Lenin and the Bolsheviks in 1919 that aimed to spread communist revolution.

Concordat   An agreement between Church and state.

Conservative   Opposing fundamental change and maintaining the traditional political order. During Weimar Germany conservatives were unsympathetic to democracy and the Republic.

Constitution   The principles and rules that govern a state. The Weimar Constitution is a good example of a written constitution.

Cult of personality   Using the power and charisma of a political leader to dominate the nation.

Democratic republic   A political system opposing a monarchy, but based on democratic principles.

Diktat   A dictated peace. The Germans felt that the Versailles Treaty was imposed without negotiation.

DNVP   German National People's Party (*Deutschenationale Volkspartei*). A right-wing party formed in 1919 from the old conservative parties and some of the racist, anti-Semitic groups. It was monarchist and anti-republican and had close ties to heavy industry and agriculture, including landowners and small farmers.

Dualism   A government system in which two forces co-exist, e.g. the Nazi Party and the German state.

Edelweiss   A white alpine flower that served as a symbol of opposition.

Élites   The conservative vested interests in society, e.g. the army, the civil service and *Junkers* (landowners).

Emergency decree   In Article 48 of the Weimar Constitution the President had the right in an emergency to rule by decree and to override the constitutional rights of the people.

Federal states   In a federal system of government, power and responsibilities are shared between national and regional governments. Weimar Germany had a federal structure with 17 *Länder* (regional states), e.g. Prussia, Bavaria, Saxony.

Final Solution   A euphemism used by the Nazi leadership to describe the extermination of the Jews from 1941.

Freikorps   'Free corps' who acted as paramilitaries in Germany, 1918–19. They were right-wing, nationalist soldiers who were only too willing to use force to suppress communist activity.

Führer   (Leader) Hitler was declared leader of the Party in 1921. In 1934 he became leader of the country after the death of Hindenburg.

Führerprinzip   The leadership principle. Hitler upheld the idea of a one-party state, built on an all-powerful leader.

Gauleiters   Regional leaders of the Nazi Party.

Genocide   The extermination of a whole race.

Gestapo   *Ge*heime *Sta*ats *Po*lizei: Secret State Police.

Ghetto   Ancient term describing the area lived in by the Jews in a city. Under Nazi occupation the Jews were separated from the rest of the community and forced to live in appalling and overcrowded conditions.

Gleichschaltung   'Bringing into line' or 'co-ordination'.

GNP   Gross national product is the total value of all goods and services in a nation's economy (including income derived from assets abroad).

Gradualism   Changing by degrees; progressing slowly.

Great Depression   Economic crisis of 1929–33 marked by mass unemployment, falling prices and a lack of spending.

Guns or Butter?   A phrase used to highlight the controversial economic choice between rearmament and consumer goods.

Hegemony   Political leadership and dominance.

Holocaust   Generally used to describe mass slaughter – in the context of the Third Reich it refers specifically to the extermination of the Jews.

Horst Wessel   A young Nazi stormtrooper killed in a fight with communists in 1930. The song he wrote became a Nazi marching song and later virtually became an alternative national anthem.

Hyper-inflation   Hyper-inflation is unusual. In Germany, in 1923, prices spiralled out of control as the government increased the amount of money being printed. This displaced the whole economy.

Imperial Germany   Germany from its unification in 1871 to 1918. Also referred to as the Second Reich (Empire).

Imperialism   Rule by an emperor. It has come to mean one country taking political and economic control of another territory.

Indoctrination   Inculcating and imposing a set of ideas.

Intentionalist   Interprets history by emphasising the role (intentions) of people who shape history.

Isolationism   The foreign policy of the USA after the First World War when it withdrew from international politics. The USA decided not to join the League of Nations.

Junkers   The landowning aristocracy, especially those from eastern Germany.

Kaiser   German Emperor.

Kulturkampf 'Cultural struggle'. Refers to the tension in the 1870s between the Catholic Church and the German state, when Bismarck was chancellor.

Labour exchanges Local offices created by the state for finding employment. Many industrialised countries had labour exchanges to counter mass unemployment.

League of Nations An international body based on the idea of US President Wilson to create to encourage disarmament and to prevent war.

Lebensborn Literally, the 'spring' or 'fountain' of life. Founded by Himmler and overseen by the SS to promote doctrines of racial purity.

Lebensraum 'Living space'. Hitler's aim to create an empire and to make Germany into a great power by establishing German supremacy over the eastern lands in Europe, e.g. Poland and Russia.

Locarno Pact A series of treaties that became known as the Locarno Pact in 1925. The main points were to accept the Franco-German and Belgian–German borders and to recognise as permanent the demilitarisation of the Rhineland.

Maginot Line The name given to the extensive defence fortifications built on the Franco-German frontier by the French governments in the 1930s. It was intended to resist any German offensive military action.

March converts Those who joined the NSDAP immediately after the consolidation of power in January–March 1933.

Marxist historians A school of historians who believe that history has been deeply shaped by economic circumstances. They are influenced by the ideology of the philosopher Karl Marx.

Mass suggestion A psychological term suggesting that large groups of people can be unified simply by the atmosphere of the occasion. Hitler and Goebbels used their speeches and large rallies to particularly good effect.

Mittelstand Can be translated as 'the middle class', but in German society it tends to represent the lower middle classes, e.g. shopkeepers, craft workers and clerks. It was traditionally independent and self-reliant but increasingly it felt squeezed out between the power and influence of big business and industrial labour.

Nacht und Nebel 'Night and Fog'. Name given to a decree by Hitler in December 1941 to seize any person thought to be dangerous. They should vanish into Nacht und Nebel.

Nationalisation The socialist principle that the ownership of key industries should be transferred to the state.

Nationalism Essentially, believing that a nation should be independent. In Germany it originally grew out of the national spirit to unify Germany in the nineteenth century. However, more extreme nationalists supported an expansionist policy towards eastern Europe.

New objectivity Artists in favour of the 'new objectivity' broke away from the traditional romantic nostalgia of the nineteenth century.

New Order Used by the Nazis to describe the economic, political and racial integration of Europe under the Third Reich.

Night of the Long Knives The events of the night 29–30 June 1934 when Hitler ordered the murder of about 200 SA leaders.

Non-aggression pact An agreement signed between states that they will not fight each other. Not an alliance.

NSDAP National Socialist German Workers' Party – Nazi Party (Nationalsozialistische Partei Deutschlands).

Nuremberg Trials The international military tribunal set up by the Allies to try major war criminals.

Pact of Steel The military alliance signed between Italy and Germany in May 1939.

Phoney war Used to describe the war period from September 1939 to April 1940 because there was no real aggressive activity on the Western front.

Plebiscite A vote by the people on one specific issue – like a referendum. In the Peace Settlement 1919–20, it was decided to hold a series of plebiscites to decide the future of some territories. In this context, the Treaty of Versailles stated that a plebiscite should be held on the Saarland in January 1935.

Pogrom An organised or encouraged massacre of innocent people. The term originated from the massacres of Jews in Russia.

25-Points programme Hitler drew up the Party's 25-points programme in February 1920 with the Party's founder, Anton Drexler.

Policy of legality Hitler's political strategy after his failed armed coup in the Beer Hall putsch of 1923. He felt that the only sure way to succeed was to work within the Weimar Constitution and to gain power by legal means.

Polycracy A government system with an increasing range of competing power blocs.

Population policy In 1933–45 the Nazi government aimed to increase the birth rate.

Programme school A title given to some intentionalist historians who concentrate on Hitler's foreign policy.

Protectorate A weak state that is dependent on a stronger one.

Protestant General name for the reformed Churches created in sixteenth-century Europe that split from the Roman Catholic Church. There were 28 different Protestant Churches in Germany, of which the largest was the Lutheran (the German state Church, like the Church of England).

Putsch An uprising, although often the French phrase, *coup d'état*, is used.

Radicalisation A policy of increasing severity.

Rationalisation Decree An intended reform of the economy to eliminate the waste of labour and materials.

Real wages The actual purchasing power of income taking into account inflation/deflation and also the effect of deductions, e.g. taxes.

Reichsmark New German currency. Introduced after 1923 inflation, initially called *Rentenmark*.

Reichstag The German parliament created in 1871. From 1919 it became the main representative assembly and law-making body.

Remilitarisation of the Rhineland In the Treaty of Versailles (1919) the Rhineland was to be demilitarised from the French frontier to a line 32 miles east of the Rhine, although legally it was still part of Germany. In March 1936 German troops 're-occupied' the territory and re-established German military control.

Revisionist In general terms revisionism is the aim to modify or change something. In this context, it refers specifically to a historian who changes a well-established interpretation.

Revisionist policy The aim to modify or change an agreement. Here it refers specifically to the policy of changing the terms of the Treaty of Versailles.

Ribbentrop Bureau Name given to the office created by Joachim von Ribbentrop, who ran his own personal 'bureau' to oversee foreign affairs.

Rome–Berlin Axis An understanding signed in 1936 based on political, economic and ideological co-operation. It did not involve any military commitments.

RSHA Reich Security Office, which amalgamated all police and security organisations.

SA *Sturm Abteilung* – Stormtroopers. Also referred to as the Brownshirts after the colour of the uniform (see page 2).

Second revolution Refers to the aims of the SA, led by Ernst Röhm, which wanted social and economic reforms and the creation of a 'people's army' – merging the German army and the SA. The aims of a second revolution were more attractive to the 'left-wing socialist Nazis' or 'radical Nazis', who did not sympathise with the conservative forces in Germany.

Social Darwinism A philosophy that portrayed the world as a 'struggle' between people, races and nations. Influenced by Darwin's theories, it viewed life as 'the survival of the fittest'. Distorted into a political and social philosophy by racist thinkers.

Sonderweg Special (or peculiar) path of development. An interpretation of German history by structuralists which argues that Germany's continuity reflected the dominance of its social and economic 'structures' in the years 1848–1945.

Spanish Civil War The 1936–9 conflict between Republicans, who supported the democratic government, and the Nationalists/Fascists (financially and militarily backed by Italy and Germany).

SS *Schutz Staffel* (protection squad). Became known as the Blackshirts, after the colour of the uniform. Formed in 1925 as an élite bodyguard for Hitler. Himmler became its leader in 1929. By 1933 the SS numbered 52,000, establish a reputation for blind obedience and total commitment to the Nazi cause.

SS *Einsatzgruppen* 'Action Units'. Four of the units were launched in eastern Europe after the invasion of Russia. Responsible for rounding up local Jews and murdering them by mass shootings.

'Stab in the back' myth The distorted view that the German army had not really lost the First World War in 1918. Rather, unpatriotic elements, e.g. socialists and Jews, had undermined the war effort. It was a myth that played on certain scapegoats and severely weakened the Weimar democracy from the start.

'State within a state' A situation where the authority and government of the state are threatened by a rival power base.

Structuralist Interprets history by analysing the role of social and economic forces and structures. Structuralists, therefore, tend to place less emphasis on the role of the individual.

Tariffs   Taxes levied by an importing nation on foreign goods coming in, and paid by the importers.

Teutonic paganism   The non-Christian beliefs of the Germans in ancient history (heathens).

Third Reich   Third Empire: a term for the Nazi dictatorship, 1933–45. It was seen as the successor to the medieval Holy Roman Empire and Imperial Germany 1871–1918.

Total war   Involves the whole population in war – economically and militarily.

Totalitarianism   A system of government in which all power is centralised and does not allow any rival authorities. The term has been applied to Nazism and also to Italian Fascism and Stalin's Russia.

Treaty of Brest–Litovsk   Signed by Germany and Soviet Russia in March 1918, i.e. eight months before the end of the First World War. Germany annexed large areas of Russia, Poland and the Baltic states.

Tripartite   An agreement of three parties.

'Turn of the tide'   Used to describe the Allied military victories in the winter of 1942–3, when the British won at El Alamein in North Africa

and when the Russians forced the surrender of 300,000 German troops at Stalingrad.

Unconditional surrender   A statement made by Roosevelt and Churchill in 1943 that the Allies would not accept a negotiated peace.

Volk   Often translated as 'people', although it tends to suggest a nation with the same ethnic and cultural identities and a collective sense of belonging.

Völkisch   Nationalist views associated with racism (especially anti-Semitism).

Volksgemeinschaft   A people's community. Nazism stressed the development of a harmonious, socially unified and racially pure community. It did not support Marxism and communism.

Waffen SS   Armed SS – the number of divisions grew during the war from three to 35.

War of attrition   A long, drawn-out war aimed at wearing down the enemy.

Wehrmacht   The German army.

Zero hour   Used in German society to describe Germany's overall collapse at the end of the Second World War.

Index